1971

This boo'

RECONSTRUCTING THE UNION

Theory and Policy during the Civil War

Committee on the Albert J. Beveridge Award, 1966
American Historical Association

Alexander DeConde, *Chairman*
William J. Griffith
Eric E. Lampard
Lawrence W. Towner
David D. Van Tassel

Published under the direction of the American Historical Association from the income of the Albert J. Beveridge Memorial Fund.

For their zeal and beneficence in creating this fund the Association is indebted to many citizens of Indiana who desired to honor in this way the memory of a statesman and historian.

Reconstructing the Union

Theory and Policy during the Civil War

❋❋❋❋❋❋❋❋❋❋❋❋❋❋❋❋❋❋❋❋❋❋❋❋❋❋❋❋❋❋❋❋❋❋❋

By Herman Belz

PUBLISHED FOR THE

American Historical Association

CORNELL UNIVERSITY PRESS

ITHACA, NEW YORK

To Mary

Preface

THOUGH not necessarily a sign of progress, modern belligerent powers, as they destroy, seem to project plans for postwar reconstruction. The American Civil War, a modern war in view of the mass conscript armies which fought it, the economic mobilization which sustained it, and the goal of unconditional surrender which dominated the war aims of both sides, was modern in this respect also. For from its very start—not only after Appomattox—Union men laid plans for the restoration of peace. That they did so was in large measure due to the distinctive shape which the American constitutional structure had given to the war. Conducted under the rules of international law, between organized federations of states, the Civil War was a struggle to settle the fundamental question of the nature of the Union: Was it a single nation, possessing sovereign powers over member states, or a confederation from which individual states had the legal right to secede? In this context, to northerners planning for peace meant planning the reconstruction of the Union, or, in political and constitutional terms, providing for the return of the rebel states and determining the respective powers of federal and state governments. But the war was more than a fight to decide a constitutional issue. It soon became in addition a war against slavery, which meant that inextricably connected with reconstruction were other questions, among which the freedom and status of the emancipated slaves were the most important. The response of the Union's political leaders to this complex set of problems, from the opening of hostilities in April 1861, to their conclusion four years later, forms the subject of this book.

Despite all the attention historians have given to reconstruction in recent years, they have generally failed to see it as a problem that emerged the moment the Union was disrupted. It is true that histories of postwar reconstruction, and accounts of Lincoln and Civil War politics as well, usually discuss wartime reconstruction. But these works invariably confine themselves to an account of Lincoln's amnesty proclamation of December 1863 and the reaction it produced in Congress, culminating in the Wade-Davis Manifesto of August 1864. The result is that reconstruction during the war has been a relatively unexplored subject. Furthermore, to the limited extent that historians have dealt with it, they have concentrated so heavily on President Lincoln as to obscure the significant role played by Congress in forcing and defining the issues involved in reconstructing the Union. Lincoln's proclamation of December 1863, often viewed as the first evidence of Union reconstruction policy, was actually another in a series of executive actions undertaken in response to congressional initiative on reconstruction that began in 1861.

I wish to acknowledge the guidance and encouragement I have received from Professor Arthur Bestor of the University of Washington. The staff of the Legislative Branch of the National Archives, and especially its chief, Mr. Buford Rowland, have been most helpful in aiding my research in congressional materials. I wish to thank Mrs. Marie Windell of the Eleutherian Mills Historical Library for help in locating letters of Henry Winter Davis in the S. F. Du Pont Papers, and the Eleutherian Mills–Hagley Foundation for permission to quote from those letters. I am grateful also to my colleagues in American history at the University of Maryland who read parts of the manuscript and offered useful criticism and advice. Finally, I wish to thank the Albert J. Beveridge Committee of the American Historical Association for sponsoring the publication of this book.

HERMAN BELZ

College Park, Maryland
October 1967

Contents

RECONSTRUCTING THE UNION

Theory and Policy during the Civil War

I

Reconstructing the Union, 1861

THE American Civil War, itself the product of profound constitutional disagreement, created a constitutional crisis as difficult and significant as any ever faced by the American people. The war caused the destruction of the Union as it had existed for nearly three-quarters of a century. The task of reconstructing it, besides involving political issues of great moment, raised fundamental constitutional issues, for reconstruction involved nothing less than the arrangement and distribution of governmental power. True, reconstruction did not proceed completely *de novo*, but followed, in broad outline, the principles of the pre-existing constitutional system. Notwithstanding a heightened sense of nationalism, Union men assumed that the southern states would eventually resume their places in a federal system basically similar to that which existed in 1861. Yet certain events—above all, the end of slavery and the emancipation of four million Negroes—made the complete restoration of the pre-existing federal system impossible. Reconstruction raised anew the fundamental question: What balance ought to be struck between the power of the states and that of the federal government?

From the start of the Civil War, reconstruction was a problem of the first magnitude. Indeed, there is a sense in which reconstruction was the central issue in American politics from the moment South Carolina seceded in December 1860. That event caused a *de facto* disruption of the Union and produced a constitutional crisis that continued for the next fifteen years. Viewed in this light, the efforts made between the secession of South Carolina and the attack on Fort Sumter in April 1861, usually described as aimed at saving the Union, were in reality the first attempts to reconstruct it. In January 1861, for example, Senator R. M. T. Hunter of Virginia actually used the word "reconstruction" in a statement which insisted that the goal of establishing a new Union on terms of equality between the sections was second only to the duty of protecting the South. According to Hunter, secession did "not necessarily destroy the Union, or rather the hopes of reunion." On the contrary, he declared, "It may turn out to be the necessary path to reconstruction." [1] As an expression of this view, the Crittenden Compromise, offering a number of constitutional amendments, was the best known of several proposals for reconstructing the Union.

The opening of hostilities in April 1861 brought to an end peaceful attempts to reconstruct the Union. Reunification, if it was desired, must thereafter be accomplished by force and hence was bound to require even more drastic action than had seemed necessary in the winter of 1860–1861.

Reconstruction was a constitutional issue from the outset, for the avowed object of the North was the restoration of a Union that would include the southern states. But events early in the war also made reconstruction a question of practical policy, as when federal armies occupied and undertook to govern parts of the South. And Congress, as well as the executive, was involved in both aspects of the problem. This was evident as early as July 1861, when representatives of a loyal government of Virginia applied for seats in Congress and raised, as legislative matters, the

[1] *Congressional Globe*, Thirty-sixth Congress, second session, pp. 328–332 (Jan. 11, 1861). Hereafter citations are in the following form: *Cong. Globe*, 36 Cong., 2 sess., 328 (Jan. 11, 1861).

twin questions of the status of the rebellious states and the method of restoring them to the Union.

Obviously both the President and Congress could claim important roles in the process of reconstruction. As commander-in-chief, the executive was involved in the earliest phase of the process, since the establishment of military control in the rebellious states was the first step in restoring loyal state governments. The pardoning power of the President was also of great importance, since the war was officially viewed as a rebellion of individuals against lawful authority. On the other hand, Congress was bound to play a vital role in reconstruction. In the long run the major questions were not really military, but civil, and hence legislative in character. Congressional power also had a specific and technical basis. If the North was victorious, the states would eventually resume their places in the Union, and it was for Congress to decide ultimately whether the elected representatives of reconstructed states should be readmitted. Furthermore, Congress could initiate the process of constitutional amendment, if amendments seemed necessary for a successful restoration of the Union. Both the executive and the legislative departments were able therefore to claim control over reconstruction—a fact which invited controversy over jurisdiction, apart from any disagreements that might arise over policy.

Although the founding fathers had not anticipated civil strife on the scale now reached, the Constitution they framed was in several of its provisions relevant to the problem of reconstruction. It gave to each house of Congress the authority to judge concerning the elections, returns, and qualifications of its own members, an absolute power permitting no review or appeal from a decision, except in recourse to the people by the electoral process. This could be viewed narrowly as a merely technical power to examine the validity of writs and certificates, which is what it traditionally amounted to. But it could also be interpreted broadly as authorization to take into account the political background of elections and, by implication, under extraordi-

nary circumstances to legislate on the problems involved in electoral conflicts. The power of Congress to make or alter regulations concerning the time, place, and manner of holding elections
for senators and representatives was also pertinent to reconstruction. Even in the absence of loyal state governments, Congress
under this power might provide for federal elections in states or
parts of states recovered from the rebellion, and thereby initiate
the process of reconstruction. On the other hand, the basic executive power for dealing with reconstruction was the power to
grant reprieves and pardons for offenses against the United
States. Because secession was officially viewed as an insurrection
of individuals against the government, the pardoning power naturally became a significant instrument of presidential authority.
Although Congress could, and under Andrew Johnson did,
grant amnesty, it made no attempts under Lincoln to grant pardons, nor was there any doubt that pardoning was primarily an
executive affair.[2]

The clause providing that "the United States shall guarantee
to every state in this union a Republican form of government"
also assumed significance for reconstruction.[3] More than the
parts of the Constitution examined above, this provision was a
fruitful source of controversy because of the uncertain meaning
of "Republican" government. At the time the Constitution was
adopted, the term presented fewer difficulties: republican government then was generally understood to be nonmonarchical
government.[4] But in the nineteenth century the issue became

[2] U.S. Constitution, Art. I, sec. 5; Henry L. Dawes, *The Mode of
Procedure in Cases of Contested Elections* (New York, 1869), 2; U.S.
Constitution, Art. I, sec. 4, Art. II, sec. 2; Jonathan T. Dorris, *Pardon and
Amnesty under Lincoln and Johnson: The Restoration of the Confederates to Their Rights and Privileges* (Chapel Hill, N.C., 1953), 7, 313 ff.

[3] U.S. Constitution, Art. IV, sec. 4.

[4] See Cecelia M. Kenyon, "Republicanism and Radicalism in the American Revolution: An Old-Fashioned Interpretation," *William and Mary
Quarterly*, 3d ser., XIX (April, 1962), 165–166; and Bernard Bailyn, ed.,
Pamphlets of the American Revolution, I: *1750–1765* (Cambridge, Mass.,
1965), 176–177.

more complex, especially as the antislavery movement developed and many people began to feel that the South's peculiar institution was incompatible with republican government. In 1819, for example, when Missouri was seeking admission to the Union as a slave state, some northerners insisted, "The existence of slavery in any State is . . . a departure from republican principles." [5] While northerners began to define republican government in relation to slavery, southerners attached no specific meaning to the term. For them republican government was simply self-government. Moreover, since twelve of the thirteen original states had permitted slavery at the time the Constitution was adopted, they argued that slavery could not be considered incompatible with a republican form of government.[6]

Equally open to interpretation were the nature and extent of the power conferred upon the federal government by the constitutional guarantee of republican government to the states. On the one hand, it could mean that the federal government might act only after a state had done something to deprive its citizens of republican government, and that it could do no more than restore the pre-existing constitutional system. This was the way southerners interpreted the clause, both before and during the war. On the other hand, northerners tended to view it broadly as granting power by which the federal government might require states to fulfill specific conditions before being admitted to the Union.[7] During the war radical antislavery men carried this interpretation farther, arguing that the federal government could intervene directly in the states to provide them with republican government as guaranteed by the Constitution.

There was a good deal of uncertainty, furthermore, over which branch of the government—the executive or the legisla-

---

[5] *Annals of Congress*, 15 Cong., 2 sess., 1180 (Feb. 15, 1819), remarks of Timothy Fuller, House of Representatives; quoted in C. O. Lerche, Jr., "Congressional Interpretations of the Guarantee of a Republican Form of Government during Reconstruction," *Journal of Southern History*, XV (May 1949), 192.

[6] *Ibid.*, 193.   [7] *Ibid.*, 193–194.

tive—had the power to fulfill the guarantee. As in other questions of constitutional jurisdiction, both departments could claim
control. On the basis of the opinion of the Supreme Court in the
case of Luther versus Borden, some Republican members of
Congress held that Congress was empowered to act under the
guarantee clause. In that case the Court had been asked to decide
which of two competing governments in Rhode Island was the
legitimate one. While Chief Justice Taney declined to make a
decision, on the ground that it was "a question to be settled by
the political power," he also said:

Under this article [Art. IV, sec. 4] it rests with Congress to decide
what government is the established one in a State. For as the United
States guarantee to each State a republican government, Congress
must necessarily decide what government is established in a State
before it can determine whether it is republican or not. And when
the senators and representatives of a State are admitted into the
councils of the Union, the authority of the government under which
they are appointed, as well as its republican character, is recognized
by the proper constitutional authority. And its decision is binding
on every other department of the government, and could not be
questioned in a judicial tribunal.[8]

Taney thus designated Congress as having a specific power.
But this power might be nothing more than the authority, already clearly recognized, to judge the election and qualifications
of its own members; Taney probably intended to imply no
more than this. Yet some Republicans interpreted the opinion
more broadly. Henry Winter Davis, for example, a leader of
congressional reconstruction in 1864, said, on the basis of
Taney's opinion, "It is the exclusive prerogative of Congress—
of Congress and not the President—to determine what is and
what is not the established government of the State." Davis held
that under the guarantee clause Congress had a "supreme, unlimited political jurisdiction, paramount over courts, subject only to

[8] 7 Howard 47, 42.

the judgment of the people of the United States, embracing within its scope every legislative measure necessary and proper to make it effectual." [9]

Supporters of the President could argue, however, that the executive possessed the power to fulfill the guarantee of republican government. In the Rhode Island case Taney had also pointed out that Congress had authorized the President to execute the guarantee in the event of domestic insurrection; therefore the executive had the power to decide which was the correct, lawful government in a state.[10] In advising Lincoln during the war, at a time when the President and Congress were deadlocked on reconstruction, Montgomery Blair, former Postmaster General in the Cabinet, relied on this part of Taney's opinion to refute specifically Davis' argument for congressional power. The question in Rhode Island was a political one, to be sure; but "what was the political power which exerted itself . . . which the Court felt bound to follow?" Blair asked. "In fact," he said, "it was the recognition of the Governor opposed to Dorr by the President of the United States." [11] Thus both the executive and Congress could claim power to act under the guarantee-of-republican-government clause.

While reconstruction policy changed as the circumstances of the war changed, the problems of constitutional theory remained the same from start to finish. In defining the nature of the war there may have been disagreement, with some Union men regarding it as an uprising of individuals against their government and with others seeing it as a war between belligerents, under the law of nations. But legislative proposals for reconstruction generally eschewed both definitions and recognized the war as a conflict between elements of the federal system—the states and the federal government. The major con-

[9] *Cong. Globe,* 38 Cong., 1 sess., App., 82–83 (Mar. 22, 1864).
[10] 7 Howard 43.
[11] Montgomery Blair to Abraham Lincoln, Dec. 6, 1864, no. 39074, Robert Todd Lincoln Collection, Library of Congress.

gressional enactment on reconstruction, the Wade-Davis Bill of 1864, proposed to deal with "States declared in rebellion," not persons. As a conservative Unionist writer was forced to admit in reviewing theories of reconstruction in 1863, it was not only partisans of the Confederacy, but supporters of the administration as well, who held "that the States are the parties to the controversy." [12]

Reconstruction as a problem in constitutional theory raised one central question: What was the status of the seceded states in relation to the federal government? At the start of the war Union men advanced two distinct answers. One was that the states remained in the Union, their constitutional status and relationship to the federal government theoretically unchanged, although actually temporarily interrupted. The other basic reply was that as a result of their attempted secession, the southern states had ceased to be states of the Union and had reverted to the condition of territories.

The first view, which became the official position of the administration, rested on the theory of the Union expounded by Lincoln in his inaugural address in March 1861. His fundamental point was that the United States as a national government was meant to exist in perpetuity, and that secession was illegal. The Union was older than both the states and the Constitution, he said—proof that it was intended to exist in perpetuity. After originating in the Articles of Association in 1774, it was solidified and its perpetuity affirmed in the Declaration of Independence and Articles of Confederation. The Constitution then aimed at creating a more perfect Union. Lincoln argued further that perpetuity was implied in "the fundamental law of all national governments." Like the organic law of any nation, he said, the Constitution had no provision for its own termination. Thus in Lincoln's view the United States was "a

[12] Isaac F. Redfield, "On American Secession and State Rights," *Monthly Law Reporter*, XXVI (Dec. 1863), 83.

government proper," not "an association of States in the nature of a contract merely." It followed that "no State, upon its own mere motion, can lawfully get out of the Union," and that *"resolves* and *ordinances* to that effect are legally void." Holding that acts of violence "within any State or States, against the authority of the United States are insurrectionary or revolutionary," Lincoln concluded, "In view of the Constitution and the laws, the Union is unbroken." [13]

The theory of the Union as perpetual implied the indestructibility of the states. Lincoln made this point clearer in his message to Congress of July 4, 1861, when he said, "The States have their *status* IN the Union, and they have no other *legal status.*" [14] Since secession was of no legal effect, the states remained members of the Union. According to this view, reconstruction involved suppressing the insurrection and placing loyal citizens in control of the state governments of the South. As there had been no change in the status of the states, state laws and institutions existed as before the rebellion, and it was the duty of the federal government, in fulfillment of the guarantee of republican government, to protect their continued existence. On the basis of this theory of reconstruction, the administration at the beginning of the war adopted a policy of encouraging and recognizing the efforts of loyal citizens in the rebellious states to reorganize state governments and renew their practical relation to the federal government.

In 1861, when it seemed that the North would win a rapid victory, this view of reconstruction received wide support. But as the war continued and the strength of loyal elements in the South proved negligible, more and more Union men began to

[13] First Inaugural, Mar. 4, 1861, in *The Collected Works of Abraham Lincoln*, ed. Roy P. Basler *et al.* (9 vols.; New Brunswick, N.J., 1953–1955), IV, 264–265. Quotations from *The Collected Works of Lincoln* are from this edition.

[14] Message to Congress in Special Session, July 4, 1861, *ibid.*, IV, 434.

question it, because it seemed to lead to a policy that would permit the rebellious states to return to the Union in the same condition as when they left or place state government in the hands of a small minority of loyal citizens. Accordingly, a number of Republicans soon proposed as an alternative approach to reconstruction the theory of territorialization.

Proponents of territorialization denounced secession as illegal and insisted on the perpetuity of the Union, but concluded nonetheless that the attempt to secede, followed by armed insurrection, had caused the legal and constitutional destruction of the states and reduced them to territories. Actually territorialization suggested itself as an approach to reconstruction as soon as secession began. And ironically it was Andrew Johnson, the archenemy of radical reconstruction after the war, who on the floor of Congress first proposed to apply the territorial concept, which soon was regarded as the hallmark of radicalism. On December 19, 1860, Johnson asked, concerning the proposed secession of Louisiana, "Does she not pass back into the condition in which she was before we admitted her into the Union?" Northern editorial writers began to adopt the same view. The Trenton *Daily Gazette and Republican* asserted in January 1861 that states which had earlier been territories and tried to secede became again "Territories over which Mr. Lincoln may appoint Governors and other Territorial officers." More specifically, advocates of territorialization focused on the failure of the rebellious states to discharge the functions of local government. According to Senator James Harlan of Iowa, a state was "such a legal organization of the people . . . as will enable it to protect the rights of each and all against all intruders . . . with such officers as will enable it to enact laws and administer justice." In other words, the states existed in order to provide local government under the Constitution, and because the rebellious states were not doing this, supporters of territorialization held them delinquent. Thus Senator Charles Sumner of Massachusetts asserted, "Nobody has suggested . . . that any 'State' of our Union has, through rebellion, ceased to exist as a *civil society*, or even as a *political community*. It is only as a *State of the Union*, armed with State rights, or at least as a *local government* . . . that it can be called in question." [15]

For supporters of territorialization the chief fact about the seceded states was their status as United States territories. Five of eleven seceded states had at one time been subject to the local authority of a territorial government under the control of Congress. Then, upon the fulfillment of certain conditions, of which acceptance of the Constitution was the most important, the exercise of local authority by a state government had followed. It seemed logical to conclude that if a state government failed to fulfill its fundamental obligation of providing local government under the Constitution, the state ceased to exist, and responsibility for local government devolved upon Congress. Not all of the seceded states had passed through the territorial stage, but this did not mean that those with no territorial history could not go in the opposite direction and become simply territories under the exclusive jurisdiction of Congress. The policy toward which this theory pointed, according to Senator Harlan, was that the government must "hold and govern . . . [the seceded states] as organized Territories, or . . . acknowledge their independence." [16]

Though territorialization has often been considered an unnecessarily harsh antislavery scheme with no constitutional basis,[17]

---

[15] *Cong. Globe*, 36 Cong., 2 sess., 138 (Dec. 19, 1860); Trenton *Daily Gazette and Republican*, Jan. 18, 1861; *Cong. Globe*, 37 Cong., 2 sess., App., 318 (July 11, 1862); Charles Sumner, *Works* (15 vols.; Boston, 1870–1883), VII, 524.

[16] *Cong. Globe*, 37 Cong., 2 sess., App., 318 (July 11, 1862).

[17] See, for example, Eben G. Scott, *Reconstruction during the Civil War in the United States of America* (Boston, 1895), 255–266; and James G. Randall and David Donald, *The Civil War and Reconstruction* (2d ed.; Boston, 1961), 537.

there are other ways of looking at the concept. John Burgess, for example, criticized radical reconstruction but thought nonetheless that "holding the districts of the South under Territorial civil government until the white race in those districts should have sufficiently recovered from its temporary disloyalty to the Union to be intrusted again with the powers of . . . local government . . . was the proper and correct course." [18] Only if the Constitution is defined simply as the formal document is it true that territorialization rested on no constitutional basis. To be sure, the document contained nothing about states reverting to territories. But one could say the same about the alternative approach to reconstruction, with its emphasis on state indestructibility: the written Constitution did not expressly mention it, either. Both theories of reconstruction rested upon a structure of inference—inference from a theory of the Union or from past practices of government.

If "Constitution" refers to the actual exercise of government power as well as to the written instrument, then territorialization had a more substantial basis. Organizing territorial governments and creating new states was one of the traditions of American government, and men who for many years had been involved in the territorial system naturally relied upon it to provide a substitute for disloyal state governments. For fifteen years, moreover, the question of slavery in the territories had been bitterly contested, and it was a fundamental principle of the Republican party that the federal government had the power to prohibit slavery there. An additional reason, therefore, for regarding the seceded states as territories was that Congress might then legislate against slavery or create territorial governments capable of abolishing the institution.

At the beginning of the war, then, these two views provided the points of departure for dealing with reconstruction: the theory of state indestructibility, which regarded the states as still

[18] John W. Burgess, *Reconstruction and the Constitution, 1866–1876* (New York, 1902), vii–viii.

in the Union and needing only new officers elected by loyal citizens in order to resume their places in the Union; and the theory of territorialization, which regarded the states as having lapsed into the condition of territories, making it necessary for Congress to assume direct control over them.

II

War Aims and Reconstruction: The Congressional Session of July 1861

RECONSTRUCTION policy at the start of the war aimed at restoring the southern states to the Union with their rights and powers unchanged. This policy was practically imperative, in view of the theory of the Union according to which the government went to war. Having argued the illegality of secession, Republicans were logically committed, once hostilities began, to adhere to this principle and to hold that the eleven states were still members of the Union, even though not in their proper practical relation to the federal government. Accordingly, when the rebellion was over, the states might resume their former places in the union.

Exigencies of policy in the border states also demanded that reconstruction mean restoration of the pre-existing Union. In order to keep Maryland, Kentucky, and Missouri in the Union, it was necessary to hold up limited war aims, for to do otherwise —say, to make the abolition of slavery an objective of the war— might throw the balance to the secessionists, who were struggling for control in each of these states. The same logic made a circumspect and conservative course necessary with regard to reconstruction. To take the position, for example, that the rebel states were no longer in the Union—were reduced to territories, perhaps, or to the status of alien enemies—would have violated the principle of state rights and possibly enabled the Confederacy to win the border states to its cause. From a second point of view, then, it was necessary to regard the seceded states as members of the Union entitled to the full exercise of their traditional powers upon the end of hostilities.

Reconstruction policy at the beginning of the war rested, furthermore, on the assumption that large numbers of southerners —perhaps a majority in each state—were loyal to the Union. Accordingly, a central feature of the policy was the idea that the loyal citizens constituted the state. Officials at Washington hoped that after federal troops crushed the military power of the rebellion, southern Unionists would restore their pre-existing governments and their states' practical relations with the Union. In the first few months of the war both the President and Congress adopted this approach to reconstruction.

By the time Congress assembled in special session on July 4, 1861, nearly three months had elapsed since the attack on Fort Sumter, and a more comprehensive view of affairs was possible. President Lincoln's long-awaited message provided such a view, setting forth administration policy within the framework of the theory of the Union on which the government had based its opposition to secession. As always for Lincoln, the essential point was the perpetuity of the Union. Historically, he explained, the Union was older than the states, dating from the first cooperative efforts against Great Britain by the united colonies. According to this concept, the colonies created the Union, which in turn threw off dependence on Britain and made the colonies states. The Declaration of Independence solidified the Union, and the Articles of Confederation were further evidence that the Union was meant to be perpetual. "Having never been States, either in substance or in name, *outside* of the Union," the President said, "whence this magical omnipotence of 'State rights,' asserting a claim of power to lawfully destroy the Union itself?" He concluded, "The States have their *status* IN the Union, and they have no other legal status." [1]

Reconstruction was already an issue, and on this score Lincoln said that he would regard the loyal citizens in a rebellious state as constituting the state, and generally indicated that the administration would seek to restore the pre-existing state governments. "Lest there be some uneasiness in the minds of candid men, as to what is to be the course of the government, towards the Southern States, *after* the rebellion shall have been suppressed," he said, "the Executive deems it proper to say, it will be his purpose then, as ever, to be guided by the Constitution, and the laws." More to the point, he stated that he "probably [would] have no different understanding of the powers, and duties of the Federal government, relatively to the rights of the States, and the people, under the Constitution, than that expressed in the inaugural address." Turning his attention to the Unionist movement that had emerged in western Virginia, Lincoln announced that loyal Virginians had claimed the protection of the government. Of them he declared, "Those loyal citizens, this government is bound to recognize and protect, as being Virginia." Furthermore, Lincoln questioned whether a majority of the legally qualified voters of any State, except perhaps South Carolina, were in favor of disunion. There was reason to believe, he said, that "Union men were the majority in many, if not in every other one, of the so-called seceded States." The contrary had not, he added, been demonstrated in any of them, including Virginia.[2]

Lincoln's discussion of the constitutional guarantee of republican government reflected his view of reconstruction as restoration. "If a State may lawfully go out of the Union," he reasoned,

[1] Message to Congress in Special Session, July 4, 1861, *Collected Works of Lincoln*, IV, 433–435.
[2] *Ibid.*, 439, 428, 437.

"it may also discard the republican form of government." To prevent its going out, therefore, was "an indispensable *means* to the *end*, of maintaining the guaranty mentioned." In other words, guaranteeing republican government meant maintaining the governments in the South as they were before the war began. Finally, taking up a question that was to occupy Congress in its discussion of war aims, Lincoln denied that the action of the government in meeting secession constituted "any coercion, any conquest, or any subjugation, in any just sense of those terms." [3]

The most important business facing Congress, according to Lincoln, was to "give the legal means for making this contest a short, and a decisive one." [4] Throughout most of the session, therefore, Congress was concerned with measures authorizing and strengthening the war effort. Its most important acts provided for a volunteer army of 500,000, increased the size of the regular army and navy, and raised revenue by means of a loan of $250,000,000, a direct tax on the states, an increase in the tariff, and an income tax. [5] The President had boldly seized the initiative when hostilities began in April, and Congress, at least for the time being, tended to defer to him in matters of war. [6]

In deliberating on these measures, Congress had to consider the objectives of the war. This consideration was inextricably bound to the question of reconstruction, however, making it necessary for Congress to decide whether the government intended to restore the old Union and how, and on what terms, if any, the seceded states were to resume their places in the Union.

---

[3] *Ibid.*, 439–440.   [4] *Ibid.*, 431.

[5] Allan Nevins, *The War for the Union* (2 vols.; New York, 1959–1960) I, 190–195.

[6] The nearest Congress came to a declaration of war was an act authorizing the President, in the event of rebellion in any state, to declare the inhabitants thereof to be in a state of insurrection. Cf. Randall and Donald, *The Civil War and Reconstruction*, 279–280; J. G. Randall, *Constitutional Problems under Lincoln* (rev. ed.; Urbana, Ill., 1951), 53–55.

As in the months before the war the term "state coercion" aroused fighting sentiments, so now the slogan "state subjugation" stirred political passions to the boiling point. Although few were willing to define the word, "subjugation" was on everyone's lips and dominated the discussion of war aims. Democrats and border-state Unionists, on the one hand, denounced subjugation of states and sought to commit Congress to the limited goal of restoring the Union with the powers and privileges of the states unchanged. Republicans, on the other hand, generally opposed any such official definition of policy, and some among them were even beginning to think of territorial government for the rebellious states. Needless to say, this attitude, accompanied as it invariably was by antislavery rhetoric, differed radically from Lincoln's approach to reconstruction.

The determination of the status of southern members of Congress who had joined the Confederacy—what might be called reconstruction in reverse—illustrates how attitudes toward the rebellious states had stiffened since the start of the war. When this question had come up at the executive session of the Senate in March, William Pitt Fessenden, a Republican of Maine, expressed the prevailing sentiment, contending that the seats of departed southerners ought to be declared vacant, "to be filled by the States whenever they choose to fill them"; he thought this would be "respectful to the States themselves." Disregarding the argument of James Bayard, a Democrat of Delaware, that the seats could not be declared vacant without implicit recognition of the act of secession, the Senate approved Fessenden's resolution by a vote of 26 to 12. But when the same question came up in July with respect to ten other southern senators, and Bayard proposed following the precedent of March, the Senate refused to do so. Most Republicans now considered the Fessenden resolution too lenient. Daniel Clark of New Hampshire reflected the new view when he said that declaring the seats vacant would leave in abeyance the question whether the states have the right to go out. "I hope that no such tame measure as declaring the seats vacant will be adopted," he said, and the Senate voted, 32 to 12, to expel the southern senators.[7]

Already, in the first week of the special session, members of Congress expressed divergent views on reconstruction. In particular, the idea of treating the rebellious states as territories before readmitting them was broached on July 10 by Senator Edward D. Baker of Oregon. The occasion for Baker's suggestion was a debate on a resolution approving emergency acts of the President. Senator Anthony Kennedy, a Democrat of Maryland, denouncing Lincoln's actions as coercive, said the Union could not be reconstructed by force and proposed "any concession to bring this country back to the point where we stood one year ago." Henry Lane, an Indiana Republican, in contrast insisted that the Union could be preserved only by force and said he would march troops wherever necessary in order to suppress the insurrection. Should the rebels abandon the rebellion, however, he added, "there [would be] an end of the matter." Senator Baker, a Republican of Oregon and a close friend of Lincoln, then turned the discussion in a new direction by introducing the idea of territorialization. Arguing for a "sudden, bold, forward, determined war," Baker said he anticipated a difficult struggle. In fact, he continued, "Instead of finding within a year, loyal States sending members to Congress, and replacing their Senators upon this floor, we may have to reduce them to the condition of Territories, and send from Massachusetts or from Illinois Governors to control them." Should this need arise, he declared, "I am one of those who would be willing to do it." Baker said he "would risk even the stigma of being despotic and oppressive, rather than risk the perpetuity of the Union of these States."[8]

The next day, July 11, Lazarus Powell of Kentucky accused Baker of proposing to "restore this Union by reducing sovereign States to provinces, and sending Governors from other States to

[7] *Cong. Globe*, 36 Cong., 2 sess., 1454-1455 (March 13, 1861); 37 Cong., 1 sess., 63 (July 11, 1861).

[8] *Cong. Globe*, 37 Cong., 1 sess., 43-45 (July 10, 1861).

rule over them." Such a remedy would be worse than the disease, Powell said, for to "blot these States out of existence, and hand them over to the strong arm of the North as conquered provinces" would be the destruction of the Union. He added that "to reduce the South to conquered provinces, and give them Governors from Massachusetts and Illinois," as Baker had suggested, would be to deprive them of the republican form of government that the Constitution guaranteed. Baker replied, "A territorial form of government may be a republican form of government as well as a State government may be." Although he hoped that the rebellious states would soon return to their allegiance to the Union, he reiterated his conviction: "If they will not come here as States, we will not let them out of the Union for that reason. If they will not govern themselves in Congress, we will govern them. Rather than separate from them . . . we will govern them as Territories, and govern them a great deal better than they will govern themselves." [9]

A few days later John C. Breckinridge of Kentucky, resuming the debate, charged Baker with holding that the seceded states "must . . . be ravaged by armies, . . . their state form must be changed, and they must be reduced to the condition of Territories." Breckinridge said it was "subversive of the Constitution, . . . subversive of the public liberty, . . . to govern ten million people as if they were in a territorial condition." Like Powell, he regarded the territorialization of states as a violation of the constitutional guarantee of republican government. If states are out of the Union, he declared, "we have the power to make war on them . . . and conquer them and do as we please with them; but if they are regarded as still being States in this Union, . . . there is no pretense of argument . . . that the . . . [Constitution] contains any authority to reduce them to the territorial condition." Baker replied, amidst applause from the galleries, that if the southern states "would not send members here to govern them, it was better, for the sake of ultimate peace, for freedom, civilization, humanity, that they should be

[9] *Ibid.*, 69 (July 11, 1861).

governed as Territories are governed, rather than permit perpetual anarchy, confusion, discord, and civil war." [10]

Senator Lane of Indiana then presented what he considered to be the administration point of view. While no one sought the abolition of slavery as an objective of the war, nevertheless, Lane explained, the seceded states "may, in their madness and folly and treason, make the abolition of slavery one of the results of this war." This he understood to be "precisely the position of the Administration." As for reconstruction, Lane said, "We do not contemplate any destruction of the Republic which involves a reconstruction." The government's course would be "to protect the Union men of the border States, to foster the Union sentiment, to get up a counter-revolution, which will lay all secession and treason in ruins." According to Lane, Congress expected soon to readmit Tennessee and North Carolina into the Union, "as we have recently readmitted old Virginia." He added, "We expect to present, in six months, an unbroken front to all foreign Powers, no single star erased, the light of no star obliterated by treason in any part of the country." [11]

Yet the problem of defining war aims persisted, and on July 18 the conservative Lazarus Powell of Kentucky sought to deal with it in an amendment he offered to a bill concerning the military establishment. Powell's amendment declared, "No part of the Army or Navy of the United States shall be employed or used in subjecting or holding as a conquered province any sovereign State now or lately one of the United States, or in abolishing or interfering with African slavery in any of the States." Republican James H. Lane of Kansas at once moved to add, "Unless it shall be necessary in enforcing the laws, or maintaining the Constitution of the Union"; a lively debate ensued. [12] John Sherman of Ohio, also a Republican, considered Powell's

[10] *Ibid.*, 140–141 (July 16, 1861).

[11] *Ibid.*, 142–144 (July 16, 1861). Representatives and senators from a restored Virginia government had been admitted to Congress on July 4 and July 13; it was this to which Lane was referring.

[12] *Ibid.*, 186–187 (July 18, 1861).

proposal out of place because it wrongly implied that the purpose of the war was to subjugate the rebel states and emancipate the slaves. Revealing the pressures being exerted to clarify war aims, he added, however, that he would "go as far as . . . any other living man to uphold the Government against all rebellious citizens." Furthermore, "If . . . there is no way of conquering South Carolina, for instance, except by emancipating her slaves, I say emancipate her slaves and conquer her rebellious citizens; and if they have not people there enough to elect members of Congress and Senators, we will send people there." Still, said Sherman, it was "not the purpose of this war to subjugate a State." James McDougall, a Democrat of California, agreed that Powell's amendment was "altogether uncalled for," and John Carlile of Virginia, Orville Browning of Illinois, and James Dixon of Connecticut all opposed it for essentially the same reason.[13]

Republicans wanted to avoid a direct vote on Powell's proposal because, as Fessenden expressed it, they believed he was simply trying "to give to those Senators in the slave States, who are so disposed, a chance to argue that because we would not vote on that amendment, therefore that is the object." Sherman therefore offered a substitute amendment that stood midway between the proposals of Powell and Lane. Sherman's amendment declared, "The purposes of the military establishment provided for in this bill are to preserve the Union, to defend the property, and to maintain the constitutional authority of the Government." [14] In the complicated parliamentary maneuvering that followed, the Senate rejected both Powell's and Lane's propositions in favor of Sherman's. But on the main vote it rejected Sherman's proposal also, thereby showing its unwillingness to be bound by any specific formulation of war aims.[15]

In the House of Representatives, meanwhile, war aims and state subjugation were also issues. On July 11 the Ohio Demo-

13 *Ibid.*, 186–190 (July 18, 1861).   14 *Ibid.*, 191 (July 18, 1861).
15 *Ibid.*, 192–194 (July 18, 1861).

crat Clement L. Vallandigham proposed to amend an army appropriation bill by insisting "that no part of the money hereby appropriated shall be employed in subjugating, or holding as a conquered province, any sovereign State now or lately one of the United States; nor in abolishing or interfering with African slavery in any of the States." Like the Senate amendments, this proposal drew objections because it implied that the object of the war was to subjugate the states, and the House rejected it by a voice vote.[16] The next day, however, the House considered subjugation more fully in connection with the volunteer-army bill. On the specific issue of whether a force of 400,000 or 500,000 men should be raised, Aaron Harding of Kentucky, a Democrat, supported the proposal for the smaller number, explaining that he was "not in favor of what is termed southern subjugation." Republican John Hickman of Pennsylvania argued the advisability of the larger force, but thought that enlarging the army would not necessarily "increase the hazard of subjugating the South." Yet, while he did not himself know "whether it [was] contemplated to subjugate the South," he was certain that "it [was] fully contemplated to force the South into submission." Hickman suggested, "Perhaps, it will be necessary . . . to leave the track of the chariot wheels of war so deep on the southern soil that a century may not obliterate it." Some Republicans apparently felt this went too far. James Campbell of Pennsylvania said that for his part he would not "talk . . . about the propriety or necessity of 'forcing the South into submission,'" while Alexander Diven of New York declared, "It is just as fatal to the Constitution and to the liberties of the country to subjugate a State as it is for a State to rebel." When the rebellion should be over, Diven continued, "South Carolina, the worst of the rebel States, will be South Carolina still, with all the rights which Massachusetts has, or else the Constitution is at an end." [17]

[16] *Ibid.*, 77 (July 11, 1861).   [17] *Ibid.*, 95–99 (July 13, 1861).

Besides rejecting proposals which prohibited the use of the army for the subjugation of states, the majority in Congress also blocked the introduction of seemingly less controversial resolutions which declared that "the sole object of the Government . . . is, and ought to be, to maintain the integrity of the Union"; that "whenever the States now in rebellion . . . shall cease their rebellion and become loyal to the Union, it is the duty of the Government to suspend the further prosecution of the war"; and that it was "no part of the object of the present war against the rebellious States to interfere with the institution of slavery therein." [18]

After rejecting a variety of proposals concerning the objectives of the war, Congress in late July resolved the question of war aims—for the time being at least—by adopting the resolutions introduced by two leading border-state men, John Crittenden of Kentucky and Andrew Johnson of Tennessee. These resolutions set forth limited war aims and marked the high point of border-state influence on the formulation of Union policy.

The Battle of Bull Run was an important factor in creating a situation favorable to the passage of the resolutions on war aims. When Crittenden first tried to introduce his resolution on July 19, Thaddeus Stevens blocked it. In the next few days, however, Union forces suffered heavy losses at Bull Run, only twenty miles from Washington. Not only was the defeat greatly demoralizing to the North; in Congress it had the effect of making antislavery Republicans more amenable to border-state views. This became apparent on July 22, when Crittenden introduced his resolution on war aims and the House, chastened by defeat and aware more than ever of the necessity of holding the border states in the Union, adopted it with only two dissenting votes.[19]

The Crittenden resolution was divided into two parts. It

[18] *Ibid.*, 117 (July 13, 1861), resolution of Rep. William S. Holman, Democrat of Indiana; *ibid.*, 130 (July 15, 1861), resolution of Rep. William Allen, Democrat of Illinois.
[19] *Ibid.*, 223 (July 22, 1861).

began by declaring, "The present deplorable civil war has been forced upon the country by the disunionists of the southern States." The heart of the resolution was the second part, which stated that the war "is not waged . . . in any spirit of oppression, or for any purpose of conquest or subjugation, or purpose of overthrowing or interfering with the rights or established institutions of those States." Rather, the object of the war was "to defend and maintain the supremacy of the Constitution, and to preserve the Union with all the dignity, equality, and rights of the several States unimpaired." The resolution stated in conclusion, "As soon as these objects are accomplished the war ought to cease." [20]

Formulated to express the idea of a war limited to suppressing insurrection and restoring the pre-existing Union, the Crittenden resolution included elements on which men of diverse views could agree. It was supposed to convey the impression in some circles that slavery was not, under any circumstances, to be interfered with, nor the rebellious states divested of any of their powers or privileges. Some took the resolution to be a binding commitment and a restriction on the federal government. The best-known advocate of this view was Andrew Johnson himself, who as President cited the resolution in proclamations and veto messages. Johnson called the Reconstruction Act of March 2, 1867, for example, "a breach of our plighted honor," because it repudiated the "solemn resolution that the war was and should be carried on for no purpose of subjugation." [21] Yet the resolution yielded other interpretations. For one thing, it nowhere mentioned slavery, which meant that it need not be taken as a firm commitment against interfering with the institution. Furthermore, while the resolution disavowed any intention of interfering with state rights and institutions, it did not promise to

[20] *Ibid.*
[21] James D. Richardson, ed., *A Compilation of the Messages and Papers of the Presidents, 1789–1908* (11 vols.; Washington, 1908), VI, 509.

safeguard them under all circumstances. This distinction was well understood at the time. When the resolution was before the Senate, John P. Hale of New Hampshire, a prominent anti-slavery man, said he approved the statement of purpose it contained. But he implied that there was nothing new or startling in the resolution, recalling that most radical abolitionists as far back as the 1830's had admitted an indisposition and a want of power to interfere with slavery in the states where it existed. On the other hand, Hale said, "There may be something in the suggestion that was made by the late Mr. Adams, of Massachusetts . . . that there might be, incidental to the war power belonging to any Government, some control over this subject of slavery." [22] Similarly, Senator Ira Harris of New York agreed that the purpose of the government was not to overthrow slavery. But, he added, "If slavery shall be abolished . . . as a consequence of this war, I shall not shed a tear over the result. . . . If it comes as a consequence, let it come; but it is not an end of the war." [23]

The Crittenden resolution differed in significant respects from the earlier unsuccessful proposals of Powell, Lane, Sherman, and Vallandigham that Congress announce war aims. Whereas Powell's proviso (as well as Vallandigham's in the House) was concerned with the use of the army for specific purposes, the Crittenden resolution dealt with the purposes of the war and hence was not restrictive in the same legalistic way. Thus Republicans who could not accept Powell's proposition could accept Crittenden's. On the other hand, it was agreeable to conservatives and border-state men, where Lane's and Sherman's proposals were not. Lane's proposition, by making an exception to the prohibi-

---

[22] *Cong. Globe*, 37 Cong., 1 sess., 260 (July 25, 1861). In 1842, John Quincy Adams in the House of Representatives said that an army commander had the right to emancipate slaves in invaded territory. This was often referred to by antislavery men in discussions of the government's power over slavery. Cf. J. G. Randall, *Constitutional Problems under Lincoln*, 374-376.

[23] *Cong. Globe*, 37 Cong., 1 sess., 259 (July 25, 1861).

tion against using federal troops for subjugation, in effect would allow such a policy under certain conditions—a possibility of course unacceptable to conservatives. The Crittenden resolution, in contrast, stated that no purpose of "conquest" or "subjugation" was involved in the Union effort. Sherman's proposal was unsatisfactory to conservatives because it mentioned only the preservation of the Union and the defense and maintenance of federal property and authority. But Crittenden's resolution referred also to the preservation of the "dignity, equality, and rights of the several States unimpaired."

Despite the carefully conceived compromise features of the Crittenden resolution, some Republicans opposed it. Albert G. Riddle of Ohio and John F. Potter of Wisconsin voted against it, and ten others abstained, including James Ashley, John Bingham, Martin Conway, John Hutchins, George Julian, and Owen Lovejoy, all of whom subsequently assumed a radical position on reconstruction.[24] Riddle and Ashley later described the passage of the resolution in the House. A number of men had urged Riddle to change his vote, but he retorted: "Not a man of you believes that slavery is eternal. Not one is stupid enough, *notwithstanding his vote*, to believe that it can be abolished by convention." They all believed that slavery would be destroyed "through convulsion, fire, and blood," but Riddle differed from them in thinking, "That convulsion is upon us."[25] James Ashley too remembered that every public man he knew in Washington, as well as personal and political friends, urged him to vote for the resolution on war aims and not to assume the responsibility of separating himself from the party on such an important issue. Although he voted for the first part of the resolution, he abstained on the second part—"the blush of shame tingling my face," he recalled, "as it has every time I have thought of that act." Moments after the balloting he told

[24] *Ibid.*, 223 (July 22, 1861).
[25] Albert G. Riddle, *Recollections of War Times: Reminiscences of Men and Events in Washington, 1860–1865* (New York, 1895), 42–43.

Thomas Corwin, a Republican colleague from Ohio, that failure to vote against the Crittenden resolution was "the most cowardly act" of his life. When Corwin said that he had voted for it, Ashley, who soon became the leading advocate of territorialization, replied, "Yes, Governor, but you do not see things as I do." [26]

Two days later, on July 24, Andrew Johnson of Tennessee introduced into the Senate a resolution virtually identical to Crittenden's. While it provoked more debate than Crittenden's had in the House, opposition to it was minimal, coming mainly from Democrats who thought the resolution should condemn northern as well as southern disunionists. There was discussion of subjugation, but without the revolutionary overtones present in Senator Baker's earlier remarks on the subject. Lyman Trumbull of Illinois argued that the word "subjugation" ought to be struck out, because, though it was the intention of the government to subjugate citizens who defied the laws of the Union, "it has never been proposed . . . to subjugate States or coerce States." Republican Senator Jacob Collamer of Vermont held that in subjugating the people of a state, the Union was in a sense subjugating the state itself; but in another sense it was not, for, he said, "You do not meet it in its corporate capacity as a State, but you meet the people of the State." This view prevailed, and on July 25 the Senate passed the Johnson resolution without amendment, by a vote of 30 to 5.[27]

While debating war aims, Congress had at least one opportunity to work out the practical implications of reconstruction. The divided state of opinion in Virginia provided a test of reconstruction policy in the summer of 1861.[28]

[26] James M. Ashley, *Orations and Speeches: Duplicate Copy of the Souvenir from the Afro-American League of Tennessee to the Hon. James M. Ashley of Ohio*, ed. Benjamin W. Arnett (Philadelphia, 1894), 697 (hereafter cited as *Orations and Speeches*).

[27] *Cong. Globe*, 37 Cong., 1 sess., 257–265 (July 25, 1861).

[28] In Maryland, Missouri, and Kentucky opinion was also divided, but in none of these states did secessionists gain control. The federal govern-

The long history of sectional conflict within Virginia, which on several occasions had led to consideration of separate statehood among western Virginians, came to a climax in the popular movement which resisted secession and in the opening months of the war organized a Unionist convention at Wheeling.[29] The Wheeling convention considered two alternatives: separation from Virginia and the creation of a new state, or the reorganization of the Virginia government on a loyal basis. Choosing the more conservative course of restoring the state government, the convention constituted itself a state legislature and appointed a governor, Francis H. Pierpont, and other officers to carry on the machinery of government until regular elections could be held. United States representatives had been elected in May under the existing election laws, and on July 2 the general assembly elected John Carlile and Waitman Willey senators. Although subsequently the proposal for separate statehood gained support, for

---

ment played an important role in keeping them in the Union, relying to a considerable extent on military power. In Maryland, for example, federal forces occupied Annapolis and Baltimore, arresting members of the state legislature known to be secessionists. In Missouri, the Union military reconvened the state convention which the governor, a secessionist, had dismissed because of its Unionist majority. Under the protection of federal force, the convention then chose a Unionist governor. William B. Hesseltine sees these experiences in the border states, in which military power was used to establish loyal governments, as providing the basis for Lincoln's approach to reconstruction. Thus Hesseltine says of Maryland, "Substantially, it was the first Southern state to be conquered, and the first to be reconstructed." Because these states did not leave the Union and did not present the constitutional problem discussed in Chapter 1, they have not been considered examples of reconstruction in the present work. See Hesseltine's *Lincoln's Plan of Reconstruction* (Tuscaloosa, Ala., 1960), 21–30.

[29] On the background of the West Virginia statehood movement, see James C. McGregor, *The Disruption of Virginia* (New York, 1922); Richard O. Curry, *A House Divided: A Study of Statehood Politics and the Copperhead Movement in West Virginia* (Pittsburgh, 1964); and George E. Moore, *A Banner in the Hills: West Virginia's Statehood* (New York, 1963).

the present it was set aside as too radical.[30] The important fact was that a loyal government of Virginia had been restored.

The presence in Washington of senators and representatives from Virginia provided the first of several cases during the war in which Congress had to decide the status of a seceded state that was seeking readmission. In accordance with the policy Lincoln outlined in his message of July 4, Congress recognized the Wheeling government as the legitimate government of Virginia. Many congressmen saw Virginia as a model of reconstruction and wanted to recognize it, in order to encourage Unionists elsewhere. Moreover, if Virginia was to be divided, as some no doubt hoped, it was necessary to recognize it as a state in the Union so that it could consent to the division.[31]

On the opening day of Congress three representatives from Virginia were admitted to seats in the House. The only objection came from Henry C. Burnett, a Democrat of Kentucky, who argued that since the Richmond government had repealed the regular state election law, the Virginia representatives had been illegally elected. On the basis of Thaddeus Stevens' contention that the Virginia members-elect held certificates of election and were prima facie entitled to be sworn in, the House rejected Burnett's motion to refer the question to the Committee on Elections.[32]

---

[30] McGregor, *The Disruption of Virginia*, 208; Curry, *A House Divided*, 69–72.

[31] Art. IV, sec. 3, of the Constitution states: ". . . no new state shall be formed or erected within the jurisdiction of any other state; nor any state be formed by the junction of two or more states, or parts of states, without the consent of the legislatures of the states concerned as well as of the Congress." The decision at Wheeling to reorganize the old state government had been taken in part with an eye to this aspect of the situation. See Charles H. Ambler, *Francis H. Pierpont* (Chapel Hill, N.C., 1937), 88; Curry, *A House Divided*, 71; and Moore, *A Banner in the Hills*, 83.

[32] *Cong. Globe*, 37 Cong., 1 sess., 6 (July 4, 1861). The House acted differently on July 8 in referring to the Committee on Elections the case of Charles Upton, representative-elect from the Alexandria district. Ap-

Although this disposition of the case showed an inclination to accept the Pierpont government as the legitimate government of the state, in a strict sense it signified only that the House did not recognize the repeal of the state election law by the rebel authorities at Richmond.[33] The first true test, therefore, of the legitimacy of the restored government was the attempt of Waitman Willey and John Carlile to be admitted to the Senate.[34]

As in the House, Republicans supported the claim of the Virginia delegates while border-state men provided opposition. James Bayard of Delaware, seeking to refer the credentials to the judiciary committee, criticized any attempt to "recognize a government of the State of Virginia, which is not the regular State government." But John P. Hale, a Republican of New Hampshire, declared, "It becomes this Government to recognize the loyal and the true men that still cling to the Union and support the Constitution." Hale urged, "If there are loyal men in Virginia that are determined to stand by the cause of civil liberty . . . , let them rally; let them form a constitutional Government as they best may; and let this Federal Government pour them out men and money if necessary to sustain them in their contest." Lyman Trumbull of Illinois hoped the Senate would not "stick in the bark" on the Virginia question. Pointing out that the loyal men in the state had elected a legislature, Trum-

---

parently, however, the legitimacy of the restored government was not being challenged in this instance. S. S. Cox, the Democrat from Ohio who initiated the motion, asserted that Upton was a resident of Ohio and had voted there in 1860, a charge that Upton did not deny. For this reason, and not because of opposition to the restored government, the case seemed worth investigating. Upton was sworn in and held his seat until February 1862, when the House, in a decision that did reflect on the way in which Virginia had been restored, declared that he had not been legally elected (*ibid.*, 24 [July 8, 1861]).

[33] *Ibid.*, 6 (July 4, 1861); cf. the remarks of Carlile. Carlile was a representative from Virginia before being elected senator.

[34] Andrew Johnson of Tennessee was present at the opening of Congress, but as he had been in the Senate since 1857, no question arose concerning his credentials.

bull said, "If Virginia is in the Union, her loyal men . . . have a right to be represented here." [35]

Rejecting the argument of Lazarus Powell of Kentucky that the Wheeling government did not represent a majority of the people of Virginia, the Senate admitted Willey and Carlile by a vote of 35 to 5.[36] Some Republicans hoped the readmission of Virginia would establish the mode of reconstruction for the other states. Henry Lane of Indiana cited North Carolina as a state that would soon return, and James Doolittle of Wisconsin said, "What has transpired in this body already has shown how reconstruction may go on." Doolittle believed that Tennessee would follow the example of Virginia in "reconstructing, redeeming, regenerating herself . . . [and] taking her position once more upon the Constitution." [37]

Willingness to support Unionists in seceded states was evident also in debates concerning the military academy at West Point. Because southern representatives had failed to make appointments, there were many vacancies in the cadet corps. How they should be filled raised a question concerning policy toward Unionists living in the rebel states. One course suggested was to fill the vacancies by appointments from the loyal states. The Senate rejected this suggestion, however, in part because of the traditional dislike of some senators for the military academy, but also because such a solution would be unfair to the Union men in the South.[38] Another proposal was to allow the President to appoint cadets from among loyalists in the rebel states, a pro-

[35] *Cong. Globe*, 37 Cong., 1 sess., 103–105 (July 13, 1861).
[36] *Ibid.*, 109 (July 13, 1861).
[37] *Ibid.*, 144 (July 16, 1861); 263 (July 25, 1861).
[38] *Ibid.*, 89 (July 12, 1861), remarks of Ben Wade; 182 (July 18, 1861), remarks of Zachariah Chandler. At one point Chandler declared: "I hope these places may remain open for the appointment of good Union men when those States shall return to their allegiance. I am perfectly confident that there are sound Union men in every one of the seceded States; and I think it is but a simple act of justice to the Union men in those States that these places should remain vacant until they return to their allegiance."

cedure which would also help to promote Unionist movements in those states.[39] Most senators apparently felt that the war would soon be over, making new legislation unnecessary, and consequently rejected this proposition even though it had the backing of Henry Wilson, the Republican chairman of the Committee on Military Affairs.[40]

The House also dealt with the problem of West Point. The Committee on Military Affairs, headed by Frank Blair of Missouri, proposed to fill the vacancies by appointments from the loyal slave-holding states, but this proposal was overwhelmingly defeated as a "sectional" measure.[41] As in the Senate, Republicans attempted unsuccessfully to fill the vacancies with Unionists from the seceded states. Finally the House passed a bill authorizing the President to deal with the problem by making appointments at large. Abram Olin, the Republican of New York who introduced the measure, explained, however, "Such vacancies will be filled, wherever they can be, from the districts which are not represented." [42] The House passed a similar bill for the naval academy, but the Senate took no action on either measure, and existing arrangements for appointing cadets and midshipmen remained in effect. Nevertheless, the debates showed the interest of many members of Congress in encouraging and supporting southern Unionism.

A more important issue involving reconstruction was raised by a bill that would have established Congress as the source of authority for governing parts of the South recovered from re-

[39] *Ibid.*, 180, 183 (July 18, 1861), remarks of Ben Wade and Jacob Collamer; 182, remarks of Daniel Clark. Clark, a Republican, thought it wise to let the President "have it in his power to hold out some inducements to the Union men in the seceding States, in filling up these vacancies, and show them that there is some advantage still to be held out to the Union men in those States, and that they may have the advantage of these places."

[40] *Ibid.*, 184 (July 18, 1861). The vote was 17 to 23, with Republicans dividing, 12 for and 13 opposed.

[41] *Ibid.*, 212 (July 19, 1861). Cf. the remarks of Roscoe Conkling.

[42] *Ibid.*, 348 (July 30, 1861).

bellion. Though introduced by Senator Lyman Trumbull of Illinois, a Republican, this was no administration measure. On the contrary, it challenged the executive control over reconstruction that was implicit in control of the military establishment. This central issue in reconstruction—conflict over the authority of the executive and legislative branches—so divided the Senate that no final action on the bill was taken.

The chief significance of the bill was that it presumed, under the circumstances, to legislate on the exercise of military power. It authorized military commanders to declare territories designated by the President to be in a state of insurrection and war, suspended the writ of habeas corpus, and authorized military commanders to try persons found bearing arms against the United States and to administer an oath of allegiance to persons suspected of disloyalty. Furthermore, the bill established a form of military government over rebellious districts by authorizing military authorities to "make and publish such police rules and regulations" as might be necessary to suppress the rebellion and restore order in insurrectionary districts.[43] Because this grant of power gave no assurance that state laws would be respected, the judiciary committee, to whom the bill was referred, amended it by specifying that military commanders should make rules and regulations "conforming as nearly as may be to previously existing laws and regulations." [44] In this way the committee upheld the principle of recognizing the pre-existing governments in the seceded states.

Equally significant was the implication contained in the bill that before resuming their original places in the Union, the rebellious states would have to pass through a period of military government under the control of Congress. This proviso repre-

[43] 37 Congress, Senate Bill 33, introduced July 17, 1861, section 2. Hereafter abbreviations are used in the following form: 37 Cong., S. 33, July 17, 1861, sec. 2.

[44] *Cong. Globe,* 37 Cong., 1 sess., 336 (July 30, 1861); S. 33, amendment by Trumbull, July 26, 1861, sec. 2.

sented a new line of thought concerning reconstruction, for it meant that the states would not be restored directly by Unionist movements, as happened in Virginia, but would come under direct federal—and congressional—control during an interim period before actual reconstruction.

Debate on the bill revealed the existence of three positions: support for military government under executive control, support for such government under congressional control, and opposition to military rule in the states in any form. Jacob Collamer, a Republican of Vermont, represented the first point of view. He believed that, in reconstructing the union, it would be necessary to impose temporary military governments on the rebellious states. He opposed the bill, however, on the ground that by the laws of war the President already had the power to do what Congress was proposing to authorize him to do. Nor was the main provision of the bill, permitting a military commander to "make arrangements for the government of the civil affairs of that part of the country of which he takes possession," unprecedented; on the contrary, said Collamer, it included one of the "rights of war" which the United States had exercised in the Mexican War in setting up military governments in California and New Mexico. Collamer thought that in states which had reorganized a loyal government the military commander ought to request that government to appoint officers to regulate civil affairs. But in states where there was no recognized government, he added, "You must establish temporary governments as all people do when you go on conquering a country." In Collamer's opinion, the "rebel provinces" could again form state governments only by passing through "this transition state of constraint," the power to oversee which was inherent in the presidential office and did not derive from Congress.[45]

The second of the three positions was taken by the senator who introduced the bill, Lyman Trumbull, and by others like Edward D. Baker. They regarded military government as neces-

[45] *Cong. Globe*, 37 Cong., 1 sess., 374 (Aug. 1, 1861).

sary but thought that Congress ought to control the process. Trumbull said plainly that his object in introducing the bill was to confer the necessary power on the military authorities to suppress the rebellion and to regulate the exercise of that power. He explained that when Congress was not in session, emergency actions by the President were necessary, but that "after Congress convenes, . . . we shall be derelict in our duty if we leave our positions here without having regulated by law the action of the Executive." [46] Citing the constitutional power of Congress to declare war and raise armies, and to make rules concerning captures on land and water and for the governing of land and naval forces, Trumbull said that Congress was "necessarily clothed with all the power to make the war effective, to put the rebellion down, and restore peace to the country." Without regulation by law, Trumbull warned, a military commander might "on his own mere motion establish just such a system as he pleases." [47]

Edward D. Baker similarly argued for congressional authority over the military in the government of rebellious districts. "Look at the fact," he said. "The civil power is utterly overwhelmed; the courts are closed; the judges banished." Obviously there was a need for some kind of military government. But, granting that the President had to execute the laws through military commanders, Baker nevertheless asked, "Are they to do it with regulation, or without it? That is the only question." On this issue Baker's stand was consistent with his previously stated view that the seceded states might be regarded as territories. Refuting the charge that the bill was unconstitutional because the President had no authority to declare a state in insurrection, Baker pointed out, "The bill does not say a word about States." "In point of fact," he explained, "the Constitution of the United States, and the Congress . . . acting upon it, are not treating of States, but of the territory comprising the United States." Baker

[46] *Ibid.*, 337 (July 30, 1861).   [47] *Ibid.*, 373 (Aug. 1, 1861).

concluded that it was the government's duty "to preserve, in the terms of the bill, the liberty, lives, and property of the people of the country by just and fair police regulations." [48]

Some senators who were not prepared to vote for the bill nonetheless thought that Congress possessed authority to oversee military government in the seceded states, and were not sure that as a matter of policy it ought not to attempt to do so. John Ten Eyck, a Republican of New Jersey, could not support every provision of the measure, but he appreciated the need for "some regulation of this matter." Noting that in Virginia "all law was beaten down and disregarded," he asserted that "there ought to be some act of Congress prescribing and defining the duties" of military officers who would be acting as "conservators of the peace." The alternative was to "suffer the military to regulate the whole thing according to their own will and dictation." [49] Another Republican senator, Ira Harris of New York, advised postponing consideration of the bill until December, when the government would control "not only a belt of country along the borders of the Potomac, but we shall have the whole State of Virginia, and . . . still more territory, which will be embraced within the considerations which the bill involves." The basic problem, said Harris, was that in some areas "a perfect state of anarchy" prevailed; "civil authority has disappeared; civil government no longer exists." Though he tended to think that the military had power, without civil process, to try persons arrested for committing crimes, he said that he had come to that conclusion with much hesitation, and he had "no doubt that it will become necessary for Congress . . . to mature a bill on the subject" at its next regular session.[50] Harris later led an attempt to assert congressional authority over reconstruction, and his remarks, along with those of Baker, Trumbull, and Ten Eyck, make it clear that some congressional Republicans were already moving in this direction in the summer of 1861.

[48] *Ibid.*, 378 (Aug. 1, 1861).   [49] *Ibid.*, 342 (July 30, 1861).
[50] *Ibid.*, 372 (Aug. 1, 1861).

Voicing opposition to any form of military government over the rebellious states, John Breckinridge of Kentucky said, "It is a bill . . . which abolishes . . . all State governments, all the judicial, executive, and legislative functions of State governments, and authorizes subordinate military commanders to substitute rules and regulations at their will for the laws of the different Commonwealths of this Union." [51] Timothy Howe, a Republican of Wisconsin, argued that while the suppression of the rebel governments would destroy all local government, the Union army ought not to administer civil government, because the army was not representative of the people. Advising that federal forces be confined "to the single purpose of flinging off the scum," Howe said, "If you find underneath that a residuum of loyalty represented by a portion of the people . . . , the very necessity of the case and their old instincts will induce them and compel them to provide for that local government and to reorganize it." According to James Doolittle, a Republican of Wisconsin, the bill exceeded the power of Congress to make regulations concerning the armies of the United States. Reminding his "friends on this side of the Chamber" that the purpose of the war was "not . . . to subjugate any State of the Union" or to "subject them to the control of our armies," Doolittle avowed that it was "to enable the loyal people of the several States of this Union to reconstruct themselves upon the Constitution." [52]

These differences of opinion prevented any final action on the bill at the special session. One reason it was not revived at the next meeting of Congress was that by this time the executive department had begun to assert its authority in regulating the army in rebel districts, a process that was temporarily completed in 1863 with the publication of General Orders 100 for the government of Union armies in the field.[53] But more important, by the next session of Congress, Republican members concerned

[51] *Ibid.*   [52] *Ibid.*, 380–381 (Aug. 1, 1861).
[53] Frank Freidel, "General Orders 100 and Military Government," *Mississippi Valley Historical Review*, XXXII (March, 1946), 541–556.

with the government of occupied rebel states developed a more consistent and thoroughly legislative solution to the problem—territorialization.

Congress adjourned on August 6, after ratifying Lincoln's strong action in meeting the opening of hostilities and after enacting important measures for prosecuting the war. Hoping for a swift victory, Union authorities also considered reconstruction. Both Congress and the President recognized the reorganized government of Virginia, thereby endorsing the theory that in the rebel states loyal men constituted the state and were capable of restoring it to its position in the Union. The problem of defining war aims also involved ideas about reconstruction. The Crittenden and Johnson resolutions dealt with this issue along lines acceptable to both Democrats and Republicans, setting forth the essentially conservative goal of restoring the old Union with the rights of the states unimpaired. Despite this action by Congress, there was a tendency—which was obviously radical in its political implications—to think of reconstruction in terms of imposing territorial governments on the seceded states. This tendency reflected a constitutional understanding common to many Union men, namely, that governing the rebel districts was a legislative rather than an executive function. Already the conflict of authority between the President and Congress, which dominated the later phases of reconstruction, was foreshadowed. At the regular session of Congress in December 1861, Republican congressmen developed these ideas more fully and expressed them in concrete proposals which challenged the theory and policy of reconstruction adopted in July.

III

Reconstruction as Territorialization

WHEN Congress met in regular session on December 2, 1861, the war had been in progress for nearly eight months. Gone was any real expectation that the Union would be quickly restored by a return to the *status quo ante bellum.* Gone also was the tendency toward compromise and forbearance predicated upon such a hope or expectation. Instead, more radical ideas, which earlier had merely been broached, now came to the fore. Of these the most significant was territorialization—the idea that the seceded states had reverted to the status of territories and must be governed by Congress.

The new mood was a response to military developments since the summer of 1861 and a reflection of growing antislavery sentiment in the Republican party. In the last half of 1861 the Union navy captured a few forts along the southern coast, but the Army of the Potomac remained in camp most of the time, thereby arousing criticism of the administration's conduct of the war. This criticism turned to bitter opposition among many Republicans after the Battle of Ball's Bluff in October, a defeat nearly as disastrous as Bull Run had been. When Congress met, therefore, dissatisfaction with military policy was so keen that

40

congressional critics were able to create their own joint Committee on the Conduct of the War.[1]

Many Republicans were also dissatisfied with the attitude of the administration toward slavery. The dissatisfaction became apparent when General John C. Fremont challenged Lincoln's policy of noninterference with slavery. In August 1861, Fremont, commanding in Missouri, issued a proclamation confiscating the property and emancipating the slaves of all persons in the state who were in arms against the United States or supporting the rebellion. This order directly contradicted the government's policy of enforcing the fugitive-slave law affecting escaped slaves in loyal states, and the confiscation act of August 6, 1861, which freed slaves in rebellious states who were employed for military purposes.[2] Politically, Fremont's action was inconsistent with administration efforts to keep the border states in the Union. "There is great danger," Lincoln wrote to Fremont on September 2, 1861, that "the confiscation of property, and the liberating slaves of traiterous [sic] owners, will alarm our Southern Union friends, and turn them against us—perhaps ruin our rather fair prospect for Kentucky." He asked Fremont to modify his proclamation in accordance with the confiscation act of Congress, and after some hesitation Fremont agreed.[3]

Although public opinion in general came to support the President, there was an initial hostile reaction to his repudiation of Fremont's order, even among some conservative Republicans, and a continuing resentment on the part of more radical antislavery men. At the Massachusetts Republican state convention in October, for example, Senator Charles Sumner urged a policy of emancipation as a means of ending the war, and in December,

[1] T. Harry Williams, *Lincoln and the Radicals* (Madison, Wis., 1941), 62–66.

[2] James Ford Rhodes, *History of the United States from the Compromise of 1850 to the Final Restoration of Home Rule at the South in 1877* (7 vols.; New York, 1912), III, 467.

[3] Lincoln to John C. Fremont, Sept. 2, 1861, in *Collected Works of Lincoln*, IV, 506.

Republican Representative Thomas D. Eliot of Massachusetts criticized Lincoln's interference with Fremont's proclamation, which he called "a blow struck in the right direction, by the right man, at the right time, under the right circumstances." [4] Antislavery men, in short, were impatient with what one of them referred to as the "infernal idea of carrying on a war for the Union *upon border-state specifications* and dictation." [5]

Thus by the time Congress assembled many Republicans were critical of the conduct of the war and sought a more aggressive policy against slavery. It was clear, too, that there was disagreement within the party over reconstruction, and that this was related to the administration's slavery policy. Eliot of Massachusetts expressed the conjunction of these issues when he told the House, "Reconstruction must come, but in the rebellious and seceding States, when it comes, it shall come . . . without the presence of the slave." [6] Another Republican member of the House, Martin Conway of Kansas, said the administration was cooperating with loyal slaveholders in order to restore the seceded states with slavery intact. Referring to the reorganized government of Virginia, Conway charged, "These skeleton State organizations are nothing but the machinery of political artificers for monopolizing power" and for trying to get "the whole body of slaveholders firmly planted once more on the side of the Union." [7] Representative George S. Boutwell of Massachusetts also criticized the policy of reconstruction adopted at the start of the war. Rejecting the idea that the rebellious states were entitled to the protection of the Constitution, Boutwell said that whatever was necessary to reestablish federal authority

[4] James G. Randall, *Lincoln the President* (4 vols.; New York, 1945–1955), II, 21; James M. McPherson, *The Struggle for Equality: Abolitionists and the Negro in the Civil War and Reconstruction* (Princeton, 1964), 73–76; Sumner, *Works*, VI, 1–29; *Cong. Globe*, 37 Cong., 2 sess., 80 (Dec. 12, 1861).
[5] Quoted in Rhodes, *History of the United States*, III, 475.
[6] *Cong. Globe*, 37 Cong., 2 sess., 78 (Dec. 12, 1861).
[7] *Ibid.*, 86 (Dec. 12, 1861).

was legitimate. He reasoned, "The Constitution, if it secures any thing, secures the integrity of the territory over which and to which . . . [it] applies." Boutwell questioned the recognizing of loyal citizens as the state, warning, "We cannot stop now . . . to inquire whether, in South Carolina, or in Georgia or in Tennessee, there may be men who, if they could, would be loyal to the Union." [8]

This disagreement within the Republican party was significant, because military events were making reconstruction an important problem of policy. The capture of the Sea Islands off South Carolina in November 1861 forced consideration of this issue, and in the first six months of 1862, Union victories in North Carolina, Tennessee, Arkansas, and Louisiana presented federal authorities with the problem of governing rebellious districts.[9]

In dealing with the situation that existed following the collapse of Confederate authority, three basic courses were open. First, on the theory that the states were indestructible and that the loyal citizens constituted the state, the federal government might rely on local Unionists to restore their state government. The Wheeling government in Virginia provided the model for this kind of reconstruction. Many Union men thought the federal government could depend on Unionists in other rebel states to behave similarly, and for a brief while in 1861 hoped that North Carolina would follow the example of Virginia. Yet

[8] George S. Boutwell, *Emancipation: Its Justice, Expediency, and Necessity* . . . (Boston, 1861), 4–5.

[9] The nature of the problem was described by a constituent of Representative Henry L. Dawes of Massachusetts who wrote shortly after the Sea Islands expedition, "A portion of S.C. has been reclaimed & yet no measures as to the future decided upon. A military occupation is had— without any course fixed which shall follow such military occupation." The writer also reflected the drift toward more radical ideas, in advocating the confiscation of rebel estates and the settlement of South Carolina by "enterprising free men" of Massachusetts, who would "give another tone hereafter to Southern music" (J. E. Field to Henry L. Dawes, Dec. 1, 1861, Dawes Papers, Library of Congress).

events soon revealed that the fundamental precondition of success in Virginia—a substantial body of loyal citizens—existed in no other rebel state. Consequently this approach to reconstruction became irrelevant in 1862.

A second course open was to create, under federal authority, interim governments that would maintain peace and order until the loyal citizens could restore their pre-existing state government. Either military authority under the executive, or civil authority under Congress could perform this function, though in American constitutional history there was clearer precedent for the former, in the military government established in parts of Mexico during the Mexican War.[10] Whatever the nature of the authority, however, the central purpose was to administer civil affairs in accordance with existing laws and institutions until the loyal citizens could resume the conduct of state government.

A third approach to reconstruction was to establish plenary federal power in the occupied states, in plain disregard of state rights. This would be a temporary authority, but it would be an authority capable of altering the laws and institutions of the rebel states. Although military government could be used for such a purpose, it was not likely to be so used under Lincoln, committed as he was to restoration of the old Union with the powers of the federal government and the states unchanged. Instead, this radical attitude toward reconstruction found expression in Congress, in proposals for the establishment of provisional civil governments with full legislative power over the occupied states. Distinctive in this procedure—the reason why it may aptly be called territorialization—was the idea, based on the assumption that the states had been destroyed, of creating territorial governments and admitting new states to the Union on terms set by Congress. Far from being merely a bridge leading to the restoration of the occupied states to their previous places

---

[10] See Justin H. Smith, "American Rule in Mexico," *American Historical Review*, XXIII (Jan. 1918), 287–302; and Theodore Grivas, *Military Governments in California, 1846–1850* (Glendale, Calif., 1963).

in the Union, territorialization was a potentially revolutionary instrument.

At the start of the second session of the Thirty-seventh Congress, the House continued to uphold the first of these three methods of reconstruction by admitting Horace Maynard and Andrew Clements of Tennessee and Jacob Blair of Virginia. Each had polled a substantial number of votes and clearly seemed to be the choice of the majority of Union men in his district.[11] But this recognition of a second rebel state, Tennessee, as a member of the Union—for this was the implication of admitting a representative to a seat in Congress—did not pass unchallenged, and now it was Republicans who questioned it. Thaddeus Stevens proposed that the credentials of members-elect from states in rebellion be referred to the elections committee, since, said Stevens, "we know that their States are, so far as they can be, out of the Union." Noting that some representatives from Virginia had been chosen by as few as twenty votes,[12] Stevens called such representation "a mere mockery" and urged exclusion of members from rebel districts, at least until their cases had been investigated.[13]

Evidence that the Virginia method of reconstruction still seemed viable was the attempt to use it in North Carolina. President Lincoln called attention to this effort in his annual message

[11] Maynard and Clements had been elected on August 1, 1861, the regular election day in Tennessee. Maynard, who had about 10,000 votes, was seated on December 2. Clements, who polled about 2000 out of a total of 6000 votes—the other votes cast were for candidates to the Confederate Congress—had his case referred to the Committee on Elections and was seated, upon recommendation of the committee, on January 13, 1862. Blair, elected to fill the vacancy caused by the election of John Carlile to the Senate, received about 7000 votes in his western Virginia district and was admitted on December 2 (*Cong. Globe*, 37 Cong., 2 sess., 3 [Dec. 2, 1861]; *Reports of Committees of the House of Representatives*, 37 Cong., 2 sess., no. 9, Andrew J. Clements, 3).

[12] Stevens probably referred to Charles Upton, who was seated in July but subsequently was judged not to be the legitimate representative of his district.

[13] *Cong. Globe*, 37 Cong., 2 sess., 2 (Dec. 2, 1861).

to Congress in December. Noting the capture of Fort Hatteras, Port Royal, and other points on the southern coast, he said: "We likewise have some general accounts of popular movements, in behalf of the Union, in North Carolina and Tennessee. These things demonstrate that the cause of the Union is advancing steadily and certainly southward." The movement Lincoln referred to in North Carolina had begun in September 1861, when a limited degree of Union support became apparent along Pamlico Sound. About 250 persons took an oath of allegiance to the United States, and officials believed that many others would do so if they did not have to fear reprisals by Confederate authorities. In November a meeting was held in New York to promote support for the Unionist movement in North Carolina, and shortly thereafter a handful of North Carolinians met at Hatteras to form a provisional civil government. On November 28 the polls were opened, and Charles H. Foster, with 224 votes, was elected United States Representative.[14]

If there was any serious hope that this action might result in the restoration of North Carolina to the Union, it proved unwarranted. With Republicans like Stevens already questioning the restoration of Virginia, there was little disposition to regard Foster as a legitimate representative. Even the moderate, pro-administration New York *Times* warned against setting "dangerous precedents" by admitting to a seat someone who made "no claim to represent any defined Congressional district" and who offered "no proof that his constituency reach[ed] the numbers required as a basis of representation."[15] The House referred Foster's case to the Committee on Elections, who were unanimous against him, and on December 18 the House approved the committee's recommendation that he not be ad-

[14] Annual Message to Congress, Dec. 3, 1861, *Collected Works of Lincoln*, V, 50; J. G. DeRoulhac Hamilton, *Reconstruction in North Carolina* (New York, 1914), 82–86; Norman C. Delaney, "Charles Henry Foster and the Unionists of Eastern North Carolina," *North Carolina Historical Review*, XXXVII (July 1960), 348–366.

[15] New York *Times*, Dec. 3, 1861, p. 4.

mitted. In the next few months, elections continued to be held by the so-called provisional government of North Carolina, and Foster, with about a hundred votes, kept applying for a seat, but to no avail.[16]

In other election cases the House in effect rejected, though it did not formally repudiate, the theory that the loyal citizens were the state and were entitled to representation. Joseph Segar of Virginia was refused admission, and Charles Upton, also of Virginia, was voted out of a seat he had held since July. These cases were important because many members considered them tests of the theory of reconstruction according to which Virginia had been recognized and other states might be restored to the Union. In the first of the two cases, Segar claimed election as representative of the first district in Virginia, under an ordinance passed by the Wheeling government. Although he had only 25 votes—almost the entire district was under rebel control —he argued that because the loyal Virginia government had been recognized as legitimate, the number of votes he had received was immaterial.[17] Upton, with only 10 votes, claimed election under the regular election laws of Virginia. Supporters of these claims, such as John Noell, a Democrat of Missouri, asserted that the Union would have to be restored by some such process as that by which Upton had been chosen. Referring to Tennessee, Noell argued, "You cannot get a majority of the people . . . to unite in an effort to bring that State back into the Union as it was before." "The loyal people of the State are the State," he insisted, and if restoration of the Union was to take place, it would have to be accomplished "through the instrumentality of minorities of the people of the seceded States. . . . It will not do to say that actual majorities must elect members." Noell concluded that a decision against Segar "bars the door against reconstruction of the Union." [18] Some Repub-

---

[16] *House Reports*, 37 Cong., 2 sess., no. 118, Charles Henry Foster.

[17] *House Misc. Docs.*, 37 Cong., 2 sess., no. 29, Joseph Segar, 3.

[18] *Cong. Globe*, 37 Cong., 2 sess., 734–735 (Feb. 10, 1862).

licans agreed with this analysis. Charles Delano of Massachusetts, for example, said that the real issue was whether it was "competent for the majority . . . of the voters of that district, by actual force or submission to force, to disfranchise the minority." Delano held that only on the theory that the loyal citizens, however few, were the state, "may [we] look for a restoration of the old Union, and to a return of the thirty-four States in all their original features and identity." [19]

The Committee on Elections reported against both Virginia claimants, on the ground that neither had been freely elected by the voters of his district, rebel obstruction having prevented the great majority of people from participating in the election. Committee Chairman Henry Dawes said, however, that if Segar had been able to demonstrate the support of the legal loyal voters, he would have been admitted, no matter how few they might be. The House accepted the committee's findings and rejected both Segar and Upton. [20] The theory behind this disposition of the cases did not deny that the loyal citizens were the state and could be represented. But the theory was based on the supposition, asserted by its proponents as fact, that the loyal electorate had been prevented from voting and that it was larger than the handful who had voted. It was clear that Unionist strength in the two districts was practically nonexistent, however, and the result of the election reflected this fact, regardless of the theory. Thus by February 1862, with the failure of the Unionist movement in North Carolina and the rejection of additional representatives from Virginia, the theory of state indestructibility and of the identification of loyal citizens as the state ceased to be a viable approach to the problem of reconstruction.

If loyal citizens in the seceded states were unable to organize local governments, it was obvious that the federal government

---

[19] *Ibid.*, 1002–1003 (Feb. 27, 1862).

[20] *House Reports*, 37 Cong., 2 sess., no. 12, Joseph Segar; no. 17, Charles Upton; *Cong. Globe*, 37 Cong., 2 sess., 757 (Feb. 11, 1862); 759 (Feb. 11, 1862); 1010 (Feb. 27, 1862).

would have to do so. Any assertion of direct national power over local affairs would have been a departure from past constitutional practice of course, but there were alternative ways in which this power could be exercised. One was to create an interim government that would confine itself to maintaining order and enforcing the existing laws of the occupied state. This was Lincoln's approach. Although he eventually settled on a military solution, initially he was inclined to rely upon civil authority under congressional direction to implement his policy, as was evident in his annual message of December 1861, when he suggested that Congress deal with the administration of justice in rebellious districts. Calling attention to the same problem that several congressmen had brought up at the special session in July, Lincoln referred to "the entire suppression in many places, of all the ordinary means of administering civil justice by the officers and in the forms of existing law." He said that he had been urged "to establish, by military power, courts to administer summary justice," but had not done so, because he was "unwilling to go beyond the pressure of necessity in the unusual exercise of power." Instead, Lincoln suggested, the proper remedy lay with Congress. "The powers of Congress, I suppose, are equal to the anomalous occasion," he said; he therefore referred "the whole matter to Congress, with the hope that a plan may be devised for the administration of justice in all such parts of the insurgent States and Territories as may be under the control of this government, whether by a voluntary return to allegiance and order or by the power of our arms." He added that any such method of administration would "not . . . be a permanent institution, but a temporary substitute, and . . . [would] cease as soon as the ordinary courts can be re-established in peace." [21]

The idea of an interim civil authority also was the basis of two legislative proposals introduced into Congress at this time. On

[21] Annual Message to Congress, Dec. 3, 1861, *Collected Works of Lincoln*, V, 43-44.

December 18, 1861, Senator James Doolittle, a Republican of Wisconsin, and on January 15, 1862, Representative Frank Blair, a Republican of Missouri, introduced bills that provided for the appointment of a board of three commissioners for each rebellious state. Although their primary function would be to collect taxes, the commissioners were authorized, by and with the approval of the commanding general in each district, to "make such temporary rules for the order and government of all persons residing within the said district as shall be just and humane." Rules and regulations of the commissioners had to be approved by the President and submitted to Congress for possible revision and modification. The proposed local governments would be created upon the establishment of federal military power in any district or county and would continue "until the authority of the Federal Government and a loyal State government shall be established." [22] Explaining the scope of the interim authority, Doolittle said that the commissioners would "make police regulations for the government of the district until the civil authority of the Government is re-established." In suppressing the rebellion, he advised, "it is necessary that we should send along with the armies which destroy, a reconstructing power." [23]

These proposals for temporary federal control, limited in scope and emanating from groups generally regarded as forming the conservative wing of the party, were moderate measures. More radical, and more appealing to those who sought for a more aggressive policy toward slavery, was the concept of territorialization, which received wide expression in the winter of 1861–1862.

On December 4, 1861, John Hutchins, a Republican from Ohio, introduced a resolution declaring, "It is the duty of the government of the United States to put down said rebellion

[22] 37 Cong., S. 121, Dec. 18, 1861, secs. 11, 13; H.R. 214, Jan. 15, 1862, secs. 10, 12.

[23] *Cong. Globe*, 37 Cong., 2 sess., 2059 (May 12, 1862), 3146 (July 7, 1862).

. . . , and to exercise territorial jurisdiction in and over all States whose people have repudiated the Constitution." The next day the New York *Tribune* suggested that "Florida, as a punishment for rebellion, might be reduced from its rank as a State, and restored to its original condition of a Territory." And on December 9, John Gurley, a Republican of Ohio, introduced a confiscation-and-colonization bill that provided a provisional government for Florida "similar to those of the Territories of the United States." [24]

During the ensuing weeks a number of Republicans explained more fully the theory of territorialization. Its proponents affirmed the perpetuity of the Union, denied that the people of any state could withdraw from the Union, and held that ordinances of secession were void. But they insisted, with John Bingham of Ohio, that the "treasonable civil organization [of the seceded states], while it is void as against the Federal Government, operates an absolute forfeiture of all *their* powers and rights as States." Charles Sumner expressed the same idea in declaring that secession, "when sustained by force . . . becomes a practical *abdication* by the State of all rights under the Constitution, while the treason which it involves still further works an instant *forfeiture* of all those functions and powers essential to the continued existence of the State as a body-politic." Thus, concluded Salmon P. Chase, a rebellious state "lapsed into the condition of a Territory." Fernando Beaman of Michigan applied all this to the situation of South Carolina. Her "State officers have abdicated," he explained, "and her State government, in so far as she is connected with the Union, has been abandoned; . . . her relation to the General Government is not unlike that of an unorganized territory." According to Beaman, the term "State" was "significant not so much of the land and inhabitants, as of the character of the political organization." Again citing South Carolina, Beaman asserted: "The people . . . deny that they constitute any portion of the United States; and

[24] 37 Cong., House Joint Resolution 13, Dec. 4, 1861; New York *Tribune*, Dec. 5, 1861, p. 4; 37 Cong., H.R. 121, Dec. 9, 1861.

thus they have cast off their corporate rights and abandoned their former political condition. . . . Their political condition as a State has been extinguished." [25]

Yet, though the states as political entities had been destroyed, the areas in question could not be separated from the Union. The land occupied by South Carolina was "a part of the soil of the United States," said Thomas D. Eliot of Massachusetts, "and it cannot be separated from it. It is a part of our territory, and it must be brought back." Beaman put the matter forcefully: "The United States is a nationality, a sovereign Power, with vast territorial possessions . . . over which it is entitled to governmental jurisdiction, from which allegiance is due, and to which it owes the obligations of protection and a just administration of law. . . . It is manifest that the Federal government has sovereign power over all parts of its possessions." [26]

The problem faced by Congress, said Charles Sumner, was to re-establish "rightful jurisdiction" which the United States might recognize. Advocates of territorialization conceded that military rule must immediately follow the collapse of rebel authority, but they objected to military government as a solution to the question of reconstruction. Fernando Beaman warned against the "design of establishing military governments, for any considerable duration, over seven millions of native-born Americans." To do so, he said, would be "incompatible with the spirit of our institutions." On the other hand, the loyal citizens in the southern states were such a hopeless minority that to rely upon them was "monstrous folly and madness." Thus Beaman proposed, as an alternative, "to take control of the territory and people lately recognized as a State, and spread over them such provisional government as might be suitable to their peculiar condition." Pursuing the same objective, Salmon P. Chase sug-

[25] *Cong. Globe*, 37 Cong., 2 sess., 1205 (March 12, 1862); 737 (Feb. 11, 1862); Salmon P. Chase, *Inside Lincoln's Cabinet: The Civil War Diaries of Salmon P. Chase*, ed. David Donald (New York, 1954), 51; *Cong. Globe*, 37 Cong., 2 sess., 1552 (Apr. 4, 1862).

[26] *Cong. Globe*, 37 Cong., 2 sess., 78 (Dec. 12, 1861); 1551–1552 (Apr. 4, 1862).

gested that Congress first "organize territorial courts," then, "as soon as it became necessary, a Territorial Government." [27]

Constitutional authority for territorialization derived from the general sovereign power of the federal government over United States territory. Thus Charles Sumner, pointing out that state goverments had been vacated, asserted that the jurisdiction of the federal government was "incident . . . to that guardianship and eminent domain belonging to the United States over all its territory." He insisted, "From the necessity of the case, . . . Congress must have jurisdiction over every portion of the United States *where there is no other government.*" The scope of this authority, finally, was unlimited. Said John Bingham of Ohio, "The only limitation that is imposed upon the power of this Government in the premises is that whenever any of these Territories presents a State government organized in subordination to the Federal Constitution, and recognized as such by the Federal Government, the State authority will be again established." [28]

The leading advocate of reconstruction as territorialization was Representative James M. Ashley of Ohio. Ashley, born in Pennsylvania in 1824 the son of an itinerant preacher, early became acquainted with slavery and came to hate it, while traveling with his father through Kentucky and Virginia. With no formal education, he left home at sixteen, worked on a river boat, and returned to Virginia, which he was asked to leave, however, because of his violent denunciations of slavery. In the 1840's he worked in a printing office in Ohio, studied law, and was admitted to the bar, though he never practiced. At first a Democrat, Ashley became a Free-Soiler in 1848 and a Republican in 1854. He was elected to the Thirty-sixth Congress in 1858.[29]

---

[27] Sumner, *Works,* VII, 529; *Cong. Globe,* 37 Cong., 2 sess., 1554 (April 4, 1862); Chase, *Inside Lincoln's Cabinet,* 51.

[28] Sumner, *Works,* VII, 534; *Cong. Globe,* 37 Cong., 2 sess., 1205 (March 12, 1862).

[29] *Dictionary of American Biography,* ed. Allen Johnson and Dumas

Re-elected to the Thirty-seventh Congress, Ashley became chairman of the Committee on Territories, from which position he promoted plans of territorialization. By the time Congress met in July 1861, Ashley had prepared a bill creating territorial governments in the seceded states. But the plan was too radical, even for his Republican colleagues on the committee, who would not agree to it, so Ashley contented himself with discussing the issue with Salmon P. Chase, Charles Sumner, and Henry Winter Davis, all of whom agreed with his fundamental point: "that Congress had power under the Constitution, to legislate for the government of States and districts in rebellion." Patient and determined, Ashley, according to his own account, "went to work to convert one by one, the Republican members of [his] committee." When Congress convened in December, Ashley and Ben Wade of Ohio, chairman of the Senate Committee on Territories, conferred with Secretary Chase and found him in agreement with their view that territorial governments should be established. Evidently encouraged, Ashley persuaded William Vandever, a Republican of Iowa, to introduce a resolution charging the Committee on Territories "to inquire into the legality and expediency of establishing territorial governments within the limits of the disloyal States and districts, and to report by bill or otherwise." Late in December the House approved the resolution by voice vote.[30]

The only comment Vandever's resolution evoked was a humorous query by Horace Maynard of Tennessee as to whether it would not be in order "to amend so as to provide that we should first get into the disloyal States."[31] This caused a ripple of laughter in the House, reflecting the feeling that the problem of reconstruction was not a practical one. In view of

Malone (22 vols.; New York, 1928–1944), I, 389; *Biographical Directory of the American Congress, 1774–1961* (85 Cong., 2 sess., House Doc. no. 442), 462.

[30] Ashley, *Orations and Speeches*, 360; Chase, *Inside Lincoln's Cabinet*, 50–51; *Cong. Globe*, 37 Cong., 2 sess., 168 (Dec. 23, 1861).

[31] *Cong. Globe*, 37 Cong., 2 sess., 168 (Dec. 23, 1861).

the bitter opposition that soon appeared against any suggestion of territorializing the states, however, it was surprising that no one else in Congress objected to Vandever's resolution. The virtues of the territorial idea meanwhile seemed clear to some observers. The Washington correspondent of the New York *Times*, for example, noted the adoption of the resolution with approval and commented, "Congress [should] decide upon some *uniform* and simple plan for the reconstruction, directly or through a provisional organization, of a loyal and *Republican* government for each State as it may be reclaimed." [32]

Although reconstruction may have seemed a remote issue, military developments were soon to force it to the forefront of public attention. While McClellan still hesitated in Virginia, Grant scored important victories in the west, capturing, within a ten-day period in February 1862, Forts Henry and Donelson, thereby breaking the front line of Confederate defense in western Tennessee. The most significant Union success since the start of hostilities, Grant's achievement inspired hope that the war would soon be over and made reconstruction a practical issue. The Washington correspondent of the New York *Post* reported on February 19 that news of the victories in Tennessee "set our legislators to planning a government for the disloyal states in the future." John Forney, secretary of the Senate and publisher of two Republican newspapers, wrote that Congress would soon take up "the stupendous question, What is to be the political relation of the revolted States when they are conquered?" From the Democratic side, the Columbus *Crisis* speculated on "the tug of war, *politically*," that would follow the military struggle. "Here is the great turning point in our future," explained the *Crisis*. "If the States are permitted to come back into the Union by States, as they went out, then all may be well." [33]

[32] New York *Times*, Dec. 28, 1861.
[33] New York *Post*, Feb. 19, 1862; Philadelphia *Press*, Feb. 15, 1862; Columbus, Ohio, *Crisis*, Feb. 19, 26, 1862.

Though reconstruction now for the first time attracted considerable public attention, legislative proposals based on the theory of territorialization had already been introduced. On December 26, 1861, James Harlan of Iowa introduced into the Senate a bill for the establishment of provisional governments in the South. Then, on February 11, 1862, just after the capture of Fort Henry, Charles Sumner offered a series of resolutions "declaratory of the relations between the United States and the territory once occupied by certain States, and now usurped by pretended Governments." The mere mention of these resolutions—they included Sumner's famous "state suicide" proposition—was enough to provoke protest, and two days later Garrett Davis of Kentucky countered with a set of resolutions indicating the conservative view of the relations between the seceded states and the federal government. On February 14, Senator Ira Harris of New York introduced a bill calling for the creation of provisional civil governments in the rebellious states.[34]

In the House, where reconstruction had received somewhat more attention, two relevant measures had been introduced: a bill by John Gurley of Ohio for a provisional government in Florida, and a proposal by John Hutchins of Ohio for territorial governments in all the seceded states. In February, as interest in reconstruction mounted, Ashley brought his bill of the previous summer before the Committee on Territories, which reported it to the House on March 12. And on March 7, Hutchins of Ohio gave notice of his intent to introduce a bill to establish "a provisional government for the territory formerly occupied by the state of South Carolina."[35]

Four of the authors of proposals for territorialization were

[34] 37 Cong., S. 132, Dec. 26, 1861; *Cong. Globe*, 37 Cong., 2 sess., 736–737 (Feb. 11, 1862); 786 (Feb. 13, 1862); 37 Cong., S. 200, Feb. 14, 1862.

[35] 37 Cong., H.R. 121, Dec. 9, 1861; H.R. 236, Jan. 20, 1862; H.R. 356, March 12, 1862, MS, National Archives, RG 233, 37A–B1; *Journal of the House of Representatives*, 37 Cong., 2 sess., 418.

from the old Northwest Territory—James Ashley, John
Hutchins and John Gurley of Ohio, and James Harlan of Iowa.
Harlan was the most prominent of the group. Born in Illinois in
1820, he grew up in Indiana, attended De Pauw University, and
then moved to Iowa, where he studied law and was admitted to
the bar in 1848. In the early 1850's, Harlan served as president
of Iowa Wesleyan University. He was elected to the Senate as a
Whig in 1855, but because of election irregularities, the Senate
declared his seat vacant. He won re-election in 1857, this time as
a Republican. Harlan was a strong antislavery man and during
the war was frequently on the radical side of questions relating
to the Negro. Like Edward D. Baker of Oregon, who had first
formulated the theory of territorialization in 1861, Harlan was a
close friend of President Lincoln. In March 1865, Lincoln
appointed him Secretary of the Interior, a post which he held
until 1866, when he broke with President Johnson.[36]

John Hutchins of Ohio, a graduate of Western Reserve College, was a lawyer active in state and local politics before being
elected as a Republican to the Thirty-sixth and the Thirty-
seventh Congresses. His political views, like those of most Republicans, were characterized by a strong antislavery attitude.
The same was true of John Gurley, also of Ohio. A New
Englander by birth, Gurley grew up in Connecticut and entered
the Universalist ministry. In the late 1830's he moved to Cincinnati and began publishing a newspaper. He was elected as a
Republican to Congress in 1858 and served two terms. Defeated
for re-election in 1862, he was appointed governor of the territory of Arizona but died in August 1863, before he could assume office.[37]

Senator Ira Harris of New York, the only easterner among
those who submitted plans for territorialization, was born in
New York in 1802. A graduate of Union College, Harris earned

[36] Johnson Brigham, *James Harlan* (Iowa City, Ia., 1913).
[37] *Biographical Directory of the American Congress, 1774–1961*, 1011,
983.

a distinguished reputation as a jurist and professor at Albany Law School. He was a Whig member of the New York Assembly in the 1840's and a judge of the state Supreme Court from 1847 to 1859. In 1860 he was elected to the Senate as a Republican and served one term. Though a consistent supporter of the administration, Harris was not intensely partisan, and contemporaries usually considered him a conservative.[38]

The historical significance of the proposals introduced by these five men was in their expression of the idea of territorialization. The actual historical relationship between the bills is less clear. Why, after the first bill was submitted in December 1861, were others so similar brought in? Possibly the similarity was coincidental. Rivalries may also have been involved, especially in the House, where Hutchins' bill was introduced and referred to the Committee on Territories in January 1862. Instead of making it the basis for its reconstruction proposal, the committee brought in a new measure. This of course was the bill of Ashley, who seems to have considered reconstruction a special concern of his, and who perhaps wanted to make his own proposal the basis of House action. In the Senate it was perhaps more understandable that two separate bills should be introduced, for there were significant differences between Harlan's measure of December and Harris' of February. Meanwhile, Sumner had submitted his "state suicide" resolutions, and the territorial committees of both houses apparently were inclined to support measures equally bold and sweeping. Under the circumstances, there was reason to bring in a bill for interim governments, based on the theory of territorialization, that did not go as far as those already introduced.

Gurley's bill of December 1861 was a confiscation-and-colonization measure which dealt in part with reconstruction. Restricted to Florida alone, it provided that the state should be occupied and governed by military law. When the President believed military government was no longer needed, he was to

[38] *Dictionary of American Biography*, VIII, 310.

"communicate the fact to Congress and recommend the erection of a provisional government similar to those of the Territories of the United States." Although the bill did not outline the precise steps to be taken, it carried the territorial principle to its logical conclusion by providing that "if there be sufficient loyal white inhabitants to entitle them to a representative in Congress, [the President] shall recommend the passage of an act authorizing them to form a State government, and adopt a constitution by which slavery or involuntary servitude shall be forever prohibited." [39] Gurley's bill was important because it foreshadowed subsequent proposals in two respects: it applied the principle of territorialization, and it made the prohibition of slavery a condition of readmission to the Union.

The bills of Harlan, Hutchins, Ashley, and Harris were general measures concerned with governing states or parts of states recovered from rebel authority. Their most important feature was their authorizing of the President to establish temporary civil governments possessing full legislative power over the seceded states. Patterned directly on the model of territorial government as it had developed by 1860, the provisional governments were to consist of executive, legislative, and judicial departments, supplemented by secretaries, marshals, and district attorneys. In form and in much of their substantive content the bills were plainly territorial bills. The description of executive powers was the stock one; for example, the governor was empowered to grant pardons for offenses against the provisional government, to appoint necessary officers, to command the militia, and to enforce the laws. [40]

The radical nature of these proposals was most apparent in their extension of legislative power to "all rightful subjects of legislation, not inconsistent with the Constitution and laws of the United States." The quoted passage comprised a formula for

[39] H.R. 121, sec. 11.
[40] An exception was Harris' bill, which mentioned only the power of the executive to enforce the laws.

defining the powers of a territorial government which, according to Republican constitutional theory, permitted interference
with slavery.[41] Its inclusion marked all the bills as fundamentally radical, for it meant that the provisional government could
alter or repeal state laws protecting slavery. The bills of
Hutchins and Harlan in addition specifically stated that laws in
existence at the time the provisional government was organized
might be repealed or modified. Ashley achieved the same effect
by employing this constitutional formula and by declaring that
the state governments were extinguished, thus implying that all
state laws had also terminated. Harris' bill, though subsequently
modified, contained this all-important grant of power for interfering with slavery.[42] In broad outline, then, the bills were alike
in imposing on the rebel states territorial governments capable of
abolishing slavery.

[41] H.R. 236, sec. 4; H.R. 356, sec. 3; S. 132, sec. 4; S. 200, sec. 2. The
formula dated back to the Louisiana territorial-government act of 1804.
In the late 1840's it acquired special meaning in connection with the
dispute over slavery in the territories. The heart of the dispute concerned
the nature and extent of the power of a territorial government over
slavery. In July 1848, Senator John M. Clayton of Delaware introduced a
bill for the establishment of territorial governments in Oregon, California, and New Mexico which contained this formula as a compromise,
with no mention of slavery. Clayton's idea was to let the Supreme Court
decide whether slavery was a "rightful subject of legislation," and the
formula was employed in the same way in the Utah and New Mexico
territorial acts of 1850. Throughout the 1850's, Free-Soilers, Republicans,
and Douglas Democrats interpreted it to mean that a territorial government could legislate against slavery (*Cong. Globe*, 30 Cong., 1 sess., 1003
[July 26, 1848]; U.S., *Stat. at Large*, IX, 446, 454; *Cong. Globe*, 34 Cong.,
1 sess., App. 797 [July 2, 1856], remarks of Stephen Douglas and Lewis
Cass). See Wallace Mendelson, "Dred Scott's Case—Reconsidered," *Min-
nesota Law Review*, XXXVIII (Dec. 1953), 16–27, for a discussion of
the Judiciary and the power of a territorial government over slavery. On
the compromise of 1850 and the territorial question see Robert R. Russel,
"What Was the Compromise of 1850?" *Journal of Southern History*,
XXII (Aug. 1956), 292–309.

[42] When Harris' bill was reported out of committee in July, it had
been amended so as to restrict the provisional legislature from interfering
with pre-existing state laws and institutions.

While proposing the same general territorial approach, the bills nevertheless differed considerably on specific details. Besides providing for interim civil authority, Hutchins' and Ashley's bills carried to a logical conclusion the concept of treating the rebel states as territories by providing for their readmission to the Union. Hutchins' bill declared that whenever any district under a territorial government contained enough "free white loyal inhabitants to entitle it to a member of the House of Representatives," they could "adopt, for their government, a State Constitution, republican in form and substance, and apply for admission into the Union as a State, with such boundaries and under such name as may be fixed and agreed upon by said State and Congress." In Ashley's bill, the provisional government was to continue "until such time as the loyal people residing therein shall form new State governments, republican in form, as prescribed by the Constitution of the United States, and apply for and obtain admission into the Union as States." Originally Ashley had formulated an even stronger proposal: "The States which may be erected out of said territory, shall be formed with the express stipulation, that after their admission they shall forever remain a part of the American Union, subject to the Constitution of the United States, and such amendments as shall be Constitutionally made." Ashley also deleted from his bill the conclusion that "any act of rebellion, or alliance with one or more states or with foreign nations, for the purpose of making war on the United States, shall terminate their legal existence as State Governments and remand them to a Territorial condition subject to the Government and control of Congress." [43] Although neither Ashley nor Hutchins specified the precise steps to be taken to reconstruct state governments, both had in view the entire process of creating new states out of territories.

Harlan's and Harris' bills did not embody the territorial idea

[43] H.R. 236, sec. 12; H.R. 356, sec. 1. The manuscript copy of the bill includes the sections which were struck out.

to quite the same extent. Harlan stated only that the provisional governments should continue "until the . . . State governments shall be established under the Constitution." [44] Harlan may have had in mind an interim civil government as a means of countering and weakening rebel authority. Referring to the method of creating provisional governments, he said: "You can never suppress the rebellion in any other manner. Civilized people cannot live with each other in large numbers without a civil government. Property must be bought and sold, wills must be made, . . . debts must be collected." If the inhabitants of the southern states were not provided the means for doing these things, Harlan concluded, "even loyal men must adopt the rebel government." [45] Like Harlan, Harris did not look ahead to the final stage of reconstruction. He specified only that the provisional government should continue no longer than three months after the convening of the first session of Congress following the end of the war. Judging from views he expressed a few months later, Harris anticipated the resumption of the pre-existing state governments. But in its original form his bill made no commitments on this question; as with the other proposals, the concept of territorial control, with its obvious antislavery implications, stood out.

The bills had different provisions with respect to slavery, reflecting different degrees of radicalism. Ashley's bill, as first drafted, declared that laws and municipal institutions in conflict with the general welfare and the Constitution of the United States terminated with the destruction of the state governments. When it was introduced, it contained the stronger provision that "no act shall be passed . . . establishing, protecting, or recognizing the existence of slavery." Hutchins' bill similarly provided that "from and after taking possession of [rebel] districts, or either of them, . . . there shall be neither slavery nor involuntary servitude in said districts." Harlan's measure was more

[44] S. 132, sec. 1.
[45] *Cong. Globe*, 37 Cong., 2 sess., App., 318 (July 11, 1862).

moderate, prohibiting the interstate slave trade and freeing slaves brought into the jurisdiction of the provisional government, as well as all persons born after passage of the act. It did not propose the direct abolition of slavery, leaving this to the provisional government under its general legislative powers. Harris' bill was even more moderate; it made no specific mention of slavery but of course contained the constitutional formula permitting interference with the institution.[46]

The territorial bills, with the exception of Harris', also dealt with confiscation. Ashley and Hutchins in the House and Harlan in the Senate proposed that all public lands in the seceded states be seized and held for the use of soldiers and as compensation to loyal citizens in the rebel states who had suffered losses. Again Ashley's bill was the most radical, providing that confiscated lands be leased in limited quantities not to exceed 160 acres "to actual occupants, who are loyal"—which meant former Negro slaves, since the provision contained no racial qualification. Ashley's farther reaching social aims were also reflected in provisions instructing the provisional government to establish schools and prescribe the number of hours constituting a day's work for field hands and laborers.[47]

A final point for comparison is the stipulations concerning political privileges of the local population. Here the authors of reconstruction proposals conspicuously failed to adhere to the territorial model, for none of the bills allowed popular election of the provisional legislature.[48] Some minor privileges were permitted, and again Ashley's bill was more radical than the others. While Hutchins and Harlan restricted grand- and petit-

[46] H.R. 356, sec. 3; H.R. 236, sec. 9; S. 132, sec. 9; S. 200.

[47] H.R. 356, secs. 4, 5.

[48] Actually Harris' bill was consistent with the model it followed, the Northwest Ordinance of 1787, which provided merely for a governor and three judges appointed by the President. It contained no provision for popular election of officers, as did laws which authorized the second stage of territorial government and on which Ashley, Hutchins, and Harlan patterned their measures.

jury service to "free male white persons," Ashley omitted racial qualifications, in the interest of Negro equality. Hutchins also provided that white inhabitants should be relied on in reorganizing a state government. On the other hand, Ashley's bill was more radical in being the only one which disqualified certain groups. It excluded from political rights persons who had held civil or military office under the United States or a state government, lawyers and others who had sworn an oath to the United States, and ministers of the gospel who had supported the rebellion.[49]

Thus by February 1862 many Republicans had concluded that territorialization was the best approach to reconstruction. Obviously, the antislavery impulse was important in this development. But it was not the only factor. After all, as proponents of territorialization insisted, constitutional state governments did not exist in the rebel states. Certainly there was need of some kind of government, but there was no compelling reason why this should be military government under the executive. The problem of establishing civil government was essentially political in nature and therefore seemed to involve the legislative power. Nor could territorialization, drastic expedient though it was, be easily dismissed on constitutional grounds. The organizing of territories and creating of new states were fundamental traditional processes in American government and provided a historical and constitutional basis for dealing with the unprecedented situation in the South. Territorialization was the legislative or congressional means, just as military government was the executive method, of providing local government.

Territorialization, despite its historic basis, was constitutionally bold and innovative, and politically radical. Yet not only radical antislavery men or Republicans found its logic persuasive. This was strikingly apparent when Garrett Davis submitted resolutions answering Charles Sumner's "state suicide" proposition of February 1862. Davis, an old-line Kentucky Whig,

[49] H.R. 356, sec. 8; H.R. 236, secs. 8, 12; S. 132, sec. 8.

reiterated the substance of the Crittenden resolution as his central theme, but then concluded, to the undoubted satisfaction of radical Republicans, "If the people of any State cannot or will not reconstruct their State government and return to loyalty and duty, Congress should provide a government for such State as a Territory of the United States, securing to the people thereof their appropriate constitutional rights." [50]

[50] *Cong. Globe*, 37 Cong., 2 sess., 786 (Feb. 13, 1862).

IV

Plans for Territorialization in Congress

AS long as it was up to loyal citizens in the seceded states to start reconstruction there was no conflict of authority between President and Congress. Both could support the goal of restoring states to their place in the Union on the basis of their pre-existing constitutions and laws. By early 1862, however, it was clear that mere readmission without a period of direct federal control was no longer possible. The larger and more significant question was whether federal intervention after military victory would act as a conservative force, confining itself to administering civil affairs in accordance with state laws, or a revolutionary one, subjecting the social and political order of the rebel states to radical alteration. Though military government as instituted by Lincoln in 1862 was constitutionally radical, involving an unprecedented extension of national power into areas traditionally reserved to the states, politically it was designed to serve a conservative purpose, especially with respect to slavery.[1]

[1] There was much pressure on the administration to use military power to destroy slavery, as the Fremont incident of 1861 showed. Anti-slavery men argued that a belligerent power might confiscate enemy

66

Reconstruction planners in Congress challenged the general policy of the administration, first with Ashley's radical territorial bill in March 1862, and then in July with a more moderate plan which especially challenged the authority of military governments to interfere in local affairs.

The Mexican War furnished precedents for the establishment of American military government, but whether imposing military rule on United States territory was the same as imposing it on foreign territory was a question which disturbed many Republicans. Stronger even than the tradition of creating territorial government was the principle of resorting to civil as opposed to martial law, a concept based on the idea that civil authority should always be superior to military authority. There was much to be said for the view that military rule over even part of the American people was inconsistent with republican government, and that the loyal citizens in the seceded states, though few in number and unable by themselves to restore their state

property, including property in slaves, under international law. There was ample authority for this view in the law of belligerent occupation. In his general treatise on international law published in 1861, for example, General Henry W. Halleck declared that according to the general theory of war, all private property might be taken by the conqueror, and the occupying power could suspend or change municipal laws as necessary. In 1863, Francis Lieber, in preparing General Orders 100 under Halleck's supervision, was at pains to show that emancipation of enemy slaves was sanctioned by the laws of war. Throughout the war William Whiting, the solicitor in the War Department, vigorously advanced this point of view in a series of essays on the war powers of the President and Congress. Yet in the first half of 1862, Lincoln resisted military emancipation. In May 1862, Benjamin F. Butler, commanding in occupied Louisiana, issued an order emphasizing that "all rights of property, of whatever kind, will be held inviolate, subject only to the laws of the United States." And in the same month Lincoln countermanded an order for military emancipation issued by General Hunter in South Carolina (Henry W. Halleck, *International Law, or Rules Regulating the Intercourse of States in Peace and War* [New York, 1861]; William Whiting, *War Powers under the Constitution of the United States* [43d ed.; Boston, 1871]; Frank Freidel, "General Orders 100 and Military Government," *Mississippi Valley Historical Review*, XXXII [March 1946], 546).

governments, were entitled to the protection of the federal government, even if not to representation. Many agreed with Senator James Harlan who said, in accordance with the theory of territorialization, "The people [in the rebel states] are citizens of the United States; they have a right to claim the protection of the laws of the United States." [2]

The imposition of military government also raised the question of the status of the rebel states. Officially the administration considered them to be in the Union. Yet the implications of military rule seemed inconsistent with this conclusion. Many Republicans doubted, as Owen Lovejoy of Illinois put it, "that we can consider that precisely in the character of a State where we even temporarily establish a government deriving its power from the Federal Government." [3] The theory of territorialization, which regarded the states as having been destroyed, seemed, in contrast, to accord more with the objective situation in the South. It could also be adapted to the antislavery purpose that was gaining strength in Congress and that was stimulated by the conservative character of Lincoln's military governments in their dealings with Negroes. For these reasons congressional reconstruction planners in 1862 sought to establish provisional civil governments based on the theory of territorialization.

Proposals in Congress reflected not only growing public awareness of the importance of reconstruction, but widespread interest as well in the territorial idea. The German Republican Central Committee of New York endorsed Sumner's "state suicide" resolutions, calling them "the only true basis upon which the Union can be permanently reconstructed," while an antislavery Unionist rally at Cooper Institute urged the government "to recover the territories heretofore occupied by certain States recently overturned and wholly subverted as members of the Federal Union." From western New York came petitions, signed by ninety-one persons, urging Congress to reduce South

[2] *Cong. Globe*, 37 Cong., 2 sess., App. 318 (July 11, 1862).
[3] *Ibid.*, 1796 (Apr. 23, 1862).

Carolina, Georgia, and Florida to territories, to be reserved for Negro settlement. The New York *Post*, edited by former Democrat William Cullen Bryant, saw military occupation of the South as a temporary expedient "which must be quickly followed by more permanent arrangements, under the authority of Congress, to which body the unhappy people of those states have a right to look for protection." The *Post* noted with apparent approval plans "to apply to the rebelling states the territorial government which has worked so well in our new regions." Under such a policy, meanwhile, those states "would receive the civilizing boons of free speech and a free press," Bryant's journal asserted. Even before the Committee on Territories had reported Ashley's bill, the New York *Tribune* endorsed it as "not a whit too severe upon the Rebels," while amply protective of the property and rights of all loyal people. The *Tribune* declared, "Its adoption by Congress would furnish a fitting climax to the military power which is crushing the rebellion." [4]

If some Republicans supported territorialization, Democrats and other Republicans opposed it. Calling attention to "radical measures in Congress," the Democratic Columbus *Crisis* observed, "The great question with politicians, who profess to be opposed to the SUMNER and LOVEJOY confiscation measures is, will they or will they not go for the 'territorial question'?" Sumner's "state suicide" resolutions had been tabled, but there was still cause for concern, said the *Crisis*, because "Mr. HARRIS . . . from New York, considered among the *conservatives*, has . . . introduced a bill to establish Territorial Governments over the seceded States . . . [which] is a measure not a whit less absurd than the resolutions of Mr. SUMNER, and must work all the injurious consequences of the most extreme abolition measure." The New York *World* at-

[4] Sumner, *Works*, VI, 378, 381; 37 Cong., petitions referred to the House of Representatives Judiciary Committee, March 31, 1862, MS, National Archives, RG 233, HR 37A–G7.15; New York *Post*, Feb. 20, 1862; New York *Tribune*, Feb. 26, 1862.

tacked Ashley's bill for embodying "the fallacy that, by rebellion against the United States, the rebels have overthrown and destroyed the States," and for completely reversing the previous position of the government in dealing with the rebellion. The New York *Times*, a Republican paper, condemned Sumner's resolutions as "certain to end . . . in rendering peace impossible" and in "a centralized despotism,—in which everything like freedom will be extinguished." And from within the administration itself Montgomery Blair, the Postmaster General and a leading Republican in Maryland, publicly scored the idea that the seceded states had been reduced to territories or destroyed.[5] Thus by March 1862 reconstruction, and especially territorialization, had become a controversial issue.

Attention in Congress meanwhile turned to Ashley's bill for territorial governments in the rebel states, which the Committee on Territories had approved by a 4 to 3 vote.[6] The measure was so controversial, however, that Ashley, the chairman of the committee, had difficulty in merely reporting it to the House. When he sought to do so on February 27, Clement Vallandigham of Ohio, a prominent Democrat, protested and declared that he would continue to question the bill whenever Ashley tried to introduce it.[7]

Two weeks later Ashley finally got the bill before the House. But by this time Lincoln, spurred to action by the threat of territorialization and the rising antislavery protest, had initiated a policy of installing military governments which effectively undercut the appeal Ashley's bill might have had as a solution to

[5] Columbus, Ohio, *Crisis*, Feb. 26, 1862; New York *World*, March 4, 1862; New York *Times*, Feb. 26, 1862; William E. Smith, *The Francis Preston Blair Family in Politics* (2 vols.; New York, 1933), II, 200.

[6] Republicans voting for the bill were Ashley, Fernando Beaman, Owen Lovejoy, and A. Scott Sloan. Aaron Harding and James Cravens, Democrats, opposed it, together with one Republican, William Wheeler (37 Cong., Minutes of the Committee on Territories, Feb. 24, 1862, MS, National Archives, RG 233, 35A–D21.8).

[7] *Cong. Globe*, 37 Cong., 2 sess., 986 (Feb. 27, 1862).

the problem of governing the rebel states. At the same time, Lincoln made a concession to the radical antislavery wing of the party by advocating a policy of compensated emancipation.

The evacuation of Nashville by the rebels in late February 1862, which prepared the way for the possible recovery of the entire state of Tennessee, enabled Lincoln to carry out these changed policies. Aware of the several reconstruction proposals in Congress, Lincoln met the collapse of Confederate authority by appointing Andrew Johnson of Tennessee as military governor of the state. He instructed Johnson, whose commission as brigadier general was confirmed by the Senate on March 5, "to exercise and perform . . . the powers, duties, and functions pertaining to the office of Military Governor . . . until the loyal inhabitants of that State shall organize a civil government in conformity with the Constitution of the United States." [8]

Although from their wording it was not apparent what the instructions meant with respect to such issues as slavery and confiscation, Johnson interpreted them in a conservative way.[9]

---

[8] *The War of the Rebellion: A Compilation of the Official Records of the Union and Confederate Armies*, R. N. Scott *et al.*, eds., (130 vols.; Washington, 1880–1901), ser. 1, IX, 396–397 (hereafter cited as *Official Records*).

[9] In his *War Powers under the Constitution*, William Whiting wrote: "When this work was first published (in 1862), . . . what, under this new condition of affairs, was the extent, and what were the limitations of the military power of the President or of his officers; how far he or they were bound by the local laws of the rebel States; whether those laws were still obligatory upon the inhabitants thereof; what were the legal rights of peaceable rebels, of neutrals, or of friends of the Union living there; what protection could be lawfully given to persons or property, without swerving from the purposes for which our defensive war was declared to have been commenced and carried on; whether all the laws of the United States, as, for instance, those regarding the return of fugitive slaves, were still obligatory upon our soldiers, as in time of peace; and whether citizens of the rebellious States were still entitled to all their former rights under the Constitution—were questions which embarrassed and disheartened our statesmen and jurists no less than our commanders and soldiers in the service" (1871 ed., 427).

In an address to the people of Tennessee shortly after assuming his duties, Johnson invoked the resolutions on the purposes of the war which he himself had introduced and which the Senate had approved in July 1861. He reminded his fellow Tennesseans that the war was not being waged "for any purpose of overthrowing or interfering with the rights or established institutions of these States." Regarding the constitutional status of Tennessee, Johnson also took a conservative view. "The great ship of state . . . has been suddenly abandoned," he said, avoiding any suggestion of territorialization and implying that the federal government had only to recover the ship and set it on a loyal course by placing Union men at the helm. According to Johnson, in suppressing the rebellion the government was fulfilling its guarantee of a republican government to the state, which meant restoring the pre-existing state government. Proclaimed Johnson: "I have been appointed, in the absence of the regular and established State authorities, as Military Governor for the time being, to preserve the public property of the State, to give the protection of law actively enforced to her citizens, and, as speedily as may be, to restore her government to the same condition as before the existing rebellion." [10]

The Senate's confirmation of Johnson's appointment was indicative of a favorable reaction to Lincoln's new policy, even among some who had supported territorialization. The New York *Tribune*, which had endorsed Ashley's bill, also approved of the appointment of a military governor. Though the *Tribune* said it "preferred to see a step of such moment taken with the express cooperation of Congress," it was confident that "the wisdom of the President and Cabinet is not inadequate to a happy treatment of this great question." The antislavery Cincinnati *Gazette*, pointing out that the creation of territorial governments by Congress was the alternative to military rule, nonetheless supported the administration's move in Tennessee. The

[10] Appeal to the People of Tennessee, March 18, 1862, Andrew Johnson Papers, Library of Congress.

Gazette approved of the appointment of Johnson because it would "put the States into loyal hands, whether few or many," and added that there was "gratifying evidence that the country approves this policy." John Forney wrote, "All this has been done by the Government . . . without the aid of Congress, and it is a significant evidence of the justice and expediency of this policy, that no portion of the Representatives and Senators in Congress are found to object to it." [11]

The establishment of a military government in Tennessee also seemed to cause some observers to change their position on territorialization from support to opposition. The New York *Post*, which previously had endorsed the plan for territorial governments in the South, stated on March 5, "We cannot yet persuade ourselves of the justice or policy of the scheme which proposes to disfranchise the seceding states . . . [and] proceeds . . . upon the ground that those States, by the very act of secession, have abrogated their functions as States and reverted to the condition of territories." The *Post* declared that the President, by his appointment of Johnson, had shown the "proper plan of proceeding" in governing the rebel states. Democrats, meanwhile, were pleased by the choice of the Democrat Johnson as military governor. The correspondent of the New York *World*, which was fast becoming a powerful Democratic voice, wrote that Johnson's appointment in Tennessee was "an indication of what must be done at the start in every newly conquered southern state," namely, to establish a half civil, half military authority to govern until the loyal citizens could form a state government. Such an interim government was acceptable, the *World*'s correspondent believed, because it would not offend state pride or disfranchise loyal citizens, and because "the principle of local self government will be recognized to the farthest possible limit." Predicting that Congress was not now likely to support bills for "obliterating the state governments

[11] New York *Tribune*, Mar. 8, 1862; Cincinnati *Gazette*, Mar. 8, 1862; Philadelphia *Press*, quoted in New York *Tribune*, Mar. 8, 1862.

already established in the South and converting them into territories," he said that many people thought that the problem of
restoring the southern states would solve itself.[12]

Having dealt with the immediate problem of governing Tennessee, Lincoln made a concession to radical opinion on the
slavery question which further weakened the appeal of Ashley's
territorial plan. In a special message on March 6, 1862, he urged
Congress to adopt a resolution pledging the cooperation of the
federal government "with any state which may adopt gradual
abolishment of slavery, giving to such state pecuniary aid, to be
used by such state in its discretion, to compensate for the incon-
veniences, public and private, produced by such change of system." Adhering to the traditional limitation on federal power, he
disavowed the federal government's claim to any right to interfere with slavery within the states, insisting that "absolute control of the subject" still belonged to the states and their
people.[13] Clearly, however, the message represented a major
shift in the administration's policy toward slavery, and pleased
all but the most radical antislavery zealots. The House promptly
registered its approval by adopting the resolution by a vote of 89
to 31.[14]

Thus by the time Ashley again tried to introduce the territorial committee's bill, the administration had launched a policy
of military government as an alternative to territorialization and
had shifted to a more radical position against slavery. Obviously,
both developments were obstacles to the acceptance of the
committee's territorial plan of reconstruction.

This became evident on March 12, when Ashley, after a
second unsuccessful attempt, finally reported the bill out of
committee. His strategy, in view of recent developments, was to

12 New York *Post*, March 5, 1862; New York *World*, March 4, 1862.
13 Message to Congress, March 6, 1862, *Collected Works of Lincoln*,
V, 144–145.
14 McPherson, *The Struggle for Equality*, 96–97; *Cong. Globe*, 37
Cong., 2 sess., 1149 (March 10, 1862).

order the bill to be printed and recommitted. But opponents of the territorial plan, confident of victory, tried to force a direct vote. A minority of the territorial committee launched the attack with a scathing report condemning the bill, whereupon Ohio Democrat George Pendleton, insisting that it "ought to be entitled a bill to dissolve the Union and abolish the Constitution of the United States" and adding sententiously that he was "unalterably opposed to the destruction of either, from any quarter whatsoever," moved that the measure be rejected. Pendleton's diatribe provoked Republican John Bingham of Ohio, who was sympathetic to the bill, to protest that debate was not in order. The motion to reject having been declared out of order, Pendleton moved to lay the bill on the table, and the House approved his motion by a vote of 65 to 56.[15]

An analysis of the vote reveals that fifty-six Republicans—more than two-thirds of the total in the House—opposed the motion to table, while all of the forty-three Democrats and border-state Unionists who were present supported it. The issue was decided, therefore, by twenty-two Republicans who, separating from the party majority, voted to table the bill. Because no debate was allowed, only the Democratic border-state opposition, through the minority report of the Committee on Territories, explained its position on March 12. The views of the Republican majority and minority became clear, however, from remarks made on other occasions concerning territorialization.

The argument for the territorial plan had two central points: the practical necessity of providing government for the areas reclaimed from the Confederacy, and, as a matter of principle, the inadequacy and injustice of a purely military approach to reconstruction. Fernando Beaman of the Committee on Territories developed these points in a prepared speech which he delivered in April, defending Ashley's bill. Beaman emphasized at the outset the breakdown of local government in the South. He

[15] *Cong. Globe,* 37 Cong., 2 sess., 1193 (Mar. 12, 1862); New York *Post,* Mar. 13, 1862.

argued, however, that removing the obstacles to the execution of federal laws would not in itself bring about reconstruction; the establishment of federal authority through officers such as marshals, judges, and revenue agents would not provide the kind of control needed. Rather, said Beaman, "Local government, with executive, legislative, and judicial powers, will be positively indispensable, not only for the welfare of the inhabitants, but for the preservation of the authority of the United States." Admitting that it would be necessary temporarily to impose military rule, he nevertheless rejected "the design of establishing military governments, for any considerable duration, over seven millions of native-born Americans." "Such a scheme," he said, "is incompatible with the spirit of our institutions." Equally emphatically, however, Beaman rejected the alternative of allowing the loyal citizens in a seceded state to reorganize a government and elect representatives to Congress. Though not denying that there were some loyal men in the rebellious states and that "as a legal proposition" loyal citizens might be permitted to do this, he considered such a course "monstrous folly and madness." He believed that "Federal authority should intervene, not to disfranchise loyal men, but to establish and regulate government, because of their inability to govern themselves." As he saw it, no legislation "short of the actual establishment and officering of Government . . . through the instrumentality of territorial or provisional governments, established by Congress," would bring about reconstruction on a sound basis.[16]

Constitutional authority for the territorial bill, according to Beaman, derived from the position of the United States as "a sovereign Power, with vast territorial possessions . . . over which it is entitled to governmental jurisdiction, from which allegiance is due, and to which it owes the obligation of protection and a just administration of law." The federal government was obliged, moreover, to establish justice, promote the general

[16] *Cong. Globe*, 37 Cong., 2 sess., 1554–1555 (Apr. 4, 1862).

welfare, and insure domestic tranquility in all its territory. Ordinarily these were a state's duties, but should a state fail to discharge them, the federal government had to do so itself and carry on local government. "I cannot doubt," Beaman concluded, "that cases may arise, or that such now exist, in which the General Government has the unquestionable right to take control of the territory and people lately recognized as a State, and spread over them such provisional government as may be suitable to their peculiar condition." [17]

The Democratic border-state opposition, represented by the minority report of James Cravens of Indiana, Aaron Harding of Kentucky, and George K. Shiel of Oregon, of the Committee on Territories, insisted that Ashley's bill was nothing less than a secessionist document which would destroy the Union. Cravens, Harding, and Shiel called the bill "revolutionary, unconstitutional, and monstrous, if not palpably treasonable," and said that it proposed "to enact (in substance) that the . . . State governments be abolished." In their view the bill, in plain violation of the constitutional obligation to guarantee to each state a republican form of government,

at a single blow, strikes out the existence and names of eleven States of the Union. It is virtually an Ordinance of secession by which the hitherto loyal States secede from the Eleven. It consummates the work begun by the rebels but which they were too feeble to accomplish. It proposes to extend a helping hand to them just when their failure is manifest. What one or even eleven States could not do, it is now discovered, can be done by a greater number of States by reason of their greater strength.

At the very least, the territorial bill was an attempt "to alter the whole form and construction of the American Union as at present organized by prescribing terms for the readmission of the rebellious States into the Union, with new constitutions, upon certain new terms and subject to certain new regulations."

[17] *Ibid.*, 1552 (Apr. 4, 1862).

It was based on the false assumption that Congress might "exclude certain States from the Union and hold them in colonial dependence and vassalage." The provisions in the bill for emancipation and land distribution, Cravens, Shiel, and Harding said, were designed to change the whole policy of the government by holding lands taken from the rebellious states and giving them "to actual occupants whom we think it fair to infer would be the present slaves." Thus the bill did not stop with the legal destruction of the states, "but with an unforgiving and relentless spirit [proposed] to pursue the inhabitants of those States outside of the Constitution and the Union." It would govern them by laws enacted by a few irresponsible men who had not been chosen by the people themselves. "In short," the minority of the committee asserted, "in all its absurd and impracticable details, . . . [the bill] shows that it is a cruel scheme of subjugation, Negro emancipation, and tyranny, equally repugnant to the principles of Justice, Humanity, and the Constitution." At a time when Union victories were inspiring the hope of a speedy restoration of order, the bill "has been thrust upon us seemingly for fear that peace and harmony might be restored to the land before the abolition scheme of Negro emancipation could be inaugurated." [18]

The Republicans who joined with Democrats and border-state Unionists to defeat Ashley's territorial bill seem to have objected not so much to its substantive policy provisions, though these probably seemed excessively radical, or to its assumption of congressional authority, which they in fact endorsed, as to the theory of the Union they considered implicit in the measure. Samuel Shellabarger of Ohio, for example, was opposed to territorialization because in effect it conceded validity to the seces-

[18] 37 Congress, Minority Reports of the Committee on Territories on the Resolution concerning Territorial Government in Disloyal States, March 12, 1862, National Archives, RG 233, House of Representatives Collection, 1861–1867, Box 162. There were actually two reports, one signed by all three committeemen and one signed only by Cravens and Harding.

sion ordinances of the rebellious states. Said Shellabarger, "Those words of the Constitution—'THE UNION'—take into their high import not the idea of unimpaired *territorial* domination alone, but involve as well the indestructibility of the States themselves." Attacking a favorite notion of radicals, he said that by admitting "that a State can do, by rebellion or secession, an act which can destroy a 'State,' . . . you admit that the rebellion or secession can destroy what the Constitution has guarantied to protect." Shellabarger asserted that any proposal "which gives to void State action validity for the purpose of destroying itself, misconceives, as its kindred error the right of secession misconceives, the very foundation principle upon which the entire structure of the Government rests." John T. Nixon, a Republican of New Jersey, argued similarly that proposals for territorialization "when carried to their logical results, recognize the right in a State to secede. They assume that South Carolina, for instance, is out of the Union." Nixon believed that because ordinances of secession were void and inoperative, "South Carolina is still in the Union, and . . . here she shall ever remain, with or without her consent." It was significant, however, that while Nixon objected to Ashley's proposal, he did not deny Congress' authority to legislate concerning reconstruction. Yet the time for legislation had not arrived. "It will be time enough for us to consider and legislate upon these questions when the subject-matter is under our control," he pointed out. Nixon hoped that after a brief period of military government the defeated rebels would resume the operation of their state governments, which he considered suspended but not destroyed. But "over every conquered territory where the people will not, of their own volition, return to their allegiance," he added, "we should authorize the President to establish provisional governments for the execution of the Federal laws." [19]

Thus, to its Republican opponents the territorial committee's

[19] *Cong. Globe*, 37 Cong., 2 sess., 934 (Feb. 24, 1862); 1630–1631 (Apr. 11, 1862).

plan of reconstruction seemed to concede to states the right of secession, or something very like it; certainly the results it listed were at variance with the idea of the Union as perpetual and with the corollary notion of state indestructibility. Ashley himself later recalled, "Even here at home, I was charged by men who called themselves Republicans, with recognizing and confirming by my reconstruction bill, the secession of all the rebel States." Though they did not spell out objections to substantive points, Republicans who voted to table the bill probably were also apprehensive about a measure that contained so many extreme propositions. Ashley may not have been far off when he said, with his usual self-conceit, "Timid men hesitated, and men who never move, or who when they do move, walk only in beaten paths, were frightened." The bill fully reflected the spirit of radicalism which Ashley personified and which he revealed a few days after the defeat of the measure in a conversation with Jacob Collamer of Vermont. Collamer, a Republican senator, came to Ashley in the House and asked where he had found precedent for establishing provisional governments in the states. Ashley, by his own account, "answered him sharply and with some feeling, by saying: 'Sir, we make precedents here.' " He told Collamer, "Before we get through with this rebellion, we will compel all loyal men in Congress to vote for measures far more radical than my bill." [20]

Important as this personal dimension was, it was less influential in defeating Ashley's reconstruction bill than the strategy of the President. In initiating military government, Lincoln had created an alternative to territorialization which both moderates and conservatives could support, but in adopting a policy of compensated emancipation, he was following a course that all antislavery men could support. Indeed, it was the more aggressive policy against slavery which was conspicuous in the ensuing weeks, as Congress enacted and the President signed into law

[20] Ashley to Benjamin W. Arnett, Nov. 1892, in Ashley, *Orations and Speeches*, 361.

several antislavery measures. But the policy of installing military governments also continued, as Lincoln made additional appointments in Arkansas and North Carolina. The result was compromise, with the proponents of territorialization accepting military government, while the administration pursued a more radical policy against slavery.

The testimony of contemporaries confirms this analysis of the situation. According to Representative William Wadsworth, a Kentucky Unionist, the defeat of the territorial bill could be explained as indicating an attempt by the administration to effect "a compromise between extreme abolitionists of the North and Unionists of the South." Wadsworth said that Lincoln's message on compensated emancipation meant that "general confiscation of property, general emancipation or abolition, degradation of States to Territories, & c., is to be abandoned by those who have advocated them hitherto." He continued: "This scheme, therefore, requires the ultras to yield. The vote to lay the territorial bill upon the table today is doubtless an indication of the policy of the Administration upon the subject." Wadsworth believed that the President would regard "every gentleman, however radical he may be, who comes to this message [on compensated emancipation] and still presses the ultra measures before alluded to, as putting himself in opposition to the policy of the Administration." Wadsworth was of course pleased that Republican members could be persuaded "to abandon the radical opinions and projects" they had previously entertained and proposed. The Washington correspondent of the New York *Post* agreed with this assessment. The vote on Ashley's bill seemed to him evidence that the administration would be against all extreme measures, especially emancipation by act of Congress. The New York *Herald*'s correspondent also linked the vote on the territorial plan with the policy of compensated emancipation. He remarked, "The disposition made of Mr. Ashley's Emancipation bill today, taken in connection with the vote on the President's resolution . . . demonstrates that there is an invincible and inflexible conservative majority in the House which will approve the right and defeat the wrong." [21]

Ashley's plan for territorialization had aroused strong emotions, and its defeat probably pleased conservatives more than the new policy of gradual emancipation pleased radical antislavery men.[22] The correspondent of the New York *Herald* reported that the failure of Ashley's "universal Emancipation bill today, under the cloak of providing provisional governments for the Territory recovered from the rebels, was a salutary lesson to the radicals. . . . The vote was a complete Bull Run disaster to the ultra faction, and has tamed them down considerably." Calling it "A Monster Quelled," the New York *Times* said that the tabling of Ashley's bill was "evidence that the House of Representatives is indisposed to legislate, without constitutional warrant." Expressing the hope that "Mr. Ashley and his faction" would be satisfied and would turn to matters over which Congress had jurisdiction, the *Times* advised, "It is no part of its [Congress'] business to dissolve a Union, we are just now trying somewhat expensively to restore." [23]

The defeat of Ashley's bill frustrated plans for territorialization for the time being. The Senate Committee on Territories, with whom Ashley had conferred and who were reported ready to bring a similar measure before the Senate, failed to act. Mean-

[21] *Cong. Globe*, 37 Cong., 2 sess., 1198 (Mar. 12, 1862); New York *Post*, Mar. 14, 1862; New York *Herald*, Mar. 13, 1862.

[22] The unusually strong resentment which its opponents felt toward the bill can be seen in the way in which they disposed of it. Ordinarily, as a matter of courtesy if nothing else, a bill was ordered printed before being acted upon; to table it without this customary procedure was an unusual rebuke. As the correspondent of the New York *Herald* observed, "To refuse to print a bill and order it to the tomb of the capulets on the table is regarded as an indignity greater than a rejection upon the first reading." When Justin Morrill, a Republican, tried to argue that the House was merely departing from its usual practice of having bills printed before considering them, Wadsworth cogently answered, "The House had such an aversion to the scheme that they would not consider it" (New York *Herald*, Mar. 13, 1862; *Cong. Globe*, 37 Cong., 2 sess., 1198 [Mar. 12, 1862]).

[23] New York *Herald*, Mar. 13, 1862; New York *Times*, Mar. 13, 1862.

while, the struggle against slavery continued, and measures that would have been scarcely conceivable a year earlier became law with little difficulty. All in the space of a month, Congress enacted an additional article of war prohibiting the use of military force in returning fugitive slaves, adopted Lincoln's resolution concerning compensated emancipation, and abolished slavery in the District of Columbia, giving compensation to slave owners. In June it achieved the long-standing Republican goal, on which the party had staked its existence in the 1850's, of prohibiting slavery in the federal territories.[24]

Though the bill prohibiting slavery in the territories offered an opportunity for the application of their theory, the advocates of territorialization did not pursue this objective. As introduced by the Committee on Territories, the bill prohibited slavery "in all territories of the United States . . . [and] in all places whatsoever where the national government is supreme, or has exclusive jurisdiction or power." If the seceded states were reduced to territories, they could be considered within the scope of the proposed act. Yet only William D. Kelley of Pennsylvania mentioned this interpretation, and he was not sure that a "[rebel] state government has . . . been so completely destroyed that we should look upon the land it embraced as territory over which the power of the United States extends." Kelley was willing "to act upon the principle that we cannot interfere with slavery in the several States as we have known them." The Committee on Territories deleted the provision referring to "all places whatsoever" where the federal government was supreme and had exclusive jurisdiction, and in its final form the act stated simply, "There shall be neither slavery nor involuntary servitude in any of the Territories of the United States." [25]

[24] *Cong. Globe*, 37 Cong., 2 sess., 1117 (Mar. 7, 1862); New York *Post*, Mar. 14, 1862; Cincinnati *Gazette*, Mar. 14, 1862; U.S., *Stat. at Large*, XII, 354; *Cong. Globe*, 37 Cong., 2 sess., 1496 (Apr. 2, 1862); U.S., *Stat. at Large*, XII, 432.

[25] 37 Cong., H.R. 374, May 1, 1862; *Cong. Globe*, 37 Cong., 2 sess., 2030, 2049 (May 9, 1862); U.S., *Stat. at Large*, XII, 432.

With emancipation gaining momentum and military government operating in conquered rebel districts, territorialization seemed less urgent. At the beginning of April, John Forney, from his position as secretary of the Senate, reported that "Congress is evidently in no mood to pass a radical confiscation bill, or to adopt the project of reducing each of the seceded States to a Territorial condition." Forney said that some of the most trusted Republican leaders, because of considerations of policy and the absence of constitutional power to enforce them, had strong objections to both measures. Much would depend on how the policy of military government worked. He believed that if Andrew Johnson succeeded in establishing a government in Tennessee, perhaps both problems would be satisfactorily solved.[26]

Willingness to accept military government proved short-lived, however, for in May a series of events began which led to renewed criticism of the administration's policy toward slavery and military rule. The upshot was another congressional effort to control reconstruction by creating provisional civil governments for the seceded states.

Lincoln's troubles began with another challenge to his slavery policy from the military. On May 9, 1862, General David Hunter, commander of the Department of the South, declared free all slaves in South Carolina, Georgia, and Florida. Not yet prepared to take this step, Lincoln issued a proclamation revoking the order and stating that he himself would decide whether the government was competent to declare slaves free and whether militarily it was necessary to do so. Antislavery men were predictably critical of Lincoln's action. Senator James Grimes of Iowa wrote on May 19, "The President has today rescinded Hunter's proclamation. The result will be a general row in the country. All the radical Republicans are indignant." [27]

26 Philadelphia *Press*, April 2, 1862.
27 Lincoln to Gen. David M. Hunter, May 19, 1862, in *Collected Works of Lincoln*, V, 222; James Grimes to his wife, May 19, 1862, in William Salter, *The Life of James W. Grimes* (New York, 1876), 196.

Shortly after the Hunter incident Lincoln's newly appointed military governor in North Carolina, Edward Stanley, provoked criticism by his handling of problems concerning Negroes. Like Andrew Johnson in Tennessee, Stanley considered it his duty as military governor to restore the state to its preexisting condition. He wrote to Secretary of War Stanton in June, "Unless I can give [the inhabitants] some assurance that this is a war of restoration and not of abolition and destruction, no peace can be restored here for many years to come." Acting on this basis, Stanley allowed inhabitants who would swear an oath of allegiance to the United States to recover their slaves. This policy was of course criticized, but what aroused the greatest protest in Congress was Stanley's closing of a school that had been established for Negro children in New Bern. He explained to Stanton, "I had been sent to restore the old order of things. I thought . . . [a] negro school, if approved by me, would do harm to the Union cause." Furthermore, he said, "by one of the cruel necessities of slavery the laws of North Carolina forbade slaves to be taught to read and write, and I would be most unsuccessful in my efforts if I encouraged the violation of her laws." [28]

The news of Stanley's actions produced an immediate and hostile reaction in Congress. On June 2, John Hickman, a Republican of Pennsylvania, introduced a resolution requesting that the President inform the House what powers had been conferred on Stanley as military governor. Hickman demanded to know also whether Stanley had "interfered to prevent the education of children, white or black" in North Carolina, and, if he had, under what instructions and for what purpose he had done so. While the House was approving Hickman's resolution by voice vote, Charles Sumner took up the issue in the Senate. Referring to Stanley's closing of the Negro school, Sumner said, "It is difficult to conceive that one of the first fruits of national victories, and the national power, should be such an enormity."

[28] Edward Stanley to Edwin M. Stanton, June 12, 1862, *Official Records*, ser. 1, IX, 400.

He introduced a resolution requesting Secretary of War Stanton
to provide copies of the orders appointing military governors in
Tennessee and North Carolina. A few days later Sumner offered
a more far-reaching resolution requesting that the President
cancel the orders under which Stanley presumed to act. The
resolution declared that any attempt "to create any person military Governor of a State is without sanction in the Constitution
and laws, and that its effect is to subordinate the civil to military
authority, contrary to the spirit of our institutions and in derogation of the powers of Congress, which, where a State government falls into the hands of traitors, can be the only legitimate
authority, except martial law." This stronger proposal met with
objection, but the Senate approved Sumner's first resolution.[29]

In a formal reply to the House, Lincoln stated that Stanley
had not been instructed to prevent the education of any children, black or white, and that the War Department had no
information that he had done so.[30] Though subsequently Stanley provided Stanton with information confirming the charge,
Congress pursued the specific issue no further. But it did not
turn away from the larger issues raised by the incident: What
kind of government should be established in the rebel states, and
who should be in control of it?

The policy of establishing military government now came
increasingly under attack. In general, critics charged that no
constitutional basis for such a policy existed, and that by
appointing military governors, the administration was itself
admitting that the rebel states were destroyed. "If the old State
governments are not destroyed by the action of their State officers and people," inquired James Ashley on May 23, "by what
constitutional authority does the Government of the United

---

[29] *Cong. Globe*, 37 Cong., 2 sess., 2495, 2477 (June 2, 1862); *ibid.*, 2596
(June 6, 1862).

[30] Stanton to Lincoln, June 4, 1862, *Official Records*, ser. 1, IX, 396;
Lincoln to the House of Representatives, June 4, 1862, in *Collected
Works of Lincoln*, V, 259.

States . . . attempt to establish governments in Tennessee and North Carolina?" Asked Owen Lovejoy of Illinois, "If these revolted States are in the Union, what right, [has] the President . . . to place Governors over them, as in the case of Tennessee?" The doubt felt by many Union men and the alternative solution they preferred were indicated by a correspondent of the Cincinnati *Gazette* when he wrote, "It would be a queer constitutional scruple which swallowed a military government in the rebel States, superseding their State Governments, but strained at the creation of the necessary Governments by Congress." In short, if the states were indestructible, the constitutionality of military government was questionable. Said Republican Theodore Sedgwick, referring to the seceded states, "They are authorized to require of us the guarantee of a republican form of government; and yet the President of the United States, as Commander-in-Chief of the Army, without any warrant of constitutional authority, by the military power, gives them instead a tyrannical, despotic military government." [31]

Toward the end of June 1862, two Republican senators, James Dixon of Connecticut and Lyman Trumbull of Illinois, debated the advisability of military government. Dixon defended the administration's policy. Though conceding that the President had erred in referring to military governors *of* the states—"They are military governors *in* those States, not of or over them," he pointed out—Dixon did not doubt the authority of the executive to appoint such governors. Nor did he see Lincoln's action as an infringement of state rights. Referring to military government, Dixon declared: "All this is no interference with State authority. That may exist or it may be in abeyance; but the authority of military governors appointed by the President . . . over a conquered enemy, is wholly aside from and irrespective of, and may be in entire harmony with the authority of the State government." Trumbull, in reply, dwelt on the issue

[31] *Cong. Globe*, 37 Cong., 2 sess., App. 227 (May 23, 1862); 1796 (Apr. 23, 1862); 2325 (May 23, 1862); Cincinnati *Gazette*, Mar. 18, 1862.

of executive usurpation. The fact that, in appointing Stanley, Lincoln had not sought Senate confirmation, as he had in the case of Johnson, was the basis of Trumbull's criticism. According to the Constitution, said Trumbull, all officers shall be appointed by the President, with the advice and consent of the Senate. Yet "what do we hear?" he asked. "We hear of a military Governor in North Carolina. Has his name been sent to the Senate? Was he appointed by the advice and consent of the Senate? Is there any law of Congress vesting the power in the President to appoint a military governor in North Carolina?" Trumbull asserted, "The President can no more make a Governor of North Carolina than the Senator from Connecticut [can]. . . . It is wholly without constitutional authority." [32]

Criticism of military government was the prelude to renewed efforts to find a legislative solution to the problem of governing rebel districts. The focus of these efforts was Senator Ira Harris' bill for provisional civil governments, as amended by the judiciary committee. In his debate with Dixon, Lyman Trumbull referred to Harris' proposal as an alternative to military government. "I think the President himself will be glad to divest himself of the exercise of this power," said Trumbull, "and I want the Senator from Connecticut [Dixon] to act with me . . . and pass a law authorizing the President . . . to appoint governors and judges and the other necessary officers in the rebellious districts." [33]

[32] *Cong. Globe*, 37 Cong., 2 sess., 2927 (June 25, 1862); 2973 (June 27, 1862). Trumbull approved of the appointment of Andrew Johnson as brigadier general and agreed that Johnson might act in that capacity as governor. Stanley, however, had no such appointment, so held no office recognized by law. Said Trumbull concerning Stanley's appointment, "It was unwarrantable for . . . [the President] to appoint any man to an office when there was no law creating the office, and it was not done by and with the advice and consent of the Senate." Trumbull held that the President might appoint "officers already in the public service to perform public duties." In this connection, it is worth noting that Lincoln appointed as military governor of Louisiana Colonel G. F. Shepley, who was on active military duty at the time (*ibid.*, 2974 [June 27, 1862]).

[33] *Ibid.*, 2974 (June 27, 1862). Indicating that interest in Harris' bill was

Harris' bill seemed to have a fair chance of passing, because in its amended form it was basically a moderate proposal. Even as originally introduced in February it had differed considerably from Ashley's plan. Harris' bill contained no specific emancipation or confiscation provisions, offered no explicit statement of the theory of territorialization or the status of the seceded states, and did not prescribe procedures for readmitting them. Though ardent state-rights men considered Harris' bill as repugnant as the most extreme plan for territorialization, Republicans saw it quite differently. In February 1862, reviewing the various approaches to reconstruction, John Forney distinguished between Harris' and Sumner's ideas. The plan of Sumner, he wrote, pointed to the reduction of the rebel States to a territorial condition, the establishment of provisional governments, and was "based upon a comprehensive emancipation idea." Harris' bill, in contrast, looked "simply to the organization of provisional governments in the revolted States, . . . to be maintained until the people of such States rally around the Constitution and form a republican government for themselves." [34]

If Harris' proposal in February seemed at variance with Ashley's plan, in its amended form it differed fundamentally from the territorial bill that the House had rejected. Despite all the

a quite recent development, Dixon reproachfully told Trumbull that if there was anyone who ought not to criticize the President for appointing military governors, it was Trumbull, "who has had that bill in his pocket for the space of four months past" (*ibid.*, 2975 [June 27, 1862]).

[34] Philadelphia *Press*, Feb. 15, 1862. The manner in which Harris' bill was committed showed that it was considered less radical. Harris succeeded in having it referred to the judiciary committee, of which he was a member, rather than to the Committee on Territories, whose chairman, Ben Wade, was known to favor a more comprehensive plan, such as Ashley's. But in the parliamentary maneuvering, the bill was at one point referred to Wade's committee, leading one newspaper correspondent to write that this was "indicative of the temper of the Senate to adopt radical bills for the government of rebel territory as fast as conquered." He said that the Committee on Territories favored a plan that "differs from Harris's bill, a substantial copy of which they have already rejected in being more thorough, and meaning subjugation more decidedly" (Cincinnati *Gazette*, Feb. 18, 1862).

dissimilarities between Harris' original bill and Ashley's measure, they were identical in one all-important respect: both created provisional governments possessing full legislative power, including the power to interfere with slavery. In the amended version of Harris' bill, however, the legislative power of the provisional government was curtailed to a significant degree, so that it would be a genuine interim government which might maintain peace and public order until the citizens of the rebellious states could reorganize loyal state governments.

One change in Harris' measure was to a greater recognition of the state-rights view. The original bill had given the President broad authority to establish provisional governments in any districts "within the territorial limits of the United States" where he might determine there was resistance to the Constitution by armed force. The revised bill gave him less sweeping authority to establish a provisional government "for [any] such State." The bill was to be effective, not, like the original bill, "within the territorial limits of the United States"—this implied rule by the sovereign power of a unitary government—but "within the territorial limits of any of the United States." This slight but significant change indicated a recognition of the continued existence of the states. Throughout the bill, moreover, the judiciary committee had substituted the word "State" for the words "district" and "territorial," thereby eliminating the implication that the states had been destroyed and were to be regarded as territories.[35]

The most important change which the judiciary committee made concerned the legislative power of the provisional governments. Harris' original measure stated that this power should extend to "all subjects of rightful legislation not inconsistent with the Constitution and laws of the United States." This constitutional formula remained in the amended bill, but a significant limitation was added: ". . . and not interfering with the laws

[35] S. 200, amendment by Harris, June 11, 1862, secs. 1, 3.

and institutions existing in such State at the time its authorities assumed to array the same against the government of the United States further than shall be necessary to carry into effect the provisions and purposes of this act." [36] While this addition did not impose an absolute restriction, it meant that the provisional governments would be primarily concerned with administering civil affairs until the inhabitants could form a government for themselves. This purpose became clearer in the course of debate.

The debate on the judiciary committee's bill, which took place on July 7, about a week before the end of the session, developed in two stages. First the proponents of the measure discussed the nature of the provisional legislative power. Then the opponents of the bill shifted the focus to the fundamental questions of the constitutionality and expediency of the reconstruction proposal in general.

At the outset the advocates of the bill sought to define precisely the degree of power the provisional government ought to have. They wanted it to have enough power to prevent a repetition of what had happened in North Carolina, that is, the enforcement of laws ancillary to slavery. Yet, thinking that the authority should be given to a basically interim government, they wanted to allow for substantial continuity by preserving pre-existing state laws. At issue was the amended bill's restriction of legislative power and how it was to be interpreted. Charles Sumner, for example, thought that although the restriction formally applied to the legislature, practically it would limit the provisional governor also and require that he enforce existing state laws relating to slavery and Negroes. Referring specifically to Stanley's actions in North Carolina, Sumner proposed an amendment leaving the provisional governor free to disregard laws such as the North Carolina code for Negroes, which he called "an outrage to civilization." To avoid having to enforce such laws, John Sherman proposed an amendment re-

[36] *Ibid.*, sec. 3.

quiring the executive to enforce laws of the United States, implying that he need not carry out existing state statutes. But Lyman Trumbull, the chairman of the judiciary committee, objected to this proposal.[37]

Trumbull illustrated the difficulty faced by essentially conservative men who were trying to preserve the traditional existence of the states yet change the fundamental element of the established order—the position of the Negro. "I think it would be well," Trumbull said, "not to interfere with the general laws of these States, or the general administration of justice." He added, "It would be very desirable that the officers who shall be sent temporarily to exercise authority in those localities which shall be brought under the jurisdiction of the United States . . . should conform, so far as possible, to the settled habits and customs and laws of the people." At the same time Trumbull believed that Congress ought not to allow the operation of such laws as those Sumner had referred to. Yet to enforce only federal laws was not a proper solution. It was "a very dangerous doctrine," Trumbull insisted, "to say that the officer charged with the execution of the laws may himself disregard them." He pointed out that "in order to preserve the peace of society, in order to carry out the purpose of this bill, you must have some other laws than the laws of the United States." What was needed, said Trumbull, was a provision that would "require the execution generally of the laws which were in existence at the time that the rebellion broke out," yet that would "exclude the particular class of laws to which allusion has been made." [38]

Senator Ira Harris further revealed the inner contradictions in a policy of providing interim government for the seceded states within the framework of the administration's policy on slavery —that is, *without* general emancipation—while at the same time trying to protect Negroes against the operation of laws supporting the slave system. The object of his bill, Harris explained, was

[37] *Cong. Globe*, 37 Cong., 2 sess., 3139 (July 7, 1862).
[38] *Ibid.*, 3140 (July 7, 1862).

"not to change the legislation of the States. It is to establish a temporary government, to execute the constitution and laws of the rebel States during the interval that may occur between the time when the rebellion shall be suppressed, and when those States shall be able to reorganize themselves and be restored to their proper position in the Union." Harris thought that some legislative power was necessary in a provisional government, but he was "very unwilling to clothe these officers with power to change the entire body of laws of those States." Laws concerning slavery were of course uppermost in his mind. On this score Harris said, "While I should be very glad to see slavery abolished, while I expect to see slavery abolished, I do not want to see it abolished by any such system of legislation as this [Sumner's] amendment contemplates, for it really goes to that." On the other hand, he could see the validity of Sumner's point concerning anti-Negro laws in the rebel states, and believed they should not be enforced. He resolved the problem, however, by arguing that only the legislature, and not the provisional governor, was prevented by the amended bill from interfering with existing state laws and institutions. "There is nothing in the bill," Harris explained, "that requires the executive power conferred by this bill upon the Governor to execute these obnoxious laws to which . . . [Sumner] has been referring." He observed that while a provisional governor might execute such laws, "if a proper man be appointed, he will not execute them. So far as this bill is concerned, it leaves that an open question." [39]

Answering the charge that the bill reduced the states to territories, Harris offered a theoretical framework fundamentally different from the framework of Ashley's plan for territorialization. Whereas Ashley had considered the seceded states reduced to territories which Congress could govern directly, either by the exercise of its territorial power or of the general power of a sovereign nation, Harris explained that his bill was

[39] *Ibid.*, 3139 (July 7, 1862).

based on the specific constitutional power of Congress to guarantee to each state in the Union a republican form of government. While there was some inconsistency in his ideas, and while
the bill still retained references to the forms of territorial government, his theories departed significantly from the concept of
territorialization and anticipated the direction that Republican
reconstruction theory would take later in the war. Harris also
delivered a critique of military government in terms of its constitutional implications.

The difference between Ashley and Harris appeared most
clearly in the latter's contention that the states were still in the
Union. The guarantee clause, Harris argued, "contemplates that
all the States are in the Union, that they are to be governed in
the Union, and that the General Government are to see that they
remain in the union, and that they are governed by a republican
form of government." Because of this constitutional requirement,
moreover, the policy of military government was plainly inadequate. "Where is the provision in the Constitution that authorizes the appointment of military Governors?" he asked. In
Harris' opinion, the installing of military government implied
that the states were conquered provinces. "The States where
these military Governors are appointed are in some sort prisoners
of war," he said, "and we hold them as conquered States, . . .
and undertake to govern them by the arbitrary government of
military law." The correct procedure was to provide civil
government until the people could restore their state governments. "See the anomaly that is presented," Harris explained:
"Here is a State, the State of North Carolina or South Carolina;
it has a constitution under the United States in the United States;
it has a body of laws; but its constitution and laws are unex-
ecuted, and the people refuse to execute them." Under the circumstances it was "the duty of the General Government to see
that these rebel States are governed as States under the Constitution. . . . and not to allow them to remain as outside the Government." According to Harris, this could be done

in no other way . . . so well and so much in accord with the spirit and provisions of the Constitution . . . as by a bill framed in some such way as this. . . . It is a bill to govern these States *ad interim* during the interval that shall elapse between the time when the rebellion is subdued and the States are conquered, and when they shall be willing to reorganize themselves and come back and govern themselves in the Union under their own constitution and laws.[40]

Having listened to proponents of the bill discuss specific details of executive and legislative powers, critics of the measure began to question its fundamental purpose. Lazarus Powell of Kentucky reflected their general attitude when he suggested, "Instead of fixing up the little details I think we had better see first whether we have authority to pass the bill or not." The leading opponents of the reconstruction bill included Powell and Garrett Davis, Democrats of Kentucky, John Carlile, a Unionist of Virginia, and John Ten Eyck of New Jersey and Edgar Cowan of Pennsylvania, Republicans. All regarded the bill as a territorialization measure pure and simple. "There is no power vested in Congress to declare sovereign States provinces," said Powell, who argued that the bill "does that virtually." In Ten Eyck's view, the bill "involves all the machinery of a territorial government, and in fact reduces these States to a territorial condition," while Carlile compared it to Sumner's resolutions of February asserting "the power in Congress to reduce States of this Union to a territorial condition." Opponents also charged that the bill was inconsistent with the clause guaranteeing republican government to each state. A republican form of government, said Garrett Davis, "must be made by the people, and the agencies by which that government is carried on and operated must be appointed or elected by them." According to Ten Eyck, the bill was the very denial of republican government, for it "contemplates a Governor, a judiciary, and a Legislature, all strangers to the district, to enact, decide upon, and execute laws

[40] *Ibid.*, 3141–3142 (July 7, 1862).

without responsibility to anyone or any power." Yet critics of
provisional civil government under Congress approved military
government under the executive. Ten Eyck summarized feeling
on this point in declaring, "If some little machinery of Government should be put on foot and established while the State government is in abeyance, let that government be established under
the military power by the Executive." [41]

Opponents of the congressional plan of reconstruction also
feared it would become an abolition measure, despite the restrictions in the bill on the provisional legislature. Lazarus Powell
argued that while the amended bill might be interpreted as subjecting the provisional government to local law, it had a qualify-
ing clause "that will utterly repudiate that idea," namely, the
provision that there should be no interference with existing state
laws "further than shall be necessary to carry into effect the
provisions and purposes of this act." "That clothes them with
the power to judge of the necessity," Powell explained, "and
you know . . . what kind of judgment you will have in a slave-
holding community if such [antislavery] men are appointed."
He concluded, "The object, the scope, and the intention of it
[Harris' bill] is to send judges and a Governor there for the purpose of indirectly abolishing the institution of African slavery,
and overthrowing the domestic institutions of those States under
the apparent shield and panoply of the law." [42]

The Senate debate revealed that supporters of the bill could
not agree on the precise extent of the provisional governments'
power, while its opponents regarded it as a radical scheme for
destroying the states. Although at one point the Senate rejected
a motion to postpone the bill by a vote of 20 to 17, indicating
that perhaps a majority of the senators supported the plan,
Trumbull and Harris were unable to bring the Senate to a
direct vote on it. It therefore was set aside informally and because of the pressure of other business was not taken up again
during the session, which ended nine days later. [43]

[41] *Ibid.*, 3140–3144 (July 7, 1862).   [42] *Ibid.*, 3141–3142 (July 7, 1862).
[43] *Ibid.*, 3146 (July 7, 1862).

In failing to pass Harris' bill, the Republican party missed a significant opportunity to reach a solution to the reconstruction question that might have been satisfactory to both the President and Congress. The bill avoided the excesses of Ashley's territorial plan and was intended to provide interim civil authority until the loyal citizens of a state could reorganize the local government. It was therefore acceptable to moderates; it was similar in purpose, though not in constitutional form, to Lincoln's policy of military government. On the other hand, the bill did not impose absolute restrictions on the policy-making power of the provisional government; employing the forms of territorial government, it established congressional authority over reconstruction; and it substituted the regular processes of civil law for the arbitrary methods of military rule. All this made it acceptable to the radical wing of the party. In short, Harris' bill, as amended by the judiciary committee, offered a moderate alternative to both the radical antislavery plan of territorialization and the conservative policy of military government under the control of the executive.

Evidence that Lincoln might have agreed to a proposal such as Harris' strengthens the impression that with the defeat of the bill, the party lost an opportunity to effect a compromise in the conflict between President and Congress that later dominated reconstruction politics. Lyman Trumbull said on June 27, in reference to Harris' bill, "I have no doubt we shall have the cooperation of the President in passing that law, and I have no doubt, when the bill is passed, he will sign it cheerfully, and regret that it was not passed earlier." [44] Whether Trumbull spoke with any authority it is impossible to say, but he may not have been far from the mark. Secretary of the Treasury Salmon P. Chase said a few months later that Lincoln had at one time been attracted to the idea of provisional civil government, of the kind Harris and the judiciary committee proposed, as a means of governing the seceded states. Writing in October 1862, Chase

[44] *Ibid.*, 2974 (June 27, 1862).

explained that he earlier tried to persuade Lincoln of the need for civil government in the South: "At first, the President and nearly the whole Cabinet were favorable to it; but the strenuous objections of one or two made the President, who disliked controversy, abandon it." [45] Though Chase was a radical who had agreed that the rebel states could be considered reduced to territories, the idea for provisional civil government which he suggested to Lincoln was closer to Harris' than to Ashley's concept.[46] Chase, in fact, supported Harris' bill, regretted that it had not been passed, and laid its failure to the "apprehensions of conservative Senators that it might somehow affect slavery." [47]

The defeat of Harris' bill left the problems of governing the rebel states and beginning reconstruction in the hands of the President. After Congress adjourned, Lincoln was able to proceed without interference to establish military governments and to implement a policy of reconstruction aimed at the rapid restoration of the states with a minimum of social or political

[45] Salmon P. Chase to N. B. Buford, Oct. 11, 1862, in J. W. Schuckers, *Life and Public Services of Salmon Portland Chase* (New York, 1874), 381.

[46] Chase said in March 1862 that while he regarded the rebel states "as having so far forfeited their rights that they may justly be treated as Territories, I have never proposed to make this opinion the basis of political measures. I much prefer to regard each State as still existing intact." He explained further that he preferred "civil, provisional government, authorized by Congress, to military government instituted by the President," and that he had prepared a bill which "provided only for provisional governments; not to destroy, but to preserve" (Chase to William P. Mellen, March 26, 1862, in *ibid.*, 365; Robert B. Warden, *An Account of the Private Life and Public Services of Salmon Portland Chase* [Cincinnati, 1874], 422).

[47] Chase said of Harris' bill: "The advantages of this plan seem to me obvious. It would interfere with no local administration, beyond insisting on loyalty; it would afford a head, in place of the State organization, acting directly on the people in the ordinary form of legislative, judicial, and executive administration; and it could give way, without any great disturbance or inconvenience, upon the reëstablishment of the State government" (Chase to Buford, Oct. 11, 1862, in Schuckers, *Life of Chase*, 381).

change or reform. So intent was he on seeking this end that even though at this time he decided on military emancipation, he was prepared to exempt rebel states from the effect of this policy if they would comply with his reconstruction program.

The failure of Harris' bill also signified the rejection of territorialization as an organizing principle of congressional reconstruction. The defeat of Ashley's plan in March had foreshadowed this result and influenced the judiciary committee to amend Harris' measure to make it more conservative. Nevertheless, the bill still adhered to the territorial concept, so was unacceptable to men whose main concern was to preserve state rights. When Harris in debate explained that the bill was based on the principle of the guarantee of republican government to each state in the Union, however, he was pointing out a new approach to reconstruction that would supersede the theory of territorialization as the basis of congressional action toward the rebel states.

V

A New Phase of Reconstruction

BY the end of July 1862 congressional challenges to the administration's policy of military government had failed, and territorialization was no longer a viable or relevant approach to reconstruction. In part this was because antislavery pressures in Congress, which had provided a major source of support for territorial plans, were resulting in numerous emancipationist steps in the spring of 1862. Hence the Republican majority and the radical wing in Congress had greater flexibility as they turned to the next phase of reconstruction—the organization of loyal state governments and their readmission to the Union.

In the second half of 1862 the President and Congress became convinced that the election of representatives to Congress was the best way to promote the reorganization of state governments. The implications of this procedure for constitutional theory were significantly different from those of territorialization. The former rested first on the principle that the loyal citizens in the rebel states were United States citizens entitled to the protection of the federal government and to representation in the national legislature. This concept in turn signified the continued existence of the states, for only states—and not territories —could elect representatives. There were practical advantages to such an approach to reconstruction, too. It could take effect in the occupied part of a rebel state; it did not require the existence of a loyal state government; and it utilized an established constitutional practice which, though usually under the control of the states, could be carried on by Congress under its undoubted power to legislate concerning the time, place, and manner of federal elections. Furthermore, reconstruction by means of congressional elections combined local Unionist activity with federal initiative and supervision, and politically it held out the promise of increased Republican strength in Congress. All this added up to a moderate policy which the vast majority of Republicans could support. Henry L. Dawes, the chairman of the House elections committee who had advocated this approach in the previous session of Congress, summed up the prevailing view when he said that the election of representatives to Congress was "the only hope of the restoration and of the continuance of this Government in the form and under the sanctions of the Constitution." [1]

The evolution of this moderate reconstruction policy, which resulted in the return of at least one seceded state to representation in Congress, was accompanied by an even more important development—Lincoln's adoption of a policy of military emancipation. Culminating in the Emancipation Proclamation of January 1, 1863, this action signified the continuation of the understanding arrived at between President and Congress in the spring of 1862: Congress would abandon territorial plans in return for Lincoln's taking stronger steps against slavery. But Lincoln's turning toward military emancipation also raised a question with radical implications: whether the abolition of slavery would be a condition for the return of the rebel states to the Union.

---

[1] *Cong. Globe*, 37 Cong., 3 sess., 833 (Feb. 9, 1863). In February 1862, though opposing the admission of a Virginia representative for want of sufficient Unionist support, Dawes asserted that in the election of representatives lay "the germs of reconstruction, reorganization, and the reappearance of this Union" (*ibid.*, 37 Cong., 2 sess., 1007 [Feb. 27, 1862]).

A second development during the next few months, less prominent at the time but in the long run more important, was the
drawing of a new line of conflict with regard to reconstruction.
Territorialization versus state indestructibility ceased to be the
central issue, and the question of executive versus congressional
control, which was to dominate controversy over reconstruction
in its later stages, began to assume greater significance. The relevant points at issue were whether the President could reorganize
state governments or whether Congress must regulate the
process by law; whether the executive could provide for elections or whether only Congress might do this; and whether the
wishes and actions of the President could effect the readmission
of the rebel states or whether Congress had the exclusive power
to decide on this course of action. Executive authority had been
questioned in the debate over Harris' territorial plan in July, and
earlier in the session Congress had on two occasions shown its
determination to play a role in reconstruction.[2] The conduct of
the war might of necessity be an executive function, but reconstruction was not, in the view of an increasing number of Republicans.

[2] In June, Congress passed an act making the "iron-clad" oath, concerned with the loyalty of a person's past conduct and not merely with
his future allegiance, a condition for holding federal office, with the
exception of the presidency. James Wilson, the Republican of Iowa who
introduced the measure into the House, said, "The sole object of this bill
is to keep out of office under the Government of the United States men
who have taken up arms against the United States, and who have en-
deavored to destroy the Government under which we live." A second act
dealing with reconstruction required the election of representatives by
single district, in order to prevent southern Unionists from using the
general ticket system to elect representatives for an entire state, only part
of which was under Union control. Henry Dawes, who introduced the
measure, said he was willing to "have men coming here representing
districts, so far as the districts become loyal," but he would not allow
that "any number, however few, may meet in any State and elect a full
delegation of Representatives for that State." The bill Dawes introduced
was identical to an act of 1842 requiring election by single district, which
had expired in 1850 (U.S., *Stat. at Large*, XII, 502; *Cong. Globe*, 37
Cong., 2 sess., 2564 [June 4, 1862], remarks of Wilson; 2911–2912 [June
25, 1862], remarks of Dawes).

After the adjournment of Congress in July 1862, Lincoln moved rapidly toward a policy of military emancipation. One powerful influence on him was the antislavery impulse in Congress, which for the present had culminated in the Second Confiscation Act of July 17, 1862. This sweeping measure declared free the slaves of all persons committing treason or supporting the rebellion, and all slaves found within Union lines whose owners were engaged in insurrection. A second influence on Lincoln was military. As McClellan's long-awaited spring offensive, known as the Peninsular campaign, turned into a series of defeats, emancipation began to seem a military necessity. Foreign-policy considerations also entered the picture. European opinion was antislavery, and a clear-cut turn against slavery would do much to align Europeans with the Union cause. The pressures appeared all the stronger in view of the manifest failure of the policy of gradual, compensated emancipation adopted by the administration and Congress in March 1862. Border-state men, it was clear, were almost unanimously opposed to emancipation in any form and were impervious to special appeals from the President.[3]

It was under these circumstances that Lincoln decided on military emancipation. On July 13, 1862, following another vain appeal to border-state representatives to accept compensated emancipation, Lincoln told Gideon Welles that he had "about come to the conclusion" that emancipation was "a military necessity, absolutely essential for the salvation of the Union."[4] On July 22, less than a week after the adjournment of Congress, he presented to the Cabinet the draft of a proclamation of emancipation. The Cabinet's response was favorable, but Seward pointed out that to issue the decree under existing circumstances would appear an act of weakness rather than strength. Lincoln

---

[3] U.S., *Stat. at Large*, XII, 590–591; Randall, *Lincoln the President*, II, 151–155; Williams, *Lincoln and the Radicals*, 169; Nevins, *The War for the Union*, II, 147–149.

[4] Gideon Welles, *The Diary of Gideon Welles*, ed. Howard K. Beale (3 vols.; New York, 1960), I, 70.

therefore decided to withhold the proclamation until the military situation was more propitious. Nevertheless, he had concluded that military emancipation was necessary.

In September 1862 the Battle of Antietam, in which Union forces halted a Confederate drive into Maryland, created a situation favorable for announcing the new policy on slavery. Accordingly, on September 22, Lincoln issued the preliminary proclamation of emancipation. He declared that on January 1, 1863, "all persons held as slaves within any state, or designated part of a state, the people whereof shall then be in rebellion against the United States shall be then, thenceforward, and forever free." The proclamation stated further that the Executive "will recognize and maintain the freedom of such persons, and will do no act or acts to repress such persons, or any of them, in any efforts they may make for their actual freedom." [5]

Radical as this step was in relation to the earlier policy of the administration toward slavery, Lincoln did not let it cause him to abandon his fundamental purpose—the restoration of the Union. If fact, he tried to use it to induce the rebel states to return to the Union. He began the preliminary proclamation, for example, by declaring, "Hereafter, as heretofore, the war will be prossecuted [*sic*] for the object of practically restoring the constitutional relation between the United States, and each of the states, and the people thereof, in which states that relation is, or may be suspended, or disturbed." To this end Lincoln set forth what amounted to minimum conditions for reconstruction. He said that on January 1, 1863, the executive would designate which states were in rebellion; "and the fact that any state, or the people thereof shall, on that day be, in good faith represented in the Congress of the United States, by members chosen thereto, at elections wherein a majority of the qualified voters of such state shall have participated, shall, in the absence of

[5] Preliminary Emancipation Proclamation, Sept. 22, 1862, in *Collected Works of Lincoln*, V, 434.

strong countervailing testimony, be deemed conclusive evidence that such state and the people thereof, are not then in rebellion against the United States." [6] In this way Lincoln connected emancipation with reconstruction.

The practical means for effecting restoration—the election of representatives to Congress—had been in the forefront of Lincoln's thinking on reconstruction for several weeks. Early in July he had written to Andrew Johnson, the military governor of Tennessee, "If we could, somehow, get a vote of the people of Tennessee and have it result properly it would be worth more to us than a battle gained." He asked Johnson, "How long before we can get such a vote?" The election of representatives was doubtless in Lincoln's mind a few weeks later, when he remarked to a prominent Democrat, "Louisiana has nothing to do now but to take her place in the Union as it was." Warning that such a course was imperative if revolutionary consequences were to be avoided, he said, "Broken eggs cannot be mended," and that the sooner Louisiana resumed her relations to the Union, "the smaller will be the amount of that which will be past mending." If southerners expected "to ever have the Union as it was," Lincoln concluded, "now is the time." [7]

In the fall of 1862, Lincoln moved decisively to carry out his policy of reconstruction. On September 29, one week after issuing the Preliminary Emancipation Proclamation, he told Edward Stanley, the military governor of North Carolina: "I shall be much gratified if you can find it practicable to have congressional elections held . . . before January. It is my sincere wish that North Carolina may again govern herself conformably to the constitution of the United States." In the following weeks Lincoln made similar requests of military governors and commanding officers in Louisiana, Tennessee, and Arkansas. He instructed them to assist all persons who "desire to

[6] *Ibid.*
[7] Lincoln to Andrew Johnson, July 3, 1862, in *ibid.*, 303; Lincoln to August Belmont, July 31, 1862, in *ibid.*, 350.

avoid the unsatisfactory prospect before them, and to have peace again upon the old terms under the constitution of the United States, to manifest such desire by elections of members to the Congress of the United States particularly, and perhaps a legislature, State officers, and United States Senators friendly to their object." State election laws should be adhered to as much as possible; "but," he emphasized, "at all events get the expression of the largest number of the people possible. All see how such action will connect with, and affect the proclamation of September 22nd." [8] Finally, Lincoln reminded General John A. Dix in Virginia that he had left himself "at liberty to exempt *parts* of states" from the Preliminary Emancipation Proclamation, and that he would "be very glad if any Congressional District" would elect a representative. [9]

Realizing how important the successful restoration of even a single state would be as a precedent, Lincoln kept close watch over reconstruction efforts. Louisiana received his special attention. In October, after issuing instructions to elect members of Congress, he established for Louisiana a provisional court, and appointed Charles A. Peabody of New York provisional judge, with the same powers and jurisdiction that belonged to judicial officers of federal district and circuit courts. Although one of the reasons for creating the court was the diplomatic problem resulting from claims filed against the United States by citizens of foreign countries who had lost or suffered injury to their property in New Orleans, Lincoln invested the provisional court with jurisdiction in all civil and criminal cases, and declared its judgments to be final and conclusive. When a month later he found out that no progress had been made in carrying out his request to hold elections, he wrote impatiently to Governor Shepley, "I am annoyed to learn . . . that . . . nothing had

[8] Lincoln to Edward Stanley, Sept. 29, 1862, in *ibid.*, 445; Lincoln to Benjamin F. Butler, George F. Shepley, and others, Oct. 14, 1862, in *ibid.*, 462–463. Identical letters were sent to General Grant and Andrew Johnson in Tennessee, and to General Steele and John Phelps in Arkansas (*ibid.*, 470–471, 500).

[9] Lincoln to John A. Dix, Oct. 26, 1862, in *ibid.*, 476–477.

been done about congressional elections." If the people of Louisiana "stand idle not seeming to know what to do," he told Shepley, "do you fix these things for them by proclamation. And do not waste a day about it; but, fix the election day early enough that we can hear about the result here by the first of January." Lincoln knew, however, that too overt an exercise of federal military power in this delicate political operation would jeopardize its success. He therefore reminded Shepley that he wanted elections, but that he wanted them to be the result of "a movement of the people of the Districts, and not a movement of our military and quasi-military, authorities there." "What we do want," he explained in another letter, "is the conclusive evidence that respectable citizens of Louisiana, are willing to be members of congress & to swear support to the constitution; and that other respectable citizens there are willing to vote for them and send them." [10]

In accordance with Lincoln's instructions, military authorities held congressional elections in December and early January in four southern states. The most impressive result was achieved in Louisiana, where approximately 7,600 citizens in and around New Orleans elected representatives from the first and second congressional districts. In eastern Virginia, 1,400 votes were cast in the Norfolk and eastern-shore district, and 400 votes in a district in western Virginia. Under Governor Stanley in North Carolina an election was held in the second district in which 864 voters participated, and in Tennessee about 1,900 votes were cast in an election in the ninth district.[11]

Lincoln apparently was satisfied with these results and intent

[10] Executive Order Establishing a Provisional Court in Louisiana, Oct. 20, 1862, in *ibid.*, 467–468; Charles A. Peabody, "United States Provisional Court for the State of Louisiana, 1862–1865," American Historical Association, *Annual Report, 1892* (Washington, 1893), 201–204; Lincoln to George F. Shepley, Nov. 21, 1862, in *Collected Works of Lincoln*, V, 504–505.

[11] *House Reports*, 37 Cong., 3 sess., no. 22, Michael Hahn and Benjamin F. Flanders; no. 23, John B. McCloud and W. W. Wing; no. 43, Christopher Grafflin; no. 41, Jennings Pigott; no. 46, Alvin Hawkins.

on having them accepted by Congress. This much he made clear when the question of exempting parts of the South from the effect of the Emancipation Proclamation came up at a Cabinet meeting in December. Replying to a question about the exemption of New Orleans and the surrounding area, he explained that he had promised the people there that he would exempt them if they would elect members of Congress. Salmon P. Chase interjected that while two representatives had been elected from Louisiana, "they have not yet got their seats, and it is not certain that they will." At this, according to John P. Usher, the Secretary of the Interior, Lincoln "rose from his seat, apparently irritated, and walked rapidly back and forth, across the room. Looking over his shoulder at Mr. Chase, he said: 'There it is, sir. I am to be bullied by Congress, am I? If I do, I'll be durned.' " [12]

So anxious was Lincoln to promote reconstruction that he exempted the states in which elections had been held, even though only one of them had fulfilled the conditions outlined in the preliminary proclamation of September. The President had therein stated that for representatives to be accepted, they had to be chosen at elections in which a majority of the qualified voters had participated. Only Louisiana had met this requirement; the 7,600 voters who had turned out were about half the number who had voted in the elections of 1859. Congress, furthermore, had not admitted any of the members-elect, as Lincoln had specified it should. Nevertheless, he excepted from the effect of the Emancipation Proclamation of January 1, 1863, all of Tennessee, though elections had taken place in only one part of the state; the parishes in and around New Orleans, in Louisiana; Norfolk and the eastern-shore section of Virginia; and all forty-eight counties of West Virginia, just then on the verge of statehood, where no elections had been held.[13] These exceptions

[12] Allen Thorndike Rice, ed., *Reminiscences of Lincoln by Distinguished Men of His Time* (New York, 1886), 93–94.

[13] Emancipation Proclamation, Jan. 1, 1863, *Collected Works of Lincoln*, VI, 29. As of January 1, elections had not been held in North Carolina and the Alexandria district of Virginia, which accordingly were not exempted from the requirements of the proclamation.

signified a shift from the idea, embodied in the preliminary proclamation, that the legitimacy of reconstruction efforts depended on the participation of a majority of the population and anticipated the policy of accepting state governments reorganized on the basis of a vote by a minority—Lincoln's "10-per-cent" plan of December 1863.[14]

An additional consideration for Lincoln was the political effect his reconstruction policy might have. Although he had written in October that the administration did "not particularly need members of congress from there [rebel states] to enable us to get along with legislation here," the results of the November congressional elections, in which Republicans suffered heavy losses, cast a new light on the elections being held in occupied southern states. In December a New York correspondent of General Benjamin F. Butler, the Union army commander in New Orleans, observed, "The Democratic press assume that the Louisiana election is an attempt on the part of the Administration to secure for themselves a majority in the next Congress, which otherwise would be Democratic." Actually the Republicans, according to most compilations, appeared to retain control of Congress, but only by a slim margin. Obviously Lincoln's reconstruction policy as it was now developing gave promise of helping to offset the recent Democratic electoral gains, since

---

[14] In discussing the West Virginia statehood bill in a Cabinet meeting in December 1862, Lincoln offered a constitutional explanation of this shift. The point at issue was whether the Pierpont government was the government of Virginia, the consent of which was necessary for a division of the state. Lincoln said that because less than a majority of the Virginia voters had participated in the choice of the legislature, it might be argued that the Pierpont government was not the legitimate government of the state. "But it is a universal practice in the popular elections in all these states," he added, "to give no legal consideration whatever to those who do not choose to vote, as against the effect of the votes of those, who do. . . . Hence it is not the qualified voters, but the qualified voters, *who choose to vote*, that constitute the political power of the state." On this basis the elections in the southern states could be accepted as valid (Opinions Concerning the Admission of West Virginia, Dec. 31, 1862, in *ibid.*, VI, 26–27).

members from occupied states would no doubt support an administration to which they owed their political existence.[15]

Thus by December 1862, Lincoln had implemented his plan for reconstruction and had created a situation in which Congress was under pressure to accept the results of executive action. For this reason, and also because it shared the same understanding of reconstruction priorities, Congress in the winter of 1862–1863 was mainly concerned with representation from seceded states and focused its attention both on election cases and on proposals for congressional elections.

The most important test of Lincoln's policy was Louisiana, where Michael Hahn and Benjamin Flanders had been elected representatives. In accordance with standard practice, the House at the start of the session referred their credentials to the elections committee. At the previous session the committee had rejected several similar claims, and observers predicted a similar disposition of the Louisiana case. House passage of a resolution requesting the President to explain what authority had been given to the military governor of Louisiana strengthened this impression, as did the decision of the Republican caucus on January 20, 1863, "to prevent the premature admission of members from those [rebel] states elected by authority of military governors." [16]

Contrary to expectation, however, the Committee on Elections reported in favor of seating Hahn and Flanders. Chairman Henry Dawes told the House that the process by which the Louisiana members had been chosen possessed "the all-important and all-essential element of securing to the people of these dis-

[15] Lincoln to George F. Shepley, Nov. 21, 1862, in *Collected Works of Lincoln*, V, 504; Charles S. Bartles to Benjamin F. Butler, Dec. 13, 1862, in *Private and Official Correspondence of General Benjamin F. Butler*, ed. Jessie Ames Marshall (5 vols; Norwood, Mass., 1917), II, 534.
[16] New York *Tribune*, Jan. 16, 1863; New York *Times*, Jan. 22, 1863; *Cong. Globe*, 37 Cong., 3 sess., 282 (Jan. 12, 1863); Julia P. Cutler, *Life and Times of Ephraim Cutler, with Biographical Sketches of Jervis Cutler and William Parker Cutler* (Cincinnati, 1890), 298.

tricts the free and untrammelled and unawed exercise of the electoral franchise." In the First District, where 4,970 votes had been cast in the last congressional election before secession, Flanders polled 2,370 of 2,643 votes; in the Second District, where 10,367 votes had been cast in 1859, Hahn received 2,799 of 5,117 ballots. Allowing for citizens absent in military service, the committee considered this a full vote and an honest expression of the views of the loyal citizens. The committee noted further that the state election laws had been followed, except that the military governor had acted in place of the regularly elected governor in ordering the election. The committee, said Dawes, "found no difficulty whatever in coming to the conclusion that these gentlemen were entitled to be admitted to seats upon this floor, except the fact that the election was called by a military governor." [17]

This was a most important exception, however, for it raised the question of the nature and extent of the powers of a military governor. Were they exclusively military, confined to the preservation of peace and order, or did they embrace the performance of civil functions as well, including the election of representatives to Congress? The law of belligerent occupation supported those who believed the latter, as proponents of the Louisiana claimants argued. It was common knowledge that Shepley had carried out civil as well as military tasks, and it seemed impossible to distinguish between these and the act of calling a congressional election. John Noell, a Democrat of Missouri, reasoned that military governors were appointed "to supply the place of the local functionaries in the performance of their civil duties," and Republican Owen Lovejoy of Illinois agreed that the military governor was supposed to "discharge the duties of the Governor regularly elected." [18] To support their position,

[17] *House Reports*, 37 Cong., 3 sess., no. 22, Michael Hahn and Benjamin F. Flanders, 9–11; *Cong. Globe*, 37 Cong., 3 sess., 832–833 (Feb. 9, 1863).

[18] *Cong. Globe*, 37 Cong., 3 sess. 833 (Feb. 9, 1863); 861, 863 (Feb. 10, 1863).

Dawes and others cited the Supreme Court decision in the case of Cross versus Harrison arising out of the Mexican War.[19] According to Dawes, the Court in that case gave "full force and effect to the acts of a military governor, when acting in a civil capacity." According to this point of view, then, Shepley was the *de facto* governor of Louisiana.[20]

The main objective in admitting Flanders and Hahn was to speed the reconstruction of one state, thereby setting a precedent for other states to follow. Dawes, the chief spokesman for the Louisiana members-elect, phrased the issue: "How are these districts and this State ever to be represented again in this Congress, except by some means entirely analogous to this case?" John Noell similarly declared, "The best means to bring the States in rebellion back into the Union will be to permit the introduction of Representatives from those States into this House, for the purpose of participating in the various measures of national legislation." Though reluctant to rely upon military authority, the elections committee saw the long-term advantages to be gained "in setting in motion the wheels of government in

[19] *Cross v. Harrison*, 16 Howard 164 (1853). In 1847, President Polk appointed a military governor over California with power to impose duties on imports and tonnage. A system of tariffs was thus set up, which continued after the war ended, even though the territory was included in a collection district created by act of Congress. Not until November 1849 did the military governor cease to collect duties. Cross was a member of a commercial firm which sought reimbursement for duties it had paid between February 1848, when the war ended, and November 1849, when a civil-appointed customs collector arrived. Cross argued that with the end of the war, the civil as well as military authority of the military governor ceased. The Supreme Court sustained Harrison, the customs collector under the military authority, holding that the military government "was the government when the territory was ceded as a conquest, and it did not cease, as a matter of course, or as a necessary consequence of the restoration of peace." Either Congress or the executive might have terminated the military government, but since neither had done so, the Court concluded that "the right inference . . . is, that it was meant to be continued until it had been legislatively changed" (16 Howard 193).

[20] *Cong. Globe*, 37 Cong., 3 sess., 832 (Feb. 9, 1863); *House Reports*, 37 Cong., 3 sess., no. 22, 11–12.

these States at the earliest possible moment." "No better method . . . [of reconstruction] is open to us," Dawes asserted, "than that which, recognizing the spontaneous voice of these electors, gives it a place here, around which the Union sentiment of the State of Louisiana may cluster, and cling, and twine itself, and grow and bear fruit." [21]

Finally, there was a tendency to support the admission of Flanders and Hahn as obligatory on the House after its approval of the Preliminary Emancipation Proclamation.[22] Lincoln had promised to exempt states which sent representatives to Congress. How then, asked John Noell, could "the majority of this House, which has indorsed the constitutionality and propriety of the President's proclamation, . . . vote that we shall repudiate the fruits of that proclamation, or . . . refuse to fulfill the promises which it held out?" [23]

The opponents of Hahn and Flanders, including both Democrats and Republicans, charged executive usurpation in the election process. They insisted, first, that only Congress or a state government could authorize federal elections, and that for the President to do so was *ultra vires*. Secondly, they held that the election in Louisiana had been controlled by the President, through the military authorities. As evidence of "moral coercion," Republican Albert Porter of Indiana pointed to an order of military governor Shepley stating that the purpose of the election was to enable loyal electors "to avail themselves of the benefits secured by the proclamation of the President." Because the election was dominated by the promise of saving their slaves,

[21] *Cong. Globe*, 37 Cong., 3 sess., 833 (Feb. 9, 1863); 861, 863 (Feb. 10, 1863).

[22] On December 15, 1862, the House voted 78 to 51 to pass a resolution declaring, "The policy of emancipation, as indicated in that proclamation, is well adapted to hasten the restoration of peace, was well chosen as a war measure, and is an exercise of power with proper regard for the rights of the States, and the perpetuity of free government" (*ibid.*, 92 [Dec. 15, 1862]).

[23] *Ibid.*, 862 (Feb. 10, 1863).

argued Daniel Voorhees, a Democrat of Indiana, it was "the grossest and most outrageous assault upon the freedom of the elective franchise ever known in a republican government." The corollary of these views was a narrow conception of the power of a military governor. Thomas D. Eliot, a Republican of Massachusetts, held that "no military governor can . . . be the 'executive authority' clothed with power under the [Louisiana] Constitution to issue writs of election." Military governors were appointed as a necessary first step in preserving peace, Eliot said, "but beyond the maintenance of good order and the preservation of law their power cannot go." John Crisfield, a Unionist Republican from Maryland, went so far as to question the authority of the President even to appoint a military governor. Said Crisfield: "There is no such officer described in American jurisprudence. . . . There is no such office. In legal contemplation it does not exist." [24]

As the debate unfolded, it appeared that the Louisiana claimants would be rejected. Henry Dawes wrote to his wife on February 11 that Flanders and Hahn "are most fiercely opposed and the prospect is that they will be defeated." Dawes felt that this would "be a sad thing for the future of the Union cause in other rebel States." When on February 14, with the Louisiana case still pending, the House voted against a representative-elect from Norfolk, its action seemed also to foreshadow the defeat of Flanders and Hahn. The Washington correspondent of the New York *Independent* concluded from the disposition of these cases, "It appears that the House very properly intends to be strict as to qualifications of its members." [25]

The House upset these predictions. however, and admitted Flanders and Hahn by a surprising 92 to 44 vote. Flanders was in New Hampshire at the time, campaigning for Union candi-

[24] *Ibid.*, 859–861 (Feb. 10, 1863); 835 (Feb. 9, 1863); App., 114 (Feb. 17, 1863).

[25] Henry L. Dawes to Electa Dawes, Feb. 11, 1863, Dawes Papers, Library of Congress; New York *Times*, Feb. 11, 1863; *The Independent*, Feb. 19, 1863, p. 8.

dates, but Hahn was present to take the oath. Upon his being sworn in, according to one correspondent, "members from all sides of the chamber congratulated him on the renewal of the representation of Louisiana in the House." The vote found the more extreme elements in both parties on the same side. Noting that such "ultra Republicans" as Eliot, Bingham, Stevens, and Ashley had voted with such "ultra Democrats" as Vallandigham and S. S. Cox, Benjamin Perley Poore of the Boston *Journal* concluded, "The lions and the (peace) lambs [were] lying down together." [26]

The admission of Louisiana representatives was a signal victory for the Lincoln administration. The state had been the chief focus of executive attention, and while no state officers had as yet been chosen, the seating of Flanders and Hahn could be expected to stimulate efforts to reorganize a loyal government. The result also vindicated the theory that the state was still in the Union. As the Boston *Commonwealth*, a radical antislavery newspaper which opposed the decision of the House, had pointed out in December, "The Constitution by all its provisions contemplates that Congress shall be composed only of the representatives, chosen according to prescribed forms, of certain well-defined political bodies known as States, existing in a prescribed form and which are in and of the Union and subject to its laws, by the consent of the people thereof." [27]

Thus Congress accepted presidential reconstruction, or the beginning of it, in Louisiana. On the other hand, the House was unwilling to give blanket endorsement to administration efforts, and in other cases rejected applicants elected under military authority.[28] Lincoln, for his part, accepted these decisions,

[26] New York *Times*, Feb. 19, 1863; *Cong. Globe*, 37 Cong., 3 sess., 1036 (Feb. 17, 1863); Boston *Journal*, Feb. 21, 1863. Twenty-one Republicans voted against the Louisiana members, along with twenty-one Democrats and border-state Unionists, while sixty-five Republicans voted for them.

[27] Boston *Commonwealth*, Dec. 13, 1862, p. 3.

[28] The most important other case was the Virginia election referred to above. In the Norfolk district, 1400 votes were cast (compared to a normal vote of about 9000), far fewer than in the elections in Louisiana. The

which meant that the executive and Congress, for the time being at least, had arrived at an understanding on reconstruction.

Cooperation on reconstruction was also evident in the admission of West Virginia to the Union in 1863. After both the President and Congress recognized the Wheeling government in 1861, the movement for separation from Virginia gained momentum. The Senate passed a West Virginia statehood bill in July 1862, the House approved it in December, and on December 31, 1862, Lincoln signed it into law. The new state then held a constitutional convention, conducted elections for a state government, and in June 1863 formally entered the Union. Though the circumstances had been unusual, the result, nonetheless, was a kind of reconstruction, which brought back a section of a seceded state into the Union. The possible effect of West Virginia's admission had been a chief concern of the Cabinet, and in the ensuing months some Republicans cited the admission as proof that the Union was being restored and as an example of how the process might continue.[29]

These instances of congressional and executive harmony were the most conspicuous feature of the session insofar as reconstruction was concerned. Yet in the long run they were less important than a second development: the forming of a new line

---

Committee on Elections considered the vote in Norfolk inadequate, but also commented on irregularities in the electoral process. Though Lincoln had specifically told General Dix to proceed with an election, the committee said it did not know under what authority Dix had acted. "He does not purport to call it as military governor, who is clothed to some extent with civil as well as military powers," the committee stated. In other cases the House rejected representatives from Virginia and North Carolina; it took no action in two more cases, one from Virginia again and one from Tennessee (*House Reports*, 37 Cong., 3 sess., no. 23, 5; *Cong. Globe*, 37 Cong., 3 sess., 1036–1037 [Feb. 17, 1863]; 1212 [Feb. 23, 1863]).

[29] G. E. Moore, *A Banner in the Hills*, 195–207; Toledo *Blade*, Jan. 26, 1864; William D. Kelley, *Speech in the Northrop-Kelley Debate, September 28, 1864* (Philadelphia, 1864), 12; New York *Times*, Aug. 25, 1863.

of conflict on reconstruction in general. With territorialization all but abandoned, the main issue was no longer whether the states had reverted to territories or were still in the Union—this was being decided in favor of the latter alternative—but whether the President or Congress ought to control reconstruction. For the moment the problem of military government provided the framework for discussing this issue. Republican Senator Ira Harris of New York put the matter squarely when he said, "The question is whether or not the President shall go on appointing Governors for the rebel States, as we get possession of them, without any authority, perhaps, of law, as a mere matter of necessity, or whether we shall regulate it by act of Congress." [30]

The arguments that most clearly indicate the existence of this jurisdictional conflict appeared in the debate on the Louisiana election, when both Democrats and Republicans raised the issue of executive usurpation of congressional powers. Daniel Voorhees of Indiana, a Democrat, said that the admission of the New Orleans representatives was tantamount to "surrendering to the Executive the branch of the government to which we belong." Republican Albert Porter of Indiana, who was regarded as belonging to the conservative wing of the party, insisted that the holding of elections was a legislative function only. "When the President assumes it," he argued, "it is, however well designed, usurpation." Said John Bingham, a Republican of Ohio, "The question . . . is, whether there shall be representation without any law upon the subject." Bingham held that Congress ought to control reconstruction through the election of representatives. If Louisiana was not represented in Congress, it was "because, duly notified of the fact that there was no existing law in the State . . . by which they could elect Representatives to Congress, we have failed to do our duty." He therefore urged the Committee on Elections to "report a bill authorizing an election for Rep-

[30] *Cong. Globe*, 37 Cong., 3 sess., 1507 (Mar. 3, 1863).

resentatives, to be held in such districts as may be designated by the President . . . within any insurrectionary district of any organized State." Albert Porter similarly declared: "The laws of Louisiana fixing the time, place, and manner of electing Representatives to Congress . . . are deprived of efficacy. . . . It is hence the solemn duty of Congress to enact a law to meet the emergency; and, indeed, to provide for all similar cases." [31]

The case for congressional action was so strong that even supporters of executive action in Louisiana favored legislation giving Congress supervision over elections. John Noell of Missouri, who had voted for Flanders and Hahn, declared: "I am in favor of the enactment of a law which will provide for the case of the loyal men in all these rebel States. . . . I want a law enacted by which the military governors shall be invested with the power to fix the time, place, and manner of holding elections in rebel States." [32] Indeed, it was the supporters of Louisiana representation, responding to the suggestions of critics like Bingham and Porter, who actually initiated legislation placing control of federal elections in the hands of Congress.

On February 12, 1863, two days after critics began to urge legislation, Horace Maynard of Tennessee introduced a bill for an election in Tennessee. On February 20, Samuel Worcester reported a similar measure from the Committee on Elections, and on February 24, Michael Hahn, one of the Louisiana members, submitted a proposal for elections in Louisiana. The Committee on Elections combined Hahn's bill with its own and reported a measure calling for the election of representatives in Tennessee and Louisiana. The bill stated that until otherwise provided by the legislatures of Tennessee and Louisiana, representatives in Congress from these states would be elected at the times, places, and in the manner prescribed in the act. The measure demarcated congressional districts for each state, called for elections in

[31] *Ibid.*, 834 (Feb. 9, 1863); 859, 862, 865 (Feb. 10, 1863); Cincinnati *Gazette*, Feb. 16, 1863.
[32] *Ibid.*, 862 (Feb. 10, 1863).

Louisiana for July, and in Tennessee for August 1863, and stated that citizens qualified as electors by the constitutions of the two states were entitled to vote. Except for prescribing an oath for election officials and voters whose loyalty might be challenged, the bill's detailed instructions for holding elections in the two states followed existing state laws.[33]

On March 2, the next to last day of the session, the House considered the elections bill. The arguments for the measure were well understood, having been spelled out in the debate on the Louisiana election cases, and the brief discussion that took place was largely a one-sided attack by a few Democrats. Their objections were that the bill unconstitutionally changed the qualifications for voting by adding an oath requirement; that it called for a specific exercise of federal power over elections aimed at just two states, rather than a general exercise; and that it failed to specify that only white men might vote. This last was the most interesting and significant charge. Wickliffe said that the bill extended the suffrage to "every free citizen," while Vallandigham argued that it gave Congress the right to prescribe who might vote in the states, without regard to color. Dawes denied these charges, pointing out that the bill was actually framed by men from Tennessee and Louisiana and relied upon the constitutions of those states in matters concerning suffrage.[34] The Louisiana constitution unqualifiedly restricted voting rights to white men only, but the opponents of the bill may have been partly right with respect to the Tennessee constitution, which seemed to leave an opening for limited Negro suffrage.[35] If it did, the elections committee's bill was one of the

[33] 37 Cong., H.R. 744, Feb. 12, 1863; H.R. 768, Feb. 20, 1863; H.R. 744, Feb. 24, 1863; H.R. 768, secs. 1–4, 16–19.

[34] *Cong. Globe*, 37 Cong., 3 sess., 1483–1484 (Mar. 2, 1863).

[35] Article IV of the Tennessee constitution stated: "Every free white man . . . being a citizen of the United States, and a citizen of the county wherein he may offer his vote . . . , shall be entitled to vote . . . : provided, That no person shall be disqualified from voting in any election on account of color, who is now, by the laws of this State, a

earliest proposals for freedmen's suffrage. Whether the bill was
so understood is doubtful, however, for if it had been, it almost
certainly would not have passed by the comfortable 104 to 27
vote that the House gave it.[36] Most members probably were not
aware of the exact provisions of the Tennessee constitution and
code.

competent witness in a court of justice against a white man." The code
of Tennessee, enacted in 1858, provided that Negroes, mulattoes, and
persons of mixed blood were incapable of being witnesses in any case
except for or against each other. But another section of the code stated,
"No person of mixed blood of any degree whatever, who has been
liberated from slavery within twelve months previous, shall be admitted
as a witness against a white man." This could be interpreted to mean that
free Negroes emancipated for *longer* than a year might be witnesses
against white men and, according to the constitution, might not be disqualified from voting. The provision that electors had to be citizens of
the United States might have presented an obstacle, in view of the Dred
Scott decision of 1857, in which the Supreme Court held that Negroes
could not be citizens of the United States. But this ruling could be and
was countered with the opinion of Attorney General Edward Bates,
issued in November 1862, that Negroes could be citizens of the United
States. Students of the Negro in Tennessee have been puzzled by this
"unusual" provision, as they have termed it, in the state constitution, one
holding that it was impossible to say how many Negroes were entitled to
vote under it. Their main point was that the Tennessee constitution of
1834 aimed at disfranchising free Negroes. One can agree with this but
conclude at the same time that the constitutional provision, in connection
with the state code, was potentially a significant means of extending
suffrage to Negroes, given state and federal officials sympathetic to the
freedmen (Francis N. Thorpe, *The Federal and State Constitutions,
Colonial Charters, and Other Organic Laws of the States, Territories,
and Colonies Now or Heretofore Forming the United States of America*
[9 vols.; Washington, 1909], III, 1412–1413, IV, 3433–3434; *The Code of
Tennessee Enacted by the General Assembly of 1857–'8*, comp. by Return J. Meigs and William F. Cooper [Nashville, 1858], secs. 3807, 3808;
Official Opinions of the Attorneys-General of the United States [10
vols.; Washington, 1868], X, 382–415; J. Merton England, "The Free
Negro in Ante-Bellum Tennessee," *Journal of Southern History*, IX
[Feb. 1943], 37–58; William Lloyd Imes, "The Legal Status of Free
Negroes and Slaves in Tennessee," *Journal of Negro History*, IV [July,
1919], 254–272).

[36] *Cong. Globe*, 37 Cong., 3 sess., 1484 (Mar. 2, 1863).

The next day the Senate considered the bill. The judiciary committee reported it with approval and after a large majority voted to consider it, its prospects for passing seemed good. But a handful of conservatives from the border states—James Bayard of Delaware, Lazarus Powell and Garrett Davis of Kentucky, and John Carlile of Virginia—strongly opposed it. In Bayard's opinion the bill was a scheme designed to secure the election of Republican congressmen. Democrats had gained considerably in the elections of 1862, and it was "to reverse that verdict," he asserted, "that the intent of this bill is to have a nominal election in two of the revolted States." Determined, in Davis' words, "to defeat this bill by any parliamentary proceeding that is allowable," Davis, Powell, and Carlile staged a filibuster. Their tactic was successful, as the session ended before a vote could be taken on the bill.[37] Thus a second moderate reconstruction measure—the first had been Harris' bill of July 1862—was defeated, mainly because of conservative opposition. In the earlier instance conservatives had feared emancipation. Now they feared that the elections bill would enable the federal government to interfere with, if not control, suffrage in the states.

Although some Republicans—the twenty-one radicals who voted against Louisiana representation—denied any role to the executive, the majority were prepared to support presidential reconstruction when it met certain minimum conditions, as it did in Louisiana. Yet, as the legislative history of the elections bill showed, the majority preferred to bring reconstruction under congressional control. Almost all Republicans agreed on two fundamental points: former rebels ought to be kept out of political office; and Congress had power to legislate concerning reconstruction, as well as exclusive power to decide on the readmission of rebel states. This agreement was the beginning of a congressional consensus which provided a basis for the subsequent struggle with the executive over reconstruction. At the same time a new constitutional basis for congressional recon-

[37] *Ibid.*, 1530, 1527 (Mar. 3, 1863).

struction also began to appear. The concept of territorialization as a framework for reconstruction gave way to the concept of a guarantee of republican government, which regarded the states as still in the Union and which derived from the express language of the Constitution.

Belief in territorialization of course did not disappear altogether. Some critics of executive reconstruction continued to endorse it, but only in a lingering and half-hearted way. James Ashley, for example, tried to introduce a bill for provisional civil governments similar to his proposal of March 1862; but when the measure was blocked, he made no further effort on its behalf.[38] In the Senate, Ira Harris revived his bill of the previous session, amending it by adding an antislavery section and by striking out all express references to territorial government as a means of defining the powers of the provisional government. The time was past for such a measure, however, and the Senate postponed consideration of it on March 3.[39]

Sensing that the territorial solution was no longer adequate, Harris meanwhile conceived a new approach to reconstruction, which directly anticipated the congressional plan adopted in 1864. Embodied in a bill he introduced in February 1863 were two central features: a reliance on the constitutional clause guaranteeing republican government as the source of congressional power, and an emphasis on reorganizing loyal state governments according to new state constitutions rather than on merely providing interim civil authority on the assumption that the people would eventually restore their state government.

Whereas Harris' earlier bill adhered to the model of territorial government, his new proposal took as its point of departure the fact of military government in occupied rebel states. Instead of a governor, judges, a secretary, and other officers appropriate to a

---

[38] *Ibid.*, 194 (Jan. 5, 1863); Boston *Commonwealth*, Jan. 10, 1863; Washington *Chronicle*, Jan. 6, 1863; *The Independent*, Jan. 8, 1863.

[39] 37 Cong., S. 200, amendment by Harris, Jan. 30, 1863; *Cong. Globe*, 37 Cong., 3 sess., 1507–1509 (Mar. 3, 1863).

territorial government, the bill provided for the appointment of a single officer—a provisional civil governor, however, rather than a military governor—who was "charged with the civil administration of the State until a State government shall be formed and recognized by the President." A further departure from the territorial pattern, and an implicit recognition of the continued existence of the states, was the provision that the governor might appoint "such officers, whose appointment is provided for by the laws of the State, as the same existed at the time such State renounced its obedience to the Constitution of the United States." As in the military governments under the executive, the provisional government was to enforce the existing laws; it was not given general legislative power, as it was in previous reconstruction bills, including Harris' own earlier proposal. The new bill provided that "the Constitution and laws of such State . . . and the laws of the United States shall continue to be the rules of judgment in all cases in such State until a new State government shall be formed." Furthermore, the governor was charged with the execution of all such laws, but "no law whereby any person has been held to labor or service in such State shall be recognized or enforced by any court or officer in such State." [40]

One major difference between Harris' new bill and previous proposals was a shift from providing interim governments for the rebellious states to creating new state constitutions according to which loyal governments might be organized. Upon the suppression of armed rebellion, declared the new bill, the provisional governor should call a convention election, at which qualified white male citizens could vote. The convention was to write a new constitution containing three minimum conditions: Confederate officeholders, both civil and military, were to be disqualified from voting or holding state office; the freedom of former slaves was to be guaranteed; and no rebel debts were to be recog-

[40] 37 Cong., S. 538, Feb. 17, 1863, secs. 1–3.

nized. If the convention adopted a constitution along these lines, the provisional governor was to inform the President, "who shall thereupon, by proclamation, recognize the State government formed by such Constitution, and the authority of the provisional governor shall cease from the date of such proclamation." [41]

The second major change in Harris' new bill was its reliance on the republican-form-of-government clause. Harris had broached the idea in July 1862; now he expressly embodied it in the proposed legislation, which he titled "A Bill to guarantee in certain States a republican form of government." The substance of the bill, moreover, aimed at creating governments that were republican in the only meaningful, practical sense of the word: governments that would meet the standards of the majority in Congress and whose constitutions would be compatible with those of the other states of the Union.

These changes promised to strengthen the appeal of a congressional plan of reconstruction. As Harris had pointed out at the previous session, the guarantee clause could be interpreted as applying only to states in the Union. This argument effectively countered any charge of territorialization that might be directed at a bill such as Harris' second measure, and satisfied the state-rights adherents. The express terms of Harris' new bill, furthermore, made impossible a territorial interpretation and implied the continuity of the pre-existing state governments. For moderates who saw the states as still in the Union but not in their proper practical relation with it, the forming of a new constitution, as prescribed by Harris' bill, would be an appropriate solution. On the other hand, the assertion of congressional authority and the insistence on minimum conditions—including emancipation—before reconstruction could take place would appeal to the more radical element in Congress. The significance of these considerations was apparent when Congress finally enacted a

[41] *Ibid.,* sec. 7.

plan of reconstruction, the Wade-Davis Bill, which was substantially similar to Harris' proposal of February 1863.

Some years later Henry Dawes aptly described the achievements of the Thirty-seventh Congress with relation to reconstruction as "progressive restoration." "There were many tentative measures resorted to during the war," Dawes wrote, "having for their object, what might be called progressive restoration—restoring states or portions of states to their original relations to the General Government, as fast as the army reclaimed them from the possession of the rebels." The "admission of Members of Congress from single districts, more or less exclusively in our possession," was an expression of this policy, he explained, as in "the carving of the state of West Virginia out of the Old Dominion." The bill for congressional elections in Tennessee and Louisiana also illustrated it.[42] Cooperation between President and Congress was a characteristic of progressive restoration. Yet perhaps more significant was congressional determination to control reconstruction. As the reorganization of state governments became a more pressing problem, this attitude grew stronger and formed a basis for the conflict with Lincoln, who was equally determined to control the process of state reorganization.

[42] Henry L. Dawes, "Reconstruction and Rehabilitation," 6–7, 14–15, MS, Dawes Papers, Library of Congress.

VI

Presidential Reconstruction

ALTHOUGH reconstruction had been recognized as an important question in Congress since the start of the war, in 1863 it
became a major political issue. Following the adjournment of
Congress in March 1863, Union armies scored decisive victories
which enabled Lincoln to proceed further with the reorganization of loyal governments in Louisiana, Arkansas, and Tennessee. Far more than in the winter of 1861–1862, military success
forced reconstruction into the public consciousness as a significant issue. Indeed, with the turning point in the war seemingly
reached, an intense debate on reconstruction began, which
formed the background for a major policy pronouncement by
Lincoln at the opening of the Thirty-eighth Congress—the
Proclamation of Amnesty and Reconstruction of December
1863. Presenting a general outline for organizing loyal state governments, the proclamation represented Lincoln's decision to
seek direct control of the process of reconstruction, instead of
relying to a considerable extent on local Unionists acting on
general advice from Washington, under the protection of federal military authorities.

At the adjournment of the Thirty-seventh Congress, Lincoln
occupied a relatively strong position with respect to reconstruction. Congress had supported executive reconstruction by seating

representatives from Louisiana who had been elected under military authority and by admitting West Virginia to the Union. Congress had also rejected territorialization and had accepted military government under the executive as a necessary stage preparatory to the actual reconstruction of a loyal government. At the same time Lincoln recognized a degree of congressional responsibility for reconstruction. Having accepted negative decisions by Congress in election cases in which he had a keen interest, he began to refer to the power of Congress to decide on the final readmission of the rebel states. Thus, he told General Banks in August 1863, "If Louisiana should send members to Congress, their admission to seats will depend . . . upon the respective Houses, and not upon the President." [1] Nevertheless, Lincoln's position seemed stronger. In the summer of 1863, testifying on executive influence, Salmon P. Chase said, referring to the possible readmission of North Carolina with slavery intact: "Much would depend on the President—all in fact, for were the President to acquiesce in her return it could not be prevented, but on the other hand, if he planted himself firmly, and with Jacksonian will on the [Emancipation] Proclamation . . . North Carolina would be excluded or refused her original place in the Union, unless she modified her constitution and abolished slavery." [2]

---

[1] Lincoln to Nathaniel Banks, Aug. 5, 1863, in *Collected Works of Lincoln*, VI, 365. This was the first of several such references to the power of Congress to determine its own membership through its constitutional authority to judge the election, qualifications, and returns of its members. It is difficult to say how broadly Lincoln interpreted this power, for he purposely avoided explicating such constitutional questions. But he believed that Congress could legislate on reconstruction, and his frequent reference to this specific power suggests that he regarded it as one source of congressional authority to deal with the rebel states, and not simply as a technical power to examine writs and certificates of election. Lincoln seemed to give it a broader interpretation than did Andrew Johnson, who defined it in the narrowest terms. See Eric McKitrick, *Andrew Johnson and Reconstruction* (Chicago, 1960), 191.

[2] Gideon Welles, *Diary*, ed. Beale, I, 410–411.

The decision of the Supreme Court in the Prize Cases, in which the central question was the legality of the Union blockade of southern ports from the time Lincoln proclaimed it until Congress authorized it in July 1861, also strengthened the President's position. The argument against the government was that Lincoln had no power to order a blockade without a congressional declaration of war. Presidential exercise of war powers was thus at issue, and an adverse decision could have been politically damaging. The Court sanctioned Lincoln's bold use of executive authority, however, ruling that the President had to meet the war as he found it, without waiting for Congress to act.[3] The result signified judicial deference to the executive and suggested that the Court would probably sustain the administration if other momentous political issues—such as the Emancipation Proclamation—came before it.

Military developments in the second half of 1863 were even more important in creating favorable circumstances for presidential reconstruction. After suffering severe defeats in the winter and spring of 1862–1863, Union armies scored major triumphs at Gettysburg and Vicksburg in July, and at Chattanooga and Lookout Mountain in the fall. These victories stopped a Confederate drive into the North, secured the Mississippi River for the Union, and cut off the western from the eastern half of the Confederacy. The implications for reconstruction were twofold. First, control of the Mississippi permitted reorganization efforts in Louisiana, Arkansas, and Tennessee to move ahead with reduced threat of rebel interference; the last two states were now almost clear of Confederate forces, as was the Louisiana delta region, which contained about half the population of the state. Second, military success made reconstruction a topic of political debate. Now, more than ever before, it was a problem to be dealt with in practical as well as theoretical terms.

In the debate that developed in 1863 concerning reconstruc-

[3] The Prize Cases, 67 U.S. 876.

tion, radicalism meant something different from what it had meant in the first year of the war.[4] Then its meaning was related to territorialization: supporters of the territorial approach were radicals, while opponents were either moderates, who rejected the idea that the states had been reduced to territories but upheld congressional authority over reconstruction, or conservatives, who denied any federal power to reconstruct state governments, believing that the government needed only to defeat the rebels and let loyal men return their states to the Union.[5] In the transitional winter of 1862–1863, however, these positions tended to shift. Whereas a majority of the Republicans had supported Ashley's territorial plan in March 1862, they now backed the Tennessee-Louisiana elections bill, which, though it rested on the principle of congressional supervision of reconstruction, was a moderate proposal calling for a gradual restoration of the rebel states and imposing no condition for readmission other than loyalty to the Union. The only real test of radicalism was the vote on Louisiana's representation, and this did not represent a positive policy but, rather, opposition to presidential reconstruction. The conservative position continued to be complete opposition to federal interference in reconstruction beyond the temporary military control incident to the collapse of Confed-

---

[4] Historians have been unable to agree on a satisfactory definition of radicalism or to agree on the identity of the radicals during the entire war and reconstruction period. I have defined radicalism in relation to specific issues on which distinct positions were taken which contemporaries described as "radical" or "conservative." The question of radicalism is dealt with in the following recent works: David Donald, "Devils Facing Zionwards" and T. Harry Williams, "Lincoln and the Radicals: An Essay in Civil War History and Historiography," in Grady McWhiney, ed., *Grant, Lee, Lincoln, and the Radicals* (Evanston, Ill., 1964), 72–117; Edward L. Gambill, "Who Were the Senate Radicals?" *Civil War History*, XI (Sept. 1965), 237–244; Glenn M. Linden, " 'Radicals' and Economic Policies: The House of Representatives, 1861–1873," *ibid.*, XIII (March 1967), 51–65; and David Donald, *The Politics of Reconstruction, 1863–1867* (Baton Rouge, La., 1965).

[5] See above, Chapter 4.

erate authority. By the middle of 1863, however, new issues had emerged. Jurisdictional conflict between the President and Congress was more obvious, but this was secondary to the crucial policy decision that events were forcing on Union officials: whether emancipation should be the basis of reconstruction— that is, whether the seceded states must adopt new state constitutions prohibiting slavery as a condition of being readmitted to the Union. On this issue there was no middle ground: the radical position was that such a condition ought to be imposed, the conservative position that it ought not.

Although in retrospect it is easy to conclude that slavery was doomed by the summer of 1863, this was not so clear to contemporaries. Although the military situation seemed to favor the North, the war was not yet over, and since emancipation depended for its effect on conquest by Union arms, few slaves had actually been freed. Moreover, should the war end with federal armies only in partial control, the freedom of slaves in unoccupied regions would be highly uncertain because of doubts concerning the legal and constitutional effect of the Emancipation Proclamation. Because it was a war measure based exclusively on military authority, its validity in peacetime was questionable; indeed, Lincoln himself on several occasions expressed concern that the courts might not uphold it. Out of this situation in the summer of 1863 the demand arose for the constitutional prohibition of slavery in the seceded states, as the reorganization of state governments proceeded. George Boutwell expressed the dominant Republican—and radical—view when he wrote in May 1863, "The return of a State with a new constitution [with slavery excluded], and by readmission into the Union, puts the question of slavery beyond the hazards of politics, and the vagaries of judges." But if the states returned with their old constitutions, said Boutwell, "the questions arising out of the President's Proclamation are left to the Courts for final action." [6]

[6] Lincoln to James C. Conkling, Aug. 26, 1863, in *Collected Works*, VI, 408; Proclamation of Amnesty and Reconstruction, Dec. 8, 1863, in *ibid.*,

Although it has sometimes been assumed that the "radicals" in the Republican party had formulated a unified set of demands concerning reconstruction in 1863,[7] those who were radical on the central issue of readmission with slavery disagreed on a number of specific problems connected with the seceded states. They differed in their views on the status of the states, the method to be used in governing and reorganizing loyal governments, and the treatment to be accorded loyal men in the rebellious districts.

In the summer and fall of 1863 three leading radicals—Charles Sumner, William Whiting, and Henry Winter Davis—advanced three distinct theories of reconstruction and the status of the seceded states. Sumner, writing in the *Atlantic Monthly* of October 1863, renewed his appeal for a territorial approach to the problem. Central in his essay was the now familiar idea that a rebellious state, though still in existence as a civil society and a political community, can have its position "as a *State of the Union* armed with State Rights, or at least as a *local government . . .* called in question." In some respects even Sumner seemed to adopt a more moderate approach after the rejection of territorial plans in the previous Congress. He did not emphasize the state-suicide metaphor nor rely on propositions such as those for the forfeiture of state rights and for state abdication; rather, he argued that the southern states should be "declared *vacated,* as in fact they are, by all local government which we are bound

---

VII, 54; George S. Boutwell to Nathaniel Banks, May 26, 1863, Banks Papers, Library of Congress. On the constitutional aspects of this question see J. G. Randall's *Constitutional Problems under Lincoln,* 382–385. William Whiting, the solicitor in the War Department and the chief exponent in the government of sweeping executive powers, wrote in November 1862: "The acts for confiscation or emancipation of enemy's slaves, and the President's Proclamation of the 22d of September, do not abolish slavery as a legal institution in the States; they . . . alter no local laws in any of the States; they do not purport to render slavery unlawful; they merely seek to remove slaves from the control of rebel masters" (Whiting, *War Powers,* 1871 ed., iv).

[7] See, for example, William F. Zornow, *Lincoln and the Party Divided* (Norman, Okla., 1954), 15–19.

to recognize." The practical result, however, would be the same as under Sumner's state-suicide resolutions of 1862: "The whole Rebel region, deprived of all local government, lapses under the exclusive jurisdiction of Congress, precisely as any other territory." [8]

William Whiting, the legal advisor of the War Department, offered a different view of the status of the seceded states. Whiting was a Boston lawyer with strong antislavery convictions who attracted much attention in 1863 with his ideas on reconstruction. Gideon Welles wrote at the time, for example, "This Solicitor Whiting has for several months been an important personage. . . . [He] is in high favor in the War and State Departments." Welles said that Whiting was "shoved forward, or permitted to go forward, as an oracle" and that some men were "already swearing their political faith" in his views on reconstruction. Lincoln, who tended toward a more radical position on reconstruction in the summer of 1863, may have been influenced by Whiting, who, according to Charles Sumner, was "in the full confidence of the President." Even Welles, who disliked Whiting intensely, admitted that Lincoln had endorsed him.[9] As solicitor in the War Department, Whiting frequently

[8] Sumner, *Works*, VII, 524, 529, 533.

[9] Welles, *Diary*, ed. Beale, I, 381, 400, 408; Edward S. Pierce, *Memoir and Letters of Charles Sumner* (4 vols.; Boston, 1877–1893), IV, 143. On at least one occasion Lincoln said that he had been influenced by Whiting's views on the constitutionality of permanent confiscation of rebel property. In 1862, Lincoln had opposed part of the Second Confiscation Act because it provided for the forfeiture of property after the death of the guilty parties, in contravention of the Constitution, which specified that no attainder of treason should impose forfeiture except during the life of the person involved. Lincoln prepared a veto message to this effect but withheld it when Congress passed a resolution giving an interpretation of this part of the act that was acceptable to the President. In 1864, however, when the same kind of proposal was before Congress, Lincoln was prepared to accept what he had earlier considered unconstitutional. He told George Julian that after reading "Solicitor Whiting's law argument" he had changed his mind on the question (Lincoln, Message to the Senate and House of Representatives, July 17, 1862, *Collected Works*, V, 330–331; Rice, ed., *Reminiscences of Lincoln*, 59).

provided members of Congress with legal opinions; Samuel S. Cox, a Democrat of Ohio, once referred to him as the "fertile brain" and "reservoir of all the Republican heresy and legislation proposed in this House." [10]

Whiting's central thesis concerning reconstruction, presented in a letter to the Union League of Philadelphia that was widely circulated and cited in 1863, was that the Civil War was a public territorial war between belligerents which caused all citizens in the seceded states—not simply those engaged in rebellion—to lose "all their rights or claims against the United States, under the constitution or laws." Whiting believed further that the conflict obliterated all state lines in the rebellious area.[11] Fearing that after the war the rebels would try to gain by state-rights arguments what they could not win by force of arms, Whiting considered the avoidance of any recognition of state rights most important. He therefore urged Unionists, "Beware of committing yourselves to the fatal doctrine of recognizing the existence in the Union, of States which have been declared . . . in rebellion." But he also criticized the belief that the insurrection had caused a forfeiture of state rights, on the ground that "such doctrines admit, by necessary implication, the validity of a code of laws, and of corresponding civil and political rights, which you deny." He added that since forfeiture could be justified only by admitting the validity of the act by which it was effected, the forfeited-rights argument conceded a degree of legitimacy to ordinances of secession. Whiting concluded that the basis of reconstruction ought to be "the strict enforcement against public enemies of our belligerent rights of civil war." In other words, the states, as alien territory, were subject to exclusive federal control.[12]

Henry Winter Davis, a former representative from Maryland who had been elected to a new term in the House and who would soon become a leader of congressional reconstruction, advanced

[10] *Cong. Globe*, 38 Cong., 1 sess., 709 (Feb. 17, 1864).
[11] Whiting, *War Powers*, 238–240, 244–246.   [12] *Ibid.*, 234–235, 246.

still another theory concerning the seceded states. In a speech at Philadelphia in September 1863 in which he considered the grounds on which Congress could legislate concerning the rebel states, Davis chose a middle position based on the clause of the Constitution guaranteeing to each state in the Union a republican form of government—the same position taken by Senator Harris in his reconstruction bill of February 1863. Davis rejected both the conservative view—that the states continued to exist with their rights unimpaired and could resume their places in the Union whenever they pleased with no conditions imposed by the federal government—and the radical theory that the southern states and their people were alien enemies. The latter doctrine was erroneous, he argued, because it admitted "that their [the rebel states'] secession was effectual to give them the right of independence in the eye of the world." Pointing out that neither the President nor Congress had referred to the rebellious states in those terms, Davis warned that any political party that adopted such a theory as the basis of reconstruction "will destroy itself, or if it be successful, it will destroy republican liberty." The trouble with the concept, he explained, was that "it recognizes what no responsible statesman has hitherto recognized or ought ever to recognize, the possession of absolute, arbitrary, despotic power in the government over a portion of the States as the result of its military operations to suppress an insurrection." On the other hand, Davis criticized the theory of territorialization, on the ground that it denied the principle, established by the framers of the Constitution, that "the States . . . [were] continuing, perpetual elements of our Union, and their citizens always beneath the Constitution." What happened to the constitutional requirement of a republican government in each state, he asked, if the states were converted into territories and subjected to the arbitrary power of the federal government? Davis believed that the correct approach was to hold that the seceded states were "by law . . . people forming a State without a political organization, called State government." Thus the states still existed, but their lack of organization prevented them from exercising political power. Finally, because in the absence of state governments "there must be either anarchy, or a legislative and executive power somewhere," and because the Constitution vested in Congress the duty to guarantee republican government to the states, Davis reasoned that "Congress is . . . charged to take every measure that is necessary to restore republican government." [13]

In addition to differing over the status of the seceded states, those who insisted on emancipation as the basis of reconstruction disagreed on what should be the policy toward loyal persons in rebel districts. Many objected, as they had for months, to giving special consideration to the loyal minority. Thus General Benjamin F. Butler, who thought that Union armies were deployed broadly in the spring of 1863 in order "to give a chance for the Union men at the South to rise," asked, "Have we not got over that absurd idea yet?" George Boutwell of Massachusetts believed that efforts to protect loyal men in the seceded states and to induce them to identify themselves with the government ought to be abandoned until the rebellion was put down. Boutwell, who with Davis would play a significant role in congressional reconstruction in the next Congress, urged the administration to "direct its military operations without regard to the existence of loyal men, discountenancing expressions of loyalty in the rebel districts rather than giving encouragement to them." Labeling "absurd" the notion that a state continued to exist in the few men who might remain loyal, he told the Massachusetts Republican convention in September that even "if there be minorities who would, if they could, have been true to the Union, they must take the fate of all minorities." [14]

---

[13] Henry Winter Davis, *Speeches and Addresses Delivered in the Congress of the United States and on Several Public Occasions* (New York, 1867), 320–323, 328.

[14] Benjamin F. Butler to Salmon P. Chase, Apr. 27, 1863, in *Correspondence of Benjamin F. Butler*, III, 62; George S. Boutwell, *Speeches*

Yet other radicals seemed to take a different view. *The Independent*, a New York abolitionist journal, held that the governments of the seceded states had lost their right to govern, a circumstance which "oblige[d] the state itself—that is, the loyal people thereof—to reconstruct their government *de novo*." Salmon P. Chase told an audience in Cincinnati that the proper approach to reconstruction was "to recognize the plain, indisputable principle, that in regards of the National Government the loyal citizens of a State constitute the State." Chase pointed out that both the President and Congress had sanctioned this principle in Virginia in 1861, and said that it would "doubtless be applied to every other State." [15]

Whether Chase was talking about the principle that underlay the recognition of the Pierpont government or whether he really meant something else depended on the interpretation of the role of Negroes. If Negroes were included in the number of loyal citizens, the idea of protecting the loyal minority would take on radical implications. At the end of the war, when suffrage for the freedmen had become an avowed objective of some Republicans, Chase said that he had all along "contemplated no distinction between colored and white loyalists." He told Lincoln that ever since reconstruction had been discussed, "it has been my opinion that the colored loyalists ought to be allowed to participate in it." But, he added significantly, "I did not however say much about the restriction" of political rights to white men only. This addition may be the key to what he meant. If Chase and others were looking toward Negro suffrage in 1863, they did not say so openly. Even abolitionists, though many of them believed Negro suffrage must come eventually, did not demand it as a condition of reconstruction at this time. The Boston *Commonwealth* and *The Independent* discussed reconstruction in

and Papers Relating to the Rebellion and the Overthrow of Slavery (Boston, 1867), 215; *National Republican*, Oct. 7, 1863.

[15] *The Independent*, Sept. 3, 1863; Boston *Commonwealth*, Dec. 18, 1863; New York *Times*, Dec. 20, 1863.

several editorials during the fall of 1863 without raising the issue of voting rights for the freedmen. This is not to say that there were no advocates of Negro suffrage; in Louisiana scores of Negroes petitioned for the right to vote, as did a scattering of free Negroes and some abolitionists elsewhere. Yet, in general, suffrage for the freedmen was not an abolitionist or radical demand in 1863. Finally, even if some radicals did support Negro suffrage indirectly in their suggestions concerning loyal citizens in the seceded states, they were at odds with those who would deny any role in reconstruction to local Unionists.[16]

Supporters of the radical view of reconstruction at this time also differed in their ideas on how, in the words of Sumner, "the transition from Rebel forms may be most surely accomplished." Some advocated military government; others urged provisional civil government under congressional authority. *The Independent*, for example, thought that military government should continue until the loyal people could, through a constitutional convention, organize a state government. William Whiting recommended allowing "the inhabitants of conquered territory to form themselves into States" by adopting constitutions abolishing slavery; if there were not enough loyal men to do this, military government should be continued until there were. On the other hand, Charles Sumner proposed the establishment of civil governments under Congress in the interval before the beginning of actual reconstruction. Similarly, Henry Winter Davis pointed to Congress as the source of the republican government he advocated for each seceded state. Probably George Boutwell best summarized the variety of views on this point when he said, "They [the rebel states] are to be governed during the state

[16] Salmon P. Chase to Stanley Matthews, Apr. 14, 1865, in "Some Letters of Salmon P. Chase, 1848–1865," ed. Annie A. Nunns, *American Historical Review*, XXXIX (Apr. 1929), 554; Chase to Lincoln, Apr. 12, 1865, in *Collected Works*, VIII, 400; Boston *Commonwealth*, Sept. 4, Oct. 30, 1863; *The Independent*, Sept. 3, 10, 1863; McPherson, *Struggle for Equality*, 239–240; Willie M. Caskey, *Secession and Restoration of Louisiana* (Baton Rouge, La., 1938), 104–105.

through which they are passing according to circumstances, but to be governed—I know not how." [17]

What united Sumner, Boutwell, Butler, Davis, Whiting and other antislavery men was their agreement on what the New York *Tribune*, in November 1863, called the fundamental question of reconstruction: "How is the Union to be reconstituted? *With* slavery or *without?* This is the remaining and momentous issue." [18] Radicals insisted that emancipation should be the basis of reconstruction, and that provisions requiring it should be written into the constitutions of the seceded states. This requirement seemed especially important inasmuch as the Emancipation Proclamation had been given little effect, and the states that had previously been in some way restored to the Union—Virginia, Tennessee, and Louisiana—had come back still permitting slavery. Even after the Emancipation Proclamation was issued, this pattern continued, for West Virginia, which some northerners regarded as exemplifying the kind of reconstruction policy that should be employed, had been admitted with provisions for slavery in its state constitution. [19] But all this was changing. As George Boutwell observed in May 1863, "The admission of Western Virginia was very well, but it is not a precedent. Public sentiment is moving rapidly towards the conclusion that the eleven states shall not be admitted to the Union with slavery. The contest on this point will be bitter." It would be "an indellible [*sic*] disgrace to the country and the source of innumerable woes," Boutwell told General Nathaniel Banks in Louisiana, "to

[17] Sumner, *Works*, VII, 494, 532; *The Independent*, Sept. 3, 10, 1863; Whiting, *War Powers*, 248–249; Davis, *Speeches and Addresses*, 323; New York *Tribune*, Oct. 21, 1863; *National Republican*, Oct. 7, 1863.

[18] New York *Tribune*, Nov. 23, 1863.

[19] Congress, in passing the West Virginia statehood bill in 1862, required that a clause be added to the state constitution providing that slaves under the age of ten should be free when they reached twenty-one; those between ten and twenty-one should be free when they reached twenty-five; and the children of slaves born after July 4, 1863, should be free at birth (Thorpe, *Federal and State Constitutions*, VII, 4031–4032).

permit these States to return under the constitutions which they had when they seceded from the Union." [20]

Throughout the summer and fall of 1863 insistence on emancipation was the common denominator of the radical position. Said Salmon P. Chase to Gideon Welles: "In order to be restored to the Union they [the seceded states] must be required to put away the cause of disturbance, the source of rebellion, disunion, and strife. . . . To admit them now to a full and equal participation with ourselves, without extinguishing slavery, would be with the aid of their sympathizing friends to place the government in the hands of the slaveholders." Boutwell told the National Union League Association in June, "One possible difficulty before us . . . is the return of the seceded States to this Union *as slave States*," while William Whiting urged the Union League of Philadelphia in July, "Do not allow old States, with their constitutions still unaltered, to resume State powers." If they did, he said, "we [should] at once invoke upon our country in all its force and wickedness, that very curse which has brought on the war and its terrible train of sufferings." Robert Dale Owen, recently returned from a visit to the South as a member of the American Freedmen's Inquiry Commission, denounced the idea of permitting the seceded states to return without emancipation as a precondition. The Union could not be reconstructed as a nation part slave and part free. "When politicians talk now of reconstruction, with the 'peculiar institution' of the South left intact," Owen asserted, "the words are nothing else but a mischievous mystification." Addressing the Massachusetts Republican convention, Representative Thomas D. Eliot declared that the destruction of slavery was essential to a successful reconstruction of the Union. Emancipation ought to be "the condition precedent" to restoring states to the Union, he argued. Early in August, Charles Sumner wrote, "Our present policy is . . . to insist that there can be no talk of admission

[20] George S. Boutwell to Nathaniel Banks, May 26, 1863, Banks Papers, Library of Congress.

into the Union except on the basis of the actual condition of the moment, with slavery abolished by the Proclamation." Indeed, according to Sumner, another aspect of the government's policy was "the admission of a Gulf State with an altered constitution abolishing slavery," which he said would be "a controlling precedent." Emphasizing the importance of emancipation for reconstruction, Ben Butler wrote to Salmon P. Chase, "If that State [Louisiana], by a change of her Constitution, abolishing Slavery . . . by the act of her own people, can ask readmission to the Union the first of any, the question which of all others is the most dangerous one now open will be *settled forever.*" Henry Raymond, editor of the New York *Times* and a constant critic of radicalism, testified in 1863 to the connection between emancipation and reconstruction when he asserted that advocates of a radical theory were held together, not so much by a conviction of the soundness of the theory itself, "as by the determination to use it as a basis for insisting that no rebel State shall come back to the Union except on the condition of abolishing Slavery in its State Constitution." [21]

The conservative position on reconstruction in 1863 was that the seceded states were in the Union and could resume their former places—with no conditions attached—the moment they laid down arms and returned to allegiance to the Constitution. Some conservatives opposed emancipation as a condition of reconstruction on the ground that slavery would be destroyed in any case, while others opposed it because they wanted gradual emancipation or no emancipation at all.

Although Democrats of course provided the main support for this conservative approach to reconstruction, the position also

[21] Welles, *Diary*, ed. Beale, I, 411; Boutwell, *Speeches and Addresses*, 222; Whiting, *War Powers*, 234, 247; Robert Dale Owen, *The Conditions of Reconstruction* . . . (New York, 1863), 6–10, 19; Charles Sumner to John Bright, Aug. 4, 1863, in Pierce, *Memoir and Letters of Charles Sumner*, IV, 143; Butler to Salmon P. Chase, Oct. 6, 1863, in *Correspondence of Benjamin F. Butler*, III, 118; Henry J. Raymond, *The Administration and the War* . . . (n.p., 1863), 10.

received backing from some Republicans. Former Republican Senator Orville Browning, for example, said in July that he was "deeply concerned, and fearful of trouble from the extreme wing of our Republicans that they will attempt to treat the *returning* States as conquered provinces, imposing terms on their *re*-admission." Secretary of the Navy Gideon Welles held that the government must act only on individuals, not on states as such. Believing that "slavery, as it heretofore existed, has terminated in all the States," Welles denied the power of Congress to require new state constitutions prohibiting slavery as a condition of readmission. The Democratic New York *Herald* struck the dominant conservative theme when it asked: "Is the 'Pope's bull against the comet,' after all, to be the supreme and inflexible law of reconstruction? Is every rebellious State to be compelled to make good the emancipation proclamation, and purge itself of African slavery at all hazards, before its rehabilitation as a member of the Union? The *Herald* urged that the states be restored either with or without slavery, as the case might be, as soon as practicable.[22]

Henry Raymond, a Republican, said in a speech at Wilmington, Delaware, that loyalty to the Union was the only test that the government could require in reconstruction. He admitted that Congress could exclude members from a rebel state, thus disfranchising the state. But in dealing with the readmission of a rebel state, Congress could not, he held, go further than insisting that "none but men who will swear allegiance to the Constitution of the United States, shall have part or lot in the conduct of its affairs." Thinking no doubt of the radical position on slavery and reconstruction, he declared, "We cannot insist upon any party test. We cannot require adhesion to any party platform, or to any specific opinions on any subject of legislative action, as a test of loyalty and a condition of exercising

[22] Edward Bates, *The Diary of Edward Bates, 1859–1866*, ed. Howard K. Beale (Washington, 1933), 301; Welles, *Diary*, ed. Beale, I, 410, 412, II, 85; New York *Herald*, Nov. 13, 1863.

political rights." As for slavery, Raymond was sure it had "already received its death-blow." However, its eventual abolition by the states, he added, "may not all be done in one year—possibly not in ten"; he thought that "even twenty would be a short term for the accomplishment of one of the grandest, most beneficent and most difficult reforms the world has ever seen." Meanwhile, Congress should not insist on the prohibition of slavery as a requirement for reconstruction.[23]

From within Republican ranks Frank and Montgomery Blair tried to prevent the party from making emancipation the basis of reconstruction policy. In August 1863, Frank Blair, who had resigned his seat in the House to become a colonel in the army but who was now seeking to return to Congress, publicly advocated gradual emancipation and cautioned against formulating reconstruction plans until after the war. A few months later his brother Montgomery, the Postmaster General in the administration and an archenemy of radicalism, attracted national notice with a stinging attack on the reconstruction ideas taking shape in what he called the "ultra-abolitionist" wing of the Republican party. In a speech at Rockville, Maryland, in October, Blair said that "the key note of the revolution" planned by radicals was "the sheer abolition of State constitutions in the regions suffering under the rod of the rebellion." This meant immediate emancipation as a minimum condition for reconstruction, and to this requirement Blair was unalterably opposed. In his view the seceded states were still in the Union; though temporarily "paralysed," they nonetheless lived "in all their vital powers, ready for resurrection in the persons of their loyal people." Indeed, Blair said, loyal citizens were prepared to put in motion "the whole machinery of the State government . . . by the election of representatives and all civil officers" the moment the rebellion was subdued. The restoration of the old state constitutions would follow, since the guarantee of republican government— the basis of federal action in suppressing insurrection—implied

[23] Raymond, *The Administration and the War*, ii, 13–14.

"A PRE-EXISTING GOVERNMENT of the form which is to be guarantied." Blair, a supporter of gradual emancipation, did not openly
advocate the return of rebel states with slavery permitted by
their constitutions, but that was the clear implication of the
policy he supported.[24]

Finally, some southern Unionists sought to restore their states
to the Union with slavery intact. In Louisiana and Arkansas, for
example, proslavery factions which were trying to control the
process of reorganization argued that the Emancipation Proclamation worked no change in the legal status of slavery. In
August a number of Georgia Unionists, meeting in New York
to consider the political future of their state, urged that the
Emancipation Proclamation be rescinded or modified, because it
discouraged southerners from supporting the Union cause.[25]

In the light of this extensive public discussion of reconstruction, administration efforts to reorganize state governments
acquired special significance in 1863. Clear alternatives were
emerging as political reorganization of the South became a major
problem of policy.

As in the previous year, Lincoln concentrated on rebuilding a
loyal government in Louisiana, whose strategic position for
reconstruction was more than ever apparent to Union men.
George Boutwell gave voice to this feeling in the spring of 1863
when he explained, "If one State even would frame a constitution and ask for admission a precedent would be established for
all the others. Louisiana is so situated, geographically and com-
mercially, that her lead will compel Texas, Arkansas, and Mississippi to follow." [26]

The admission of representatives from Louisiana to the Thirty-

[24] W. E. Smith, *The Blair Family in Politics*, II, 165–166, 253; Montgomery Blair, *Speech on the Revolutionary Schemes of the Ultra Abolitionists* . . . (n.p., 1863), 4–13.

[25] John R. Ficklen, *History of Reconstruction in Louisiana (through
1868)* (Baltimore, 1910), 47–48; *National Republican*, Aug. 11, 1863.

[26] George S. Boutwell to Nathaniel Banks, May 26, 1863, Banks Papers,
Library of Congress.

seventh Congress stimulated efforts to form a loyal state government, and in the spring and summer of 1863 two factions struggled to control the process: the Free State General Committee, strongly antislavery in outlook, and the Executive Central Committee, consisting of conservative, proslavery planters. The Free State Committee, which was the focal point of radical Unionism, proposed a constitutional convention for the purpose of drafting a new state constitution prohibiting slavery. Lincoln's military governor in Louisiana, George Shepley, was sympathetic to this aim and agreed to appoint Thomas J. Durant, the president of the Free State Committee, to organize a registry of loyal citizens as the first step in the convention process. At this stage of reconstruction the participation of a majority of citizens in each parish was not thought necessary; on the contrary, Durant believed that "if ten loyal men can be found in each parish to send a representative, they will be sufficient." [27] Representation in the convention was to be based on the white population only, and not on the slave population as well, as had been the earlier practice in Louisiana. Since the areas where reconstruction was taking place had been exempted from the Emancipation Proclamation, such an arrangement prevented the slave-owning planters from having a disproportionate influence in the convention.[28]

The Executive Central Committee, on the other hand, sought to restore the old state constitution protecting slavery. Insisting that the Emancipation Proclamation was a war measure only, they reasoned that slavery might be revived when the war ended. While the Free State Committee planned a constitutional convention, the conservative faction aimed at an election of state officers under the old constitution. To this end it tried to enlist the support of Shepley, and when it failed in this, it appealed directly to the President. In June 1863 a three-man delegation

[27] Quoted in Fred H. Harrington, *Fighting General: Major-General N. P. Banks* (Philadelphia, 1948), 142.
[28] Ficklen, *Reconstruction in Louisiana*, 45–47.

from the Executive Central Committee journeyed to Washington and informed Lincoln of the committee's desire "to seek of the General Government a full recognition of all the rights of the State, as they existed previous to the passage of an act of secession, upon the principle of the existence of the State Constitution unimpaired." Arguing that the privileges conferred by the Constitution were due them as loyal citizens, the delegation asked Lincoln to order an election for state and federal officers, to be held on the regular state election day in November.[29]

Confronted with a choice between rival Unionist factions, Lincoln supported the radical group. He told the conservative delegation that he would not order the requested election, because it might embarrass military operations and because "a respectable portion of the Louisiana people, desire to amend their State constitution, and contemplate holding a convention for that object." Aligning himself with the Free State Committee, Lincoln said that he would not commit himself to the existing state constitution. In formulating his reply, Lincoln rejected a more conservative approach suggested to him by Secretary of State Seward. Seward, who consistently adopted a more conciliatory attitude on reconstruction than was acceptable to most Republicans, had urged the President to say that if the military situation were more favorable, "so that the people of Louisiana could now practically enter upon the enjoyment of their rights under the present and National Constitutions, [the] request would stand before [him] in a different aspect." By refusing to endorse the old state constitution, Lincoln gave implicit approval to the plan of the radical faction in Louisiana.[30]

Early in August, Lincoln endorsed unequivocally the pro-

29 Caskey, *Secession and Restoration of Louisiana*, 74–75; E. E. Mahliot, Bradish Johnson, and Thomas Cottman to Lincoln [June, 1863], in *Collected Works of Lincoln*, VI, 287–288.
30 Lincoln to E. E. Mahliot, Bradish Johnson, and Thomas Cottman, June 19, 1863, in *Collected Works of Lincoln*, VI, 287–288; Memorandum [June 19, 1863], in *ibid.*, 289.

gram of the Free State Committee. According to Gideon Welles, Salmon P. Chase, the most radical member of the Cabinet, was seeing the President daily at this time and discussing reconstruction with him. Possibly this was having an effect. Chase at any rate thought Lincoln was "becoming firm and more decided in his opinions," a judgment that seemed to be borne out by events. But while he supported the radical plan, Lincoln still left much of the initiative with the Free State General Committee. On August 5 he wrote to General Banks, the commander of the Department of the Gulf, "While I very well know what I would be glad for Louisiana to do, it is quite a different thing for me to assume direction of the matter." He "would be glad," he told Banks, "for her to make a new Constitution recognizing the emancipation proclamation, and adopting emancipation in those parts of the state to which the proclamation does not apply." Lincoln said that registration in preparation for a constitutional convention "appears proper," adding, "If such convention were to ask my views, I could present little else than what I now say to you. I think the thing should be pushed forward, so that if possible, it's [*sic*] mature work may reach here by the meeting of Congress." He suggested that Banks confer with Durant, Michael Hahn, and Benjamin Flanders, "intelligent and trusty citizens of the State," in furthering the work of reconstruction.[31]

When he wrote his letter to Banks, Lincoln officially instructed Military Governor Shepley to hold a constitutional convention. The instructions, issued through Secretary of War Stanton, corresponded closely to the program of the Free State General Committee, which Shepley, who at the time was either still in Washington or had just recently departed, doubtless had outlined to Lincoln. Stanton ordered Shepley to conduct a regis-

[31] Welles, *Diary*, ed. Beale, I, 413; Lincoln to Nathaniel Banks, Aug. 5, 1863, in *Collected Works of Lincoln*, VI, 364–365. Copies of this letter were sent to Flanders, Hahn, and Durant, all members of the Free State General Committee.

tration "in each parish of all the loyal citizens of the United States" as soon as the military situation permitted. The registry was "to include only such as shall have taken or shall take an oath of allegiance to the United States, accompanied by a declaration that the oath was taken freely and voluntarily for the purpose of reorganizing a state government in Louisiana loyal to the United States." Shepley was to carry the registration "as far as practicable," then order an election "for the purpose of forming a constitution and establishing a civil government in the State, loyal to the United States, and in conformity with the Federal Constitution and laws, and for the passage of all needful ordinances and laws." In accordance with the plan of the Free State General Committee, Shepley's instructions called for representation in the convention on the basis of one delegate for every 2500 loyal white citizens. Finally, Shepley was authorized to appoint all officers necessary for carrying on the convention.[32]

In Louisiana, as in the country generally, the paramount issue was whether the rebel states could be readmitted without being subject to any conditions—and possibly with slavery intact—or whether they must first prohibit slavery. By supporting the Free State party in Louisiana, Lincoln endorsed the latter alternative. A short while later, at a Unionist rally in Springfield, Illinois, he renewed his commitment to emancipation, and thus to a policy of reconstruction based on the prohibition of slavery.

With the increased interest in reconstruction after Gettysburg and Vicksburg, there had been speculation that Lincoln would deal specifically with this problem. The Democratic New York *Herald*, for example, had predicted that the President's message to the Springfield rally would contain the substance of a reconstruction proclamation conciliatory toward the South.[33] The

[32] Edwin M. Stanton to George F. Shepley, Aug. 5, 1863, *Official Records*, ser. I, XXVI, Pt. I, 694–695.

[33] The *Herald* said, September 1, 1863, that Lincoln had prepared a proclamation with the assistance and under the inspiration of Seward, but

New York *Tribune* called this prediction "ridiculous" and "false," but there is reason to believe that Lincoln had not only considered raising the issue of reconstruction directly, but had contemplated taking a more conservative position than he had before. Yet, as in the choice between rival Louisiana factions in June, he preferred the more radical alternative. In what was evidently an earlier draft of the Springfield letter, Lincoln wrote, "Suppose those now in rebellion should say: 'We cease fighting: re-establish the national authority amongst us—customs, courts, mails, land-offices—all as before the rebellion—we claiming to send members to both branches of Congress, as of yore, and to hold our slaves according to our State laws, notwithstanding anything or all things which has [*sic*] occurred during the rebellion.'" Should that happen, Lincoln said in this draft version, he would take the view that "if questions remain, let them be solved by peaceful means—by courts, and votes." He added that Congress had given him broad powers to remit forfeiture and personal penalties, and said that he would "exercise these to the greatest extent which might seem consistent with the future public safety." [34] Had Lincoln included all this in the Springfield letter, it would have marked an important change in his outlook on reconstruction—a change toward the conservative position. Yet he rejected this conciliatory approach.

In its final form the Springfield letter denied that "a com-

---

had not issued it because of the opposition of Chase and other Republicans. According to the *Herald*, the proclamation would contain an offer of amnesty, a declaration that only those slaves who had moved within Union lines or had tried to comply with the terms of the emancipation edict would be considered free, and a promise to receive the seceded states back into the Union if they would institute gradual emancipation.

[34] New York *Tribune*, Sept. 2, 1863; Fragment [c. Aug. 26, 1863?], in *Collected Works of Lincoln*, VI, 410–411. Robert Todd Lincoln assigned this date to the fragment. The similarity in formal structure between the sentences in the fragment and the part of the letter in which Lincoln made his supposition about a compromise involving southern refugees strongly suggests that they were drafted for use in the Springfield letter.

promise, embracing a restoration of the Union," was possible.[35] Lincoln's other main point was a reaffirmation of the Emancipation Proclamation. Defending it first as a military necessity, he went on to say that if Negroes "stake their lives for us, they must be prompted by the strongest motive—even the promise of freedom. And the promise being made, must be kept." As slavery was central to the debate on reconstruction, Lincoln's pledge to support emancipation assumed significance for that issue. The abolitionist Boston *Commonwealth* hailed the letter as evidence that the administration would not retreat on its antislavery policy and that emancipation would be a condition of reconstruction. Yet for others Lincoln's message yielded a different meaning. The Springfield *Republican* said that it knew "no better than before what would be done with the slaves of a state which should ask to come back into the Union, and where the negroes have not already been freed by the advance of our armies." The New York *Herald* saw evidence of Lincoln's desire to end the war by some conciliatory measure toward the South. "It will be noticed," declared the *Herald*, "that he carefully refrains from committing himself against any measure of accommodation." Finally, Lincoln's willingness to let the Emancipation Proclamation come before the courts seemed to the *Herald* an "abandonment of the whole radical programme of a war of extermination against the South." [36] Lincoln was leaning toward the radical solution but was not yet prepared to make his position unequivocally clear.

[35] Lincoln to James C. Conkling, Aug. 26, 1863, in *Collected Works of Lincoln*, VI, 407. Although Lincoln rejected a more conservative course, he did not completely abandon that point of view. Having denied that a compromise was possible, he said that if those who controlled the rebel army offered a peace compromise, he would not reject it. But then he went on to recommit his administration to emancipation, thereby cutting the ground from under the conservative position on reconstruction. Lincoln also indicated, presumably for conservatives, that he was willing to have the Emancipation Proclamation tested in the courts.

[36] *Ibid.*, 409; Boston *Commonwealth*, Sept. 11, 1863; Springfield *Weekly Republican*, Sept. 5, 1863; New York *Herald*, Sept. 3, 1863.

In Louisiana, meanwhile, reconstruction efforts were floundering. The Free State Committee, finding little popular support for a constitutional convention, had decided to postpone its registration of loyal citizens, a development which disturbed Lincoln so much that it led him to take a more active role in supervising the reorganization process. Returning from a visit to Washington in October 1863, Benjamin F. Flanders, a leader of the Free State party, reported that the President wanted results and would recognize and sustain a state government organized by any part of the population that was under federal control. On November 5, Lincoln wrote to General Banks that the failure to hold a convention "disappoints me bitterly." "I wish him [Military Governor Shepley]—these gentlemen and others cooperating," Lincoln explained, "without waiting for more territory, to go to work and give me a tangible nucleus which the remainder of the State may rally around as fast as it can, and which I can at once recognize and sustain as the true State government." Instructing Banks "to give them a hearty sympathy and support," he emphasized that speed was important. "There is danger, even now," he pointed out, "that the adverse element seeks insidiously to pre-occupy the ground." Lincoln feared that "a few professedly loyal men . . . [might] draw the disloyal about them, and colorably set up a State government, repudiating the emancipation proclamation, and re-establishing slavery." [37]

Lincoln's apprehension was justified, for the conservative planter faction was moving ahead with plans for an election despite the President's rejection of their appeal for support. In October the Executive Central Committee publicly urged loyal citizens to vote for state and local officers and members of Con-

[37] *American Annual Cyclopaedia and Register of Important Events of the Year 1863* (New York, 1871), 591 (hereafter cited as *American Cyclopaedia 1863*); Lincoln to Nathaniel Banks, Nov. 5, 1863, in *Collected Works of Lincoln*, VII, 1.

gress on the regularly appointed election day, November 2. Should the opportunity to form a state government be lost, they declared, Louisiana and the other seceded states would be "subject to the danger of being thrown as 'vacated' territory, into the hands of Congress." The Committee also said, "We think we can assure you that your action in [electing representatives] will meet with the approval of the National Government." [38] Although Governor Shepley halted electoral proceedings in New Orleans, in the outlying parishes representatives were elected in three congressional districts.

Concerned that the conservatives might gain control, Lincoln made a final effort to achieve concrete results through the Free State faction. On November 9 he suggested to Benjamin Flanders that "as a preliminary step, a vote be taken, yea or nay, whether there shall be a State convention to repeal the ordinance of secession, and remodel the State constitution." Though such a step would implicitly recognize the *de facto* validity of the secession ordinance, since if the ordinance was illegal it would of course need no repealing, Lincoln was prepared to accept the risk. He told Flanders that his interest "was, not so much [in] the

[38] *American Cyclopaedia 1863*, 591. The confidence of the Executive Central Committee that representatives would be approved at Washington may have been related to the so-called "Etheridge plot," a plan by which Democrats hoped to gain control of the House in the Thirty-eighth Congress. The plan depended on the circumstance that Emerson Etheridge of Tennessee, a Democrat and the clerk of the House in the Thirty-seventh Congress, would be acting clerk at the start of the next Congress and would make up the roll of regularly elected members prior to the organization of the House. It was widely reported that Etheridge, by an interpretation of an act passed March 3, 1863, instructing the clerk on the composition of the roll, would exclude some regularly elected Republicans and place on the roll the names of the Louisiana representatives chosen in November. The threat was serious enough to prompt Lincoln to write several letters to Republican senators and representatives alerting them to the scheme (Boston *Commonwealth*, Nov. 6, 1863; Boston *Journal*, Dec. 7, 1863; Cincinnati *Gazette*, Dec. 7, 1863; *Collected Works of Lincoln*, VI, 546–553).

questions to be voted on, as [in] the effect of chrystallizing [*sic*], so to speak, in taking such popular vote on any proper question." [39] Nevertheless, this proposal proved fruitless too. Throughout November, reconstruction in Louisiana remained at a standstill.

Louisiana was one of three states in which Lincoln attempted to reorganize loyal governments in 1863. Arkansas and Tennessee were also the scene of executive efforts, but because of a less favorable military situation, Lincoln moderated his approach in these states. In Arkansas he tried first to have a former senator resume his place in Congress. To General Stephen A. Hurlbut, commanding in Arkansas, he wrote in late July, "Senator Sebastian of Arkansas thinks of offering to resume his place in the Senate." Pointing out that "the Senate, and not I, would decide whether to admit or reject him," Lincoln said that he would "feel great interest in the question. It may be so presented as to be one of the very greatest national importance." As in Louisiana, Lincoln tied reconstruction to emancipation. He reminded Hurlbut that the proclamation applied to Arkansas, said that he would not retract or repudiate it, and stated that if Sebastian could propose a plan of emancipation, even one for gradual emancipation, he himself "at least should take great interest in his case." [40]

In September the capture of Chattanooga drove the Confederates out of eastern Tennessee and spurred hopes for reorganizing a loyal state government. On September 11, Lincoln wrote to Andrew Johnson, Military Governor of Tennessee, "You need not to be reminded that it is the nick of time for reinaugerating [*sic*] a loyal State government. Not a moment should be lost." Emphasizing this point, he added with prophetic irony, "It is something on the question of *time*, to remember that

[39] Lincoln to Benjamin F. Flanders, Nov. 9, 1863, in *Collected Works of Lincoln*, VII, 6.
[40] Lincoln to Stephen A. Hurlbut, July 31, 1863, in *ibid.*, VI, 358.

it cannot be known who is next to occupy the position I now hold, nor what he will do." As in Louisiana, Lincoln was eager for results but not yet ready to assume overt direction of reconstruction efforts himself. "You, and the cooperating friends there," he told Johnson, "can better judge of the ways and means, than can be judged by any here. I only offer a few suggestions." The obvious necessity was to keep control firmly in the hands of Union men. But Lincoln also urged a new state constitution prohibiting slavery. "Get emancipation into your new State government—Constitution—and there will be no such word as fail in your case," he wrote. This was the crucial point in the current debate on reconstruction, and Lincoln was careful to make his position clear. A week later he explained to Johnson that he had so formulated his instructions concerning reconstruction as to avoid committing himself to the existing Tennessee constitution. The extent to which Lincoln had moved in a more radical direction can be seen by comparing these directives with instructions he had issued to Johnson five months earlier. Then, at Johnson's request and employing a formula suggested by him, Lincoln had ordered him to restore to the citizens of Tennessee "their civil and political rights under . . . the Constitution of the State of Tennessee and the laws made in pursuance thereof." Now in September, Lincoln was unwilling to let the old constitution be the basis of the new state government.[41]

As the opening of Congress drew near, attention focused on the position Lincoln would take on reconstruction in his annual message. Both radicals and conservatives pressed their views on him. The conservative Republican Senator James Dixon of Connecticut advised Lincoln, "Whatever may be said by the radical abolitionists, who demand the adoption of their revolutionary schemes, I beg leave to assure you that the great body of the calm, thinking, judicious men who uphold and support your

[41] Lincoln to Andrew Johnson, Sept. 11, 19, 1863, in *ibid.*, 440, 468–469; Lincoln to Edwin M. Stanton, Apr. 25, 1863, in *ibid.*, 187.

administration, are conservative in their views." Such men would resort to all necessary means to crush the rebellion, said Dixon, "but they will never consent to the annihilation of the State governments, and the wild revolutionary doctrines of Mr. Sumner and his school." Said Dixon, "They look with confidence to you as the defender of the Constitution; and they hope to see something in your message to Congress, which shall prove that this confidence in you is not misplaced." From the radical side Isaac Arnold of Illinois wrote that as the rebel military power grew weaker, "the question of the treatment of the territory in rebellion will necessarily press itself upon the consideration of the approaching Congress." "The people are looking to your message with the most intense solicitude," Arnold pointed out to Lincoln and urged, "*Complete the work you have begun. End slavery during your administration.* To that end I beg you will speak such decided words as will satisfy all friends and enemies of this institution, that so far as you have the power, *its days are numbered.*" [42]

Not only were events creating interest in what the President might say about reconstruction; they were also forcing him to take more decisive action. It was clear that the Free State General Committee, on which Lincoln had relied, was unable to generate much Unionist sentiment or make progress toward a constitutional convention. The conservative faction, moreover, was trying to place representatives in Congress and gain control over Louisiana reconstruction. The logic of the situation demanded a more positive assertion of executive power, and judging from Lincoln's actions in the summer of 1863, this seemed to mean a radical rather than a conservative solution. So far was Lincoln from being grouped with the conservatives at this time that Andrew Johnson could write apprehensively to Montgomery Blair in late November, "I hope that the President will not be

[42] James Dixon to Lincoln, Nov. 14, 1863, no. 28015, and Isaac Arnold to Lincoln, Dec. 4, 1863, no. 28422, Robert Todd Lincoln Collection, Library of Congress.

committed to the proposition of States relapsing into territories and held as such." [43]

Lincoln's response to the situation that had developed by the end of 1863 was to do what he had several times said he would not do—assume direct control of the process of reconstruction. Having tried various methods, none of them successful, that allowed Southern Unionists to take the initiative in reorganization, Lincoln issued a Proclamation of Amnesty and Reconstruction on December 8, 1863, and shortly afterward placed control of reconstruction in the key state of Louisiana in the hands of his military commander there.

For the present his larger purpose was expressed in the proclamation and in his annual message to Congress.[44] Lincoln said that his intention was "to present the people of the States wherein the national authority has been suspended, and loyal

[43] Andrew Johnson to Montgomery Blair, Nov. 24, 1863, in Edward McPherson, ed., *The Political History of the United States of America during the Period of Reconstruction* (Washington, 1871), 199.

[44] Lincoln had been considering a proclamation of amnesty for some time. As early as December 1862 he told Fernando Wood, the New York Democrat, that he would offer a full and general amnesty if the South gave up the war. As has been noted previously, he contemplated saying something about amnesty in connection with the Springfield letter in September, but decided against doing so. However, in October, replying to an inquiry from General Rosecrans concerning a general amnesty, Lincoln said he intended "doing something like what you suggest, whenever the case shall appear ripe enough to have it accepted in the true understanding, rather than as a confession of weaknesss and fear." By the end of November, Lincoln had decided to include in his message a plan of reconstruction. Salmon P. Chase wrote to him on November 25, "The conclusion you have come to concerning the reconstruction of the rebel States gives me very great satisfaction, in which I am sure almost all loyal men will share." The Washington correspondent of the New York *Tribune* predicted on November 26 that the President would embody in his message to Congress the main features of his plan for restoration (Lincoln to Fernando Wood, Dec. 12, 1862, in *Collected Works of Lincoln*, V, 553; Lincoln to William S. Rosecrans, Oct. 4, 1863, in *ibid.*, VI, 498; Salmon P. Chase to Lincoln, Nov. 25, 1863, no. 28217, Robert Todd Lincoln Collection, Library of Congress; New York *Tribune*, Nov. 26, 1863).

State governments have been subverted, a mode in and by which the national authority and loyal State governments may be re-established within said States, or in any of them." The reason for the proclamation was that "in some States the elements for resumption seem ready for action, but remain inactive, apparently for want of a rallying-point—a plan of action." Moreover, if the elements seeking to reconstruct a loyal government should agree to a course of action, "how can they know," he asked, "but that the general government here will reject their plan?" Accordingly, the aim of the proclamation was to present a plan "which may be accepted by them as a rallying point, and which they are assured in advance will not be rejected here." Lincoln hoped that "This [might] bring them to act sooner than they otherwise would." [45]

The proclamation consisted of two parts: an offer of amnesty to individual southerners, and the outline of a method by which loyal governments might be reorganized in the rebellious states. With certain exceptions, Lincoln offered a full pardon to all persons who had directly or by implication participated in the rebellion. To such persons property rights would be restored, except as they applied to slaves and involved the rights of third parties. In order to regain the right to hold property, former rebels had to subscribe to an oath to "support, protect and defend the Constitution of the United States, and the Union of the States thereunder." Furthermore, amnesty seekers had to swear that they would "abide by and faithfully support all acts of Congress . . . and proclamations of the President made during the existing rebellion having reference to slaves, so long and so far as not modified or declared void by decision of the Supreme Court." [46] This provision was necessary, Lincoln said, because the purpose of the laws and proclamations on slavery

---

[45] Proclamation of Amnesty and Reconstruction, Dec. 8, 1863, in *Collected Works of Lincoln*, VII, 56; Annual Message to Congress, Dec. 8, 1863, in *ibid.*, 52.

[46] Proclamation of Amnesty, in *ibid.*, 54.

was to aid in suppressing the rebellion, and in order to "give them their fullest effect, there had to be a pledge for their main-tenance." To abandon emancipation would be to give up a lever of power and would be "a cruel and an astounding breach of faith" toward Negroes. Therefore, declared Lincoln, "while I remain in my present position I shall not attempt to retract or modify the emancipation proclamation; nor shall I return to slavery any person who is free by the terms of that proclama-tion, or by the acts of Congress." [47]

Lincoln excepted six classes of persons from the benefits of the proclamation. The most significant groups excluded were civil and diplomatic officers and agents of the Confederate govern-ment, and military and naval officers above the rank of colonel in the army or of lieutenant in the navy. Also banned were those who had left judicial posts in the United States to aid the rebel-lion, those who had left seats in Congress or resigned commis-sions in the army or navy for the same purpose, and "all who had engaged in any way in treating colored persons or white persons, in charge of such, otherwise than lawfully as prisoners of war." [48]

The second part of the proclamation dealt with the restora-tion of the seceded states to the Union. Here Lincoln specified that the number of persons participating in the re-establishment of a state government was to be not less than one-tenth the number of votes cast in the state in the presidential election of 1860. Each participant had to be a qualified voter according to the pre-existing state election law and had to take the same oath required of persons involved in the rebellion. Moreover, the new government had to be established in accordance with that oath; that is, it had to recognize emancipation. When a state govern-ment was organized "which shall be republican, and in no wise contravening said oath," Lincoln continued, "such shall be rec-ognized as the true government of the State, and the State shall

[47] Annual Message, Dec. 8, 1863, in *ibid.*, 51.
[48] Proclamation of Amnesty, in *ibid.*, 55.

receive thereunder the benefits of the constitutional provision which declares that 'The United States shall guaranty to every State in this union a republican form of government.'" He added that he did not regard it "as . . . improper, that, in constructing a loyal State government in any State, the name of the State, the boundary, the subdivisions, the constitution, and the general code of laws, as before the rebellion, be maintained, subject only to the modifications made necessary by the conditions hereinbefore stated, and such others, if any, not contravening such conditions, and which may be deemed expedient by those framing the new State government." [49]

Having imposed stringent conditions, Lincoln tempered them by allowing the states to shape policies concerning former slaves. He said, "Any provision which may be adopted by such State government in relation to the freed people of such State, which shall recognize and declare their permanent freedom, provide for their education, and which may yet be consistent, as a temporary arrangement, with their present condition as a laboring, landless, and homeless class, will not be objected to by the national executive." [50] He told Congress that he chose this course "with the view of possibly modifying the confusion and destitution which must, at best, attend all classes by a total revolution of labor throughout whole States." He hoped that the people of the South would give up slavery more readily "if, to this extent, this vital matter be left to themselves." Lincoln added, however, that "no power of the national Executive to prevent an abuse is abridged by the proposition." [51]

Although the proclamation signified Lincoln's decision to direct the reconstruction process, he did not claim exclusive authority. As on previous occasions, he acknowledged the role of Congress in reconstruction. "To avoid misunderstanding," he pointed out, "it may be proper to say . . . that whether members sent to Congress from any State shall be admitted to seats

[49] *Ibid.*, 55–56.   [50] *Ibid.*, 55.
[51] Annual Message, Dec. 8, 1863, in *ibid.*, 55.

constitutionally rests exclusively with the respective Houses, and not to any extent with the Executive." Furthermore, Lincoln did not rule out other solutions to the problem. He noted, for example, that "while the mode presented is the best the Executive can suggest, with his present impressions, it must not be understood that no other possible mode would be acceptable." [52] He reiterated the point in his message to Congress: "Saying that reconstruction will be accepted if presented in a specified way, it is not said it will never be accepted in any other way." [53]

Analysis of the Proclamation of Amnesty and Reconstruction may begin by observing that it was based on the constitutional power of the President "to grant reprieves and pardons for offences against the United States." [54] Although the granting of a pardon is essentially a man-to-man transaction, and therefore it might be argued that the power does not extend to a general amnesty, Lincoln assumed the opposite.[55] A second authority that Lincoln relied on was the Confiscation Act of July 1862, according to which the President was "authorized at any time thereafter, by proclamation, to extend to persons who may have participated in the existing rebellion, in any State or part thereof, pardon and amnesty, with such exceptions and at such times and on such conditions as he may deem expedient for the public welfare." [56] But while invoking congressional authority, Lincoln seemed to reduce its importance by saying, "The congressional declaration for limited and conditional pardon accords with well-established judicial exposition of the pardoning power." [57]

[52] Proclamation of Amnesty, in *ibid.*, 56.
[53] Annual Message, Dec. 8, 1863, in *ibid.*, 52.   [54] *Ibid.*, 53.
[55] Edward S. Corwin, *The President: Office and Powers, 1787–1957* (4th rev. ed.; New York, 1957), 159.
[56] Proclamation of Amnesty, in *Collected Works of Lincoln*, VII, 54; U.S., *Stat. at Large*, XII, 592.
[57] Proclamation of Amnesty, in *Collected Works of Lincoln*, VII, 54.

Though the pardoning power was unquestionably valid in
dealing with individuals—for the task, in Lincoln's words, of
separating "the opposing elements, so as to build only from the
sound" [58]—its validity for imposing conditions on the rebel
states was less obvious. Apparently, however, Lincoln felt that it
extended to this process as well, for he cited no other constitutional authority under which he presumed to act. It is true that
in his message he referred to the clause guaranteeing republican
government; but he used it to justify federal protection of state
governments after they had been re-established, not as authority
for stipulating, as he had in the amnesty proclamation, that the
state governments "shall be republican, and in no wise contravening said oath." [59] Thus the pardoning power was the sole
constitutional authority for making emancipation a condition of
reconstruction.

Lincoln's message and proclamation agreed more with the radical than with the conservative position of December 1863. To
be sure, the proclamation in some respects was congenial to conservative views. To accomplish reconstruction by means of the
pardoning power, by making it a matter of individual loyalties,
was consistent with the conservative view of the war as a rebellion of individuals against their government. Lincoln furthermore regarded the rebellious states as still in the Union and
indicated that state boundaries, constitutions, and laws were to
remain unaltered, except with respect to slavery. It was consistent with the conservative position to hold that the Emancipation
Proclamation and the oath of the amnesty proclamation were
subject to repeal or modification by the Supreme Court and to
allow the southern states to work out arrangements for the
freedmen. Finally, the granting of pardon was itself an essentially conciliatory act. Higher-ranking civil and military officers
were excluded from the amnesty, but not the mass of southern

[58] Annual Message, Dec. 8, 1863, in *ibid.*, 51.   [59] *Ibid.*, 50–51.

fighting men nor the population in general. In several respects, then, Lincoln was in agreement with conservative views.

In its most important provisions, however, the Proclamation of Amnesty and Reconstruction was consistent with the radical position. Lincoln's statement that the southern state governments had "for a long time been subverted" seemed close to the radical view that constitutional state governments had been destroyed. Terms such as "subverted," "re-establish," and "revive," which Lincoln used in referring to the rebellious states, might mean that they had ceased to be states in a constitutional sense. Charles Sumner, for example, said, "The language of the proclamation and of the accompanying message plainly assumes that the rebel States have lost their original character as States of the Union." Referring to the descriptive terms used by Lincoln, Sumner declared, "If subverted, . . . [the rebellious states] are no longer States. . . . We do not *reestablish* a government which continues to exist." [60] Furthermore, Lincoln's commitment to retaining existing state boundaries and laws was couched in curiously negative language. Such a commitment, Lincoln remarked, "was suggested as not improper." As Sumner again pointed out, "The President does not insist that even the name and boundary of a State shall be preserved. . . . Of course this suggestion of what is not improper implies necessarily that in his opinion these great changes were within the discretion of the *revived* community." [61] Lincoln's support of the traditional political framework in the states, moreover, seemed to rest on strictly practical grounds, not on a firm commitment to the principle of state rights or state indestructibility. The suggestion was made, Lincoln explained, "in the hope that it may do good without danger of harm. It will save labor and avoid great confusion." [62]

---

[60] *Cong. Globe*, 38 Cong., 1 sess., 2899 (June 13, 1864). [61] *Ibid*.
[62] Annual Message, Dec. 8, 1863, in *Collected Works of Lincoln*, VII, 52.

Lincoln omitted from his message a warning against theorizing about reconstruction which would probably have implied a criticism of radicals. In the preliminary draft of the message he had written:

The question whether these States have continued to be States in the Union, or have become territories, out of it, seems to me, in every present aspect, to be of no practical importance. They all have been States in the Union; and all are to be hereafter, as we all propose; and a controversy whether they have ever been out of it, might divide and weaken, but could not enhance our strength, in restoring the proper national and State relations.[63]

According to John Hay, one of his private secretaries, Lincoln omitted these words after considering that the guarantee clause "empowers him to grant protection to States *in* the Union and it will not do ever to admit that these States have at any time been out." [64] If Lincoln had retained this warning, it probably would have seemed to be aimed more at radicals than at conservatives, for the former tended more to engage in theorizing on this question. Indeed, for conservatives the elaboration of theories to fit the circumstances in the South was less vital, since according to their way of thinking the states had undergone no essential change requiring a new understanding of their status.

It was in their substantive content, however, that Lincoln's proclamation and message most signficantly agreed with the radical position of December 1863. Clearly the main import of both papers was that emancipation would be a condition of reconstruction: slave property would not be restored, and central in the amnesty oath was a promise to abide by all future as well as past laws and proclamations concerning emancipation. The emancipation requirement was a matter both of military expediency and moral commitment—to abandon the policy would be a breach of faith to the Negro, explained Lincoln. Although he

[63] *Ibid.*

[64] John Hay, *Lincoln and the Civil War in the Diaries and Letters of John Hay*, ed. Tyler Dennett (New York, 1939), 135.

said that the Emancipation Proclamation was subject to modification by the judiciary, the longer the war lasted, the greater the likelihood that the courts would not oppose the President on this issue. Lincoln, moreover, imposed emancipation as a condition directly on the states. Re-established governments had to be "in no wise contravening the oath," he declared, and insisted that they "be republican." Though he did not define the word "republican," from its context it seemed to refer to a government prohibiting slavery, as radicals were insisting. Lincoln did not expressly require new state constitutions; the old constitutions amended in accordance with the Emancipation Proclamation presumably would be satisfactory. However, nothing he said indicated that he had altered his policy of encouraging new state constitutions.

The loyalty-oath element of Lincoln's plan also was more in keeping with the radical than the conservative position. To require the oath of all persons was to disregard the distinction between loyal and disloyal citizens that was basic to the conservative view. The requirement implied that all citizens in a seceded state occupied the same status. What that status was Lincoln did not explain, but he seemed to approximate the opinion of radicals such as William Whiting, saying that the oath would serve "as a test of admission to the political body." [65] Just as Whiting had held that all citizens of the seceded states were public enemies, Lincoln seemed to imply that as a result of the rebellion, they had acquired a lower status than citizens of the loyal states or of the nation.

Reaction to the oath provision in the next few weeks showed how radical it seemed to southern Unionists. General Banks reported in January 1864 that conservative men in Louisiana felt that they had already had their rights as citizens established by virtue of participation in the election of representatives in 1862 and ought not to have to take an additional oath in order to vote

[65] Annual Message, Dec. 8, 1863, in *Collected Works of Lincoln*, VII, 51.

at future elections. A Louisiana Unionist wrote to Lincoln, "Citizens who have not sinned cannot honorably accept a pardon," while from Tennessee, Horace Maynard reported that the element of the proclamation most frequently criticized was "its placing in the same category repentant rebels & men always loyal." "It is galling in the extreme to many of our best Union men," Maynard said, "to be transmitted to posterity, as they express it, on the same record with men reeking with treason." [66] Thus the oath requirement of the presidential plan reflected radical rather than conservative ideas.

The 10-per-cent feature of the executive plan—the requirement that a number of men equal to 10 per cent of a state's prewar voting population might form a state government—has usually been considered proof of Lincoln's leniency toward the South and a source of the conflict that developed between Congress and the President. It is true that this plan was a cause of disagreement a few months later, but at first most Republicans, including radicals, supported it, even to the extent of incorporating it in the first reconstruction bill they introduced in the new Congress.[67] Democrats, fearful of the political consequences of the 10-per-cent requirement, were its most vocal critics when it first appeared.

Though Lincoln said nothing specific about the proviso, his reason for relying on a minority was clear enough. As he told Congress, "An attempt to guaranty and protect a revived State government, constructed in whole, or in preponderating part, from the very element against whose hostility and violence it is to be protected, is simply absurd." [68] Gideon Welles said later

[66] Nathaniel Banks to Lincoln, Jan. 22, 1864, no. 29710, Jacob Bowker to Lincoln, Jan. 22, 1864, no. 29729, Robert Todd Lincoln Collection, Library of Congress; Horace Maynard to Lincoln, Feb. 2, 1864, in *Collected Works of Lincoln*, VII, 183–184; John G. Nicolay and John Hay, *Abraham Lincoln: A History* (10 vols.; New York, 1890), VIII, 444.

[67] See below, Chapter VII.

[68] Annual Message, Dec. 8, 1863, in *Collected Works of Lincoln*, VII, 51.

that the Cabinet, in discussing the number of voters who might initiate reorganization, agreed on one-tenth, but he did not explain why.[69] Probably the answer lies in the elections that had been held in parts of the South under Union control, where in most cases voter participation had been about 10 per cent. In Louisiana, it is true, about 50 per cent of the prewar voters had gone to the polls in 1862, but this was an exception; 10 percent could reasonably be expected in most elections. Nevertheless, the favorable result in the Louisiana election case seems to have caused Lincoln to believe that the 10-per-cent plan was feasible. According to James G. Blaine, in 1863 a first-term representative from Maine, the admission of Flanders and Hahn from Louisiana "misled [Lincoln] as to the temper and tendency of Congress on the whole subject of re-establishing civil government in the insurrectionary States." [70] Lincoln also believed, according to John Hay, that "the only question is, who constitutes the State," and that "when that is decided the solution of subsequent questions is easy." [71] Holding this view, and influenced by the outcome of the Louisiana case, Lincoln probably thought that Congress would agree to reconstruction according to the 10-per-cent plan, as long as the right Unionists controlled the process on the local level.

The Proclamation of Amnesty and Reconstruction pointed ahead to a period of direct control of reconstruction by the executive and set forth a policy that has usually been considered lenient toward the South, and therefore conservative.[72] Yet in its historical context—the debate on reconstruction that devel-

[69] Gideon Welles, *Lincoln's Administration,* ed. Albert Mordell (New York, 1960), 116. The essays in this volume originally appeared in *The Galaxy.*

[70] James G. Blaine, *Twenty Years in Congress: From Lincoln to Garfield* (2 vols.; Norwich, Conn., 1884–1886), II, 37.

[71] Hay, *Lincoln and the Civil War,* 135.

[72] See, for example, Benjamin P. Thomas, *Abraham Lincoln: A Biography* (New York, 1952), 405; and McPherson, *Struggle for Equality,* 241.

oped in the second half of 1863—and in terms of the central issue in that debate—reconstruction with, or without, emancipation—Lincoln's proclamation was radical. As the Boston *Commonwealth* pointed out on December 18, 1863, "The Conservatives set out with the theory that the rebel States could return at any time, *of right*. The radicals held and now hold that they must come back on such terms as our Government chooses to impose." This was precisely what Lincoln had demanded. The *Commonwealth* asserted, "The President has fully made up his mind that as far as he is concerned, during his occupancy of the Presidential chair, . . . no rebel State shall be again received into the Union as a slave State, or with slavery existing as a political and social element." [73] The *Commonwealth* correctly observed, "If the Federal Government assumes the right to prescribe, by one jot or tittle, the conditions of re-admission, the exercise of that right is fatal to the whole conservative theory." Not without reason did the journal refer to "the President's conversion to the radical programme." [74]

As the reaction of the *Commonwealth* indicated, and as we shall see in greater detail below, most Republicans—radicals included—responded favorably to Lincoln's message and proclamation. For the time being, the lines of opposition within the party were obscured. Indeed, it was by no means clear what shape the solution of the question of reconstruction would ultimately assume. As Lincoln himself said, "It must not be understood that no other possible mode [of reconstruction] would be acceptable." Charles Sumner's reaction to the executive plan seems to illustrate the openness of the situation. According to Edward Pierce, his friend and biographer, Sumner had long insisted on the power of Congress to regulate reconstruction. But he did not enter into a controversy over this issue in December 1863, thinking it wiser to await developments in the South. Sumner wrote to John Bright in mid-December, "Any plan which fosters emancipation beyond recall will suit me." The

[73] Boston *Commonwealth*, Dec. 18, 11, 1863.   [74] *Ibid.*, Dec. 18, 1863.

Washington correspondent of the Chicago *Tribune* reported a conversation with Sumner in which the Massachusetts senator said that he was "fully and perfectly satisfied" with Lincoln's proclamation and message. Though Sumner thought that there might be differences about details in admitting some of the states, he said, "These will drop out of sight and nothing remain but the irrevocability of the [emancipation] proclamation." The journalist wrote, "Senator Sumner is prepared fully to cooperate with the President in his proposed plan." Similarly indicative of the tendency to subordinate differences within Unionist ranks, the Boston *Commonwealth* observed that the most obvious criticism of Lincoln's proclamation was that Congress ought to initiate and guide the work of reconstruction, that the President lacked the power to determine the status of the rebel states. Yet this criticism was "based on proprieties of a peaceful time," explained the radical journal, and "may be said to be now out of place." [75]

Lincoln's secretaries later wrote, "This reception of the message was extremely pleasing to the President. A solution of the most important problem of the time, which conservatives like [James] Dixon and Reverdy Johnson thoroughly approved, and to which Mr. Sumner made no objection, was of course a source of profound gratification." According to Nicolay and Hay, Lincoln interpreted the entire episode "as proof of what he had often said, that there was no essential contest between loyal men on this subject if they would consider it reasonably." [76] Whether or not Lincoln was correct in his analysis, however, depended on what Congress would do about reconstruction.

[75] Pierce, *Memoir and Letters of Charles Sumner*, IV, 215–216; Sumner to John Bright, Dec. 15, 1863, in *ibid.*, 216; Chicago *Tribune*, Dec. 14, 30, 1863; Boston *Commonwealth*, Dec. 11, 1863.
[76] Nicolay and Hay, *Abraham Lincoln*, IX, 110–111.

VII

Congressional Reconstruction

CONGRESSIONAL involvement in reconstruction during the Civil War reached a climax with the passage of the Wade-Davis Bill in July 1864. Though it stood in contrast to the plan of reconstruction announced by Lincoln in December 1863, the Wade-Davis Bill was in the broadest sense not a response to the executive plan, but the logical conclusion to Congress' own concern with reconstruction since the start of the war. From the time it had first become an issue, many, if not most, members of Congress regarded reconstruction as an issue for the legislature rather than the executive to resolve. In 1862, Congress passed acts requiring the election of representatives by single districts and making the "iron-clad" oath a condition of holding federal office—measures which, though not constituting a frontal assault on the problem, nevertheless signified congressional determination to shape Union policy on this all-important question. A more direct and far-reaching attempt to control reconstruction was the Louisiana and Tennessee elections bill of February 1863, which failed only narrowly in the Senate after passing in the House by an overwhelming majority. From a restricted point of view, one might observe that these proposals all dealt with Congress and hence reflected the traditional idea that each branch of the government should decide on matters relating specifically to itself. Yet under the circumstances—with the old Union shattered and in process of reconstruction—questions affecting Congress possessed significance far beyond the orthodox constitutional concern for preserving the integrity of the legislative branch. In dealing with problems such as the admission of members from rebel states, Congress was not simply protecting itself; it was using specific powers broadly, to determine the reconstruction policy of the federal government. And when Congress in December 1863 established a Select Committee on the Rebellious States and six months later passed a reconstruction bill providing a uniform federal policy for all the seceded states, it was in part influenced by what the President had done, but its actions were based on the belief that reconstruction was fundamentally a civil and political process that properly should be controlled by the legislature.

Although by midsummer of 1864 the President and Congress were locked in conflict on the question of reconstruction policy, this discordant situation was slow in developing. Indeed, the publication of Lincoln's Proclamation of Amnesty and Reconstruction in December 1863 found the great majority of Republicans and Unionists supporting the President. The Washington correspondent of the New York *Times* wrote that "conflicting theories and speculations" concerning the restoration of the rebellious states had been "happily blended" into a practical measure by the President. "The great object of one class of persons was to secure the abolition of Slavery," he said, "and of the other, to maintain the ancient landmarks, and in some sort, the continued existence of the States. Both these ideas are embodied in the plan of the President." John Forney, the secretary of the Senate and the publisher of the Philadelphia *Press*, remarked that he had never witnessed "a more cordial and enthusiastic unity in any party." In a similar vein the correspondent of the Springfield, Massachusetts, *Weekly Republican* observed: "The president seems to have made friends among the radicals and conservatives with his new plan of reconstruction. . . . Henceforth, the republican party is a unit, and no quarrels between radicals and conservatives will be in order." [1]

Because Lincoln had committed himself to emancipation as the basis of reconstruction, radical antislavery men greeted the message and proclamation warmly. "Whatever may be the results or the verdict of history," John Hay recorded in his diary after hearing the proclamation read in Congress, "the immediate effect of this paper is something wonderful. I never have seen such an effect produced by a public document. Men acted as if the millennium had come." "Chandler was delighted, Sumner was beaming," Hay wrote of two well-known radical leaders. Another Massachusetts radical, Henry Wilson, said, "The President has struck another great blow"; still another, George Boutwell, remarked, "It is a very able and shrewd paper. It has great points of popularity: & it is right." Indicating the importance of the antislavery content of the executive plan, Owen Lovejoy of Illinois exclaimed, "I shall live to see slavery ended in America." Praising Lincoln, Henry T. Blow of Missouri announced, "I am one of the Radicals who have always believed in the President." [2]

The New York *Tribune* saw Lincoln's plan as effecting a balance between severity and weakness which, while it was not perfect, was essentially right and which deserved the support of all loyal men. The Chicago *Tribune*, expressing the sentiments of most radicals emphasizing emancipation, editorialized, "*Let slavery be destroyed* and other things will give but transitory difficulty." Relating Lincoln's proclamation to the debate on reconstruction that had preceded it, the Boston *Commonwealth* observed that most conservative journals "meekly accept the fact of the President's conversion to the radical programme." The *Commonwealth* declared, "As every man who is not an incorrigible dunce must see, the President's plan ignores com-

[1] New York *Times*, Dec. 13, 1863; Philadelphia *Press*, Dec. 11, 1863; Springfield, Mass., *Weekly Republican*, Jan. 2, 1864.
[2] Hay, *Lincoln and the Civil War*, 131–132.

pletely the present political existence of the rebel States and
subverts all their constitutions, and regulations as to suffrage,
boundaries, and everything else, where subversion is necessary or
important to secure the main object constantly held in view."
Lincoln's refusal to insist on the preservation of existing state
boundaries seemed to prove the newspaper's point. So satisfactory seemed the executive plan that the *Commonwealth*
compared it to the proposal of William Whiting. Whiting had
written: "Allow the inhabitants of conquered territory to form
themselves into States, only by adopting constitutions such as
will forever remove all cause of collision with the United States,
by excluding slavery therefrom, or continue military government over the conquered district until there shall appear therein
a sufficient number of loyal inhabitants to form a Republican
government." The *Commonwealth* concluded: "If anybody can
discover a particle of difference between this proposition, which
in July last, was denounced as the quintessence of radicalism,
and the spirit of the plan announced by the President in his
Proclamation and Message, he can see what is not to be seen.
The ideas of the solicitor and the President are identical." *The
Independent*, though it disliked Lincoln's reference to the
Supreme Court and the fact that a reorganized government
might rest on a minority of the population, considered such objections "incidental and remediable" and asserted: "The great
fact remains that the President has presented to the country a
practical issue, instead of a sentiment or a theory." The abolitionist journal declared, "We are all stronger to-day, and happier,
because the President has again solemnly said that the Nation's
Word must be kept, and that those set free shall not be abandoned again to bondage." [3]

Though radical in its most significant feature, Lincoln's reconstruction plan also received the support of moderate and conservative Republicans and Unionists. The New York *Times*,

[3] New York *Tribune*, Dec. 11, 1863; Chicago *Tribune*, Dec. 14, 1863;
Boston *Commonwealth*, Dec. 18, 1863; *The Independent*, Dec. 17, 1863.

which had not insisted on emancipation as a condition for the readmission of the seceded states, nevertheless approved of the executive plan as "simple and yet perfectly effective." The *Times* was especially pleased that Lincoln had given "no countenance to the project . . . of reducing the redeemed States to a territorial condition." Rejecting now the possibility of "a restoration which [would] be simply an emergence from the war, and resumption of the old *status* without any new limitations or conditions," the *Times* declared itself committed to Lincoln's policy. *Harper's Weekly*, ranging itself on the side of those who demanded that "no State shall be readmitted to the Union until it shall have purged its borders of slavery," supported the President's reconstruction proposal as "simple and radical" and "inevitable." Underscoring an idea that was becoming central in the thinking of an increasing number of Union men, *Harper's* said, "The initiative of political action in the seceded States . . . must proceed from the National Government." The Springfield *Weekly Republican* approved of Lincoln's plan because it rejected the "radical and destructive notions" advanced by some Union men yet adhered "inflexibly to the desire and purpose to destroy slavery with the rebellion." The Washington *Evening Star* endorsed Lincoln's proclamation as a guarantee of the right of the rebellious states "to resume their places in the Union at will, with all their State rights unimpaired, which the exigencies of this war . . . may not have destroyed." Even the conservative Unionist Washington *National Intelligencer* gave mild support to the President's policy, mainly because it denied "that pestilent political heresy which proposes to obliterate State lines in the South, and to throw all the civil as well as social institutions of that section into hotch-potch." [4]

While Republicans and Unionists generally approved Lin-

[4] New York *Times*, Dec. 10, 11, 1863; *Harper's Weekly*, Dec. 19, 26, 1863; Springfield, Mass., *Weekly Republican*, Dec. 19, 26, 1863; Washington *Evening Star*, Dec. 10, 1863; Washington *National Intelligencer*, Dec. 10, 1863.

coln's plan, Democrats criticized it. The New York *World* commented that the President would gain electoral votes, his main desire, by having some southern states admitted, but that "as a means of recovering the South and reconstructing the Union, his scheme is simply absurd." The 10-per-cent plan was unsound, said the *World*, because it would create governments based on minority rule, which could hardly be considered republican. The New York *Herald*, doubting that enough loyal men could be found to establish 10-per-cent governments, speculated that Lincoln might have been trying to conciliate the radicals in his party by proposing to receive the seceded states only as free states. The Cleveland *Plain Dealer* felt that the Proclamation of Amnesty and Reconstruction announced as policy to all the rebel states what the President had told the Louisiana conservatives in June: "Recognize my edict regarding your chattel property, and come back; fail to do it, and stay out until we subjugate you!" The *Plain Dealer* said that this policy had had no results thus far and had only prolonged the war. The Washington correspondent of the Cincinnati *Commercial* summed up opposition feeling, stating that while Lincoln's proclamation "gives general satisfaction to the Unionists, . . . the most Democrats have to say about it is that it is a bid for the next Presidential term." [5]

"Everybody abounds in schemes for settling the troubles in the rebel states, and at least six plans a day are offered in the House in the shape of a Bill," remarked Henry Dawes, describing the activity in Congress during the first weeks after Lincoln's proclamation and message on reconstruction.[6] The first concrete step the House took after organizing was to appoint a select committee on reconstruction.[7] Although it is

[5] New York *World*, Dec. 10, 1863; New York *Herald*, Dec. 10, 11, 1863; Cleveland *Plain Dealer*, Dec. 10, 1863; Cincinnati *Daily Commercial*, Dec. 14, 1863.

[6] Henry L. Dawes to Electa Dawes, Dec. 16, 1863, Dawes Papers, Library of Congress.

[7] During the organization of the House the acting clerk, Emerson Etheridge, a Democrat of Tennessee, tried to give control to the Demo-

sometimes seen as the first in a series of radical moves against the executive plan of reconstruction, the creation of the select committee was actually a routine response to the emphasis on reconstruction in the President's proclamation and message.[8] It was important, not because it was an antiadministration step, but because it revealed congressional thinking on reconstruction and suggested the general position Congress would subsequently take on the question.

Following standard House procedure, Thaddeus Stevens, the chairman of the Committee on Ways and Means, proposed on December 15 that the parts of the President's message dealing with the condition and treatment of the seceded states be referred to a special committee of nine. Asserting himself on the issue that he would make especially his own, Henry Winter Davis promptly offered a substitute resolution giving the constitutional position he had stressed in his Philadelphia speech in September. Davis proposed that "so much of the President's message as relates to the duty of the United States to guaranty a republican form of government to the States in which the governments recognized by the United States have been abrogated or overthrown, be referred to a select committee . . . , which shall report the bills necessary and proper for carrying into execution the foregoing guarantee." Explaining his position further, Davis

---

crats by keeping out fourteen Republicans on a technicality involving the act of March 3, 1863, directing the clerk in the procedure of making the roll of members-elect. Etheridge also placed on the roll the names of the three Louisiana representatives who claimed election under the auspices of the Executive Central Committee of Louisiana. Republicans were alert to the "Etheridge plot," however, and moved swiftly to prevent it from succeeding. The names of the Republicans omitted by Etheridge were added to the roll, and the credentials of the Louisiana members were referred to the Committee on Elections (*Cong. Globe*, 38 Cong., 1 sess., 4-8 [Dec. 7, 1863]).

[8] Hesseltine (*Lincoln's Plan of Reconstruction*, 100–101), for example, sees anti-Lincoln maneuvering in the appointment of the select committee.

said he thought that there had been "no destruction of the Union"; therefore he avoided the use of the word "reconstruction." "The fact, as well as the constitutional view of the condition of affairs in the States enveloped by the rebellion," he continued, "is that a force has overthrown, or the people, in a moment of madness, have abrogated the governments which existed in those States, under the Constitution." Having established a moderate position in contrast to that of the territorializers by implicitly regarding the states as still in the Union, Davis proposed a constitutional remedy that was equally moderate, again in contrast to territorialization, by saying that the United States ought to "see, when armed resistance shall be removed, that governments shall be restored in those States republican in their form." [9] These ideas were central in congressional thinking on reconstruction in 1864.

Davis became Lincoln's chief opponent on reconstruction, but this opposition did not take shape until later. Lincoln had recently rejected an appeal by Montgomery Blair, based on the argument that Davis would oppose the administration, to support Davis' rival as the Unionist candidate in the contest for representative from the Baltimore district. This was of course known to the Maryland radical, who, while not enthusiastic about the President and critical of the idea of his having a second term, did not regard himself as opposed to the administration at this time. Only if Blair represented the administration, Davis wrote to his political confidant Admiral S. F. Du Pont in November, could he be so described. Despite Blair's claim in his Rockville speech that he spoke for the President, Davis believed that this was not so, and that Lincoln's "eyes [were] opening" to the true worth of Blair's counsel. Davis let it be known that he and other newly elected Republicans would not be "tame or subservient" toward the administration; the Republican majority, he warned, "will hold the Adm[inistration] responsible—or

[9] *Cong. Globe*, 38 Cong., 1 sess., 33–34 (Dec. 15, 1863).

revolt." But Davis and his colleagues had no quarrel with respect to reconstruction.[10]

If Davis was starting an anti-Lincoln revolt, the vote on his resolution did not show it. The House approved the proposal, 91 to 80, with only 3 Republicans opposed and with proadministration men such as Isaac Arnold, Henry Dawes, and Elihu Washburne voting for it. The select committee appointed by the speaker maintained a fair balance between the radical and the conservative. Representing the radical wing were Davis, who was named chairman, James Ashley of Ohio, the leading advocate of territorialization in the preceding Congress, and Henry T. Blow of Missouri. Republicans of more moderate views were Daniel Gooch of Massachusetts, Reuben Fenton of New York, and Nathaniel Smithers of Delaware. Gooch and Fenton had taken solid antislavery positions in the Thirty-seventh Congress but had been moderates on the Louisiana election issue, voting to admit the Louisiana representatives. Smithers, a first-term member, had no particular political reputation, but because Lincoln had appointed him provost marshal of Delaware the year before, he could be expected to support the administration. At the conservative pole were Democrats James English of Connecticut, William Holman of Indiana, and James C. Allen of Illinois.[11]

Of several reconstruction proposals offered in the opening weeks of the session, the most important was a bill introduced from the radical faction by James Ashley on December 21, 1863.[12] Far from being a reaction against the executive plan of

[10] Henry Winter Davis to Samuel F. Du Pont, Nov. 4, Dec. 11, 1863, S. F. Du Pont Papers, Eleutherian Mills Historical Library; Hay, *Lincoln and the Civil War*, 105.

[11] *Cong. Globe*, 38 Cong., 1 sess., 37 (Dec. 16, 1863); Harry J. Carman and Reinhard Luthin, *Lincoln and the Patronage* (New York, 1943), 241.

[12] 38 Cong., H.R. 48, Dec. 21, 1863, MS, National Archives, RG 233, 38A–B1. From the extreme conservative side, Joseph Edgerton of Indiana proposed a resolution criticizing Lincoln's proclamation on recon-

reconstruction, Ashley's bill followed Lincoln's proclamation in many important respects; indeed, contemporary observers saw it as implementing and filling in the outline of the presidential plan contained in the amnesty proclamation. Just as significant was a shift in Ashley's bill from a purely territorial solution to reconstruction to a solution emphasizing the guarantee of a republican government as the basis of congressional legislation.

Ashley's reconstruction bill of 1862 had rested squarely on the theory of territorialization. It had stated, "Acts of nullification, rebellion, and levying war . . . have terminated and of right ought to terminate the legal existence of said State governments"; and it had authorized the President to establish temporary civil governments with such names and within such geographical boundaries as he might chose to designate. Direct federal control was to continue until new governments were formed that would "apply for and obtain admission into the Union as States." Ashley had based the bill on the general sovereign and specific territorial power of the federal government. Since the seceded states had been destroyed, their territory fell under the exclusive jurisdiction of Congress, Ashley reasoned. This conclusion was perhaps more implicit than explicit, for on

---

struction and stating, "The maintenance inviolate of the . . . rights of the States, and especially the right of each State to order and control its own domestic institutions according to its own judgment exclusively, is essential to . . . the Federal Union." This was tabled by a vote of 90 to 66. George Yeaman, a Unionist of Kentucky, offered a more moderate resolution declaring that attempted secession "does not extinguish the political franchises of the loyal citizens of . . . [rebellious] States; and such loyal citizens have the right, at any time, to administer, amend, or establish a State government without other condition than that it shall be republican in form." The House referred this resolution to the select committee on reconstruction. From the moderate Republican side, Henry Dawes introduced into the new Congress the bill for congressional elections in Louisiana and Tennessee which the House had passed the previous March, but events had caused this approach to be superseded, and the bill died in committee (*Cong. Globe*, 38 Cong., 1 sess., 45 [Dec. 17, 1863]; 70 [Dec. 21, 1863]; 19 [Dec. 14, 1863]; 38 Cong., H.R. 2, Dec. 14, 1863).

this point the bill said merely, "The sovereignty of the United States over the districts of country now in rebellion is supreme by the express terms of the Constitution—and . . . the establishment of a hostile, despotic government within any part of the Territory of the United States is incompatible with the stability, safety, and dignity of the Government of the United States." Finally, the bill in substance had proposed the creation of governments patterned explicitly on the model of a territorial government.[13]

In contrast, Ashley's bill of December 1863 rejected the theory of territorialization and regarded the states as still in existence. In the Preamble, for example, Ashley referred to "States," not to "districts of country" as in the earlier bill. A different conception of the status of the southern states was evident also in the description of the results of the rebellion. Ashley charged the "constituted authorities of said State governments" with treason, rebellion, an attempted alliance with foreign powers, and so on—charges he had made in the 1862 bill against states, instead of against individuals. But the effect of all this was no longer to be the destruction of the states. Instead, the bill declared, "The said States, have renounced their allegiance to the Constitution of the United States, and abrogated the Republican form of Government heretofore established therein." At another point the bill similarly described the seceded states as "States which have abrogated the State governments recognized by Congress" and in which there was an "absence of any constitutional State government." [14]

Ashley based his new bill on the clause of the Constitution guaranteeing to each state a republican form of government. Accordingly, the preamble stated:

Whereas the Constitution declares that the United States *shall guarantee* to every State of this Union, a Republican form of govern-

[13] 37 Cong., H.R. 356, March 12, 1862, MS, Preamble, sec. 1.
[14] H.R. 48, Preamble.

ment, therefore it is obligatory upon Congress after the rebellious States have been reduced to obedience and the citizens thereof are willing to establish State governments under the Constitution, to provide by law for eliciting the will of the loyal people of said States.

The bill directed Congress "to make such provisions and conditions as may be necessary to defend and perpetuate the Union of these States and to establish and maintain in the States, so organized, governments, Republican in form." Until loyal governments were established which the United States could recognize, it was "the duty of Congress to provide by law for the internal government of such States."[15]

In contrast to the bill of 1862, which regarded slavery as having been extinguished along with the state itself, Ashley's bill of December 1863 regarded the prohibition of slavery as an element of republican government: "Slavery is incompatible with a Republican form of government, . . . the existence of slavery in the insurrectionary States has caused and maintained the rebellion therein, and the Emancipation of said slaves and a constitutional guarantee of their perpetual freedom is essential to the permanent restoration of State governments, Republican in form."[16] The rationale of the bill, then, was not, as in 1862, that "a hostile, despotic government [whose cornerstone is slavery] . . . is incompatible with the stability, safety and dignity of the Government of the United States," but rather that an obligation was "imposed on the Congress of the United

[15] *Ibid.*

[16] *Ibid.* Some abolitionists had argued that the guarantee clause was an appropriate instrument for striking at slavery. William Goodell, for example, in 1862 called attention to "the *Constitutional* obligation to overthrow slavery, by executing its express provision—'the United States *shall* guarantee to every State in this Union, a Republican form of Government.'" "Is it not high time that this high vantage ground were occupied," he asked the Indiana radical, George Julian, "and the Constitution *itself* made the weapon of assault?" (William Goodell to George Julian, Jan. 22, 1862, Giddings-Julian Papers, Library of Congress).

States by the Constitution, to secure the rights of the States and the liberties of the people." [17]

The central purpose of Ashley's bill of December 1863 also differed from that of his earlier proposal, which had been primarily concerned with governing areas recovered from insurrection; the new bill also dealt with this problem, but was mainly concerned with developing new state constitutions as the bases of loyal state governments. Here Ashley reflected the emphasis on reorganization that had been evident in Ira Harris' reconstruction bill of February 1863, and in Lincoln's Louisiana policy in the summer and fall of that year.

In providing interim government for the seceded states, Ashley followed the lines laid out in Lincoln's policy of using military governors—another measure of the change in the radicals' position on reconstruction as territorialization was given up. The 1862 bill had been chiefly concerned with creating a provisional territorial government and outlining policies on confiscation, land redistribution, public schools, and the conditions of labor for freedmen. In contrast the bill of December 1863 directed the President to establish temporary military governments under the direction of a "Provisional Military Governor." There was also less concern with the powers of the interim government; the bill stated simply, "The Provisional Military Governor . . . shall be charged with the civil administration of such District until State governments are organized . . . [and] shall see that the Constitution and laws of the United States and the provisions of this act are maintained and obeyed, and the proclamations of the President enforced." [18] And whereas previous territorial bills had provided for a separate judicial department, Ashley's new bill authorized federal district courts to decide state cases according to existing state codes. Only with respect to the freedmen did the bill seek to prescribe policy.

[17] H.R. 356, sec. 3; H.R. 48, Preamble. The bracketed words, which are Ashley's, were included in an earlier version of the 1862 bill.
[18] H.R. 48, secs. 2, 3.

Declaring free all slaves in the rebel states, it provided "that all laws, judicial decisions, or usages which recognize or sustain slavery, or which exclude the testimony of colored persons or deny them the right of trial by jury or punish persons who may teach them to read or write . . . shall be utterly void." The bill also ordered a fine not exceeding five thousand dollars and imprisonment not in excess of twenty years for depriving freedmen of their liberty or for arresting them on a charge of indebtedness.[19]

The rest of Ashley's bill presented a detailed plan for reorganizing state governments. Reconstruction was to begin whenever military control was established in a given district and the people therein "signified to the Governor a desire to return to their obedience to the Constitution." The provisional governor was then to order an enrollment of all loyal male citizens aged twenty-one or older; when the number of enrolled men equaled 10 per cent of the aggregate vote of 1860, he was to order an election for a constitutional convention. All male citizens of the United States who had reached the age of twenty-one could vote at this election, except persons who had voluntarily borne arms against the United States or held any rebel civil or military office. And each person had to take the loyalty oath prescribed in the President's amnesty proclamation.[20]

Ashley imposed several conditions for forming a constitution. One requirement was that the new constitutions be "Republican and not repugnant to the Constitution of the United States and the President's proclamation of January 1, 1863." More specific were the stipulations that no person who had held civil or military office under a rebel government, whether state or Confederate, be allowed to vote at any election for a governor or member of the legislature or hold any office of honor or profit under the state government until pardoned by the state legislature; that no debt contracted by the rebel states or the Confederate gov-

[19] *Ibid.*, secs. 9, 10, 11.　　[20] *Ibid.*, secs. 4, 5.

ernment would be recognized or paid by those states; that the freedom of all persons previously held as slaves, who had been declared free by act of Congress or proclamation of the President, be recognized and guaranteed by the constitution; and that after the adoption of the constitution, slavery be forever prohibited in the state, except as a punishment for crime. Should a constitution meeting these conditions be agreed to, it would go to the people for ratification. If approved by them, the President was to issue a proclamation "declaring the government formed to be the constitutional government of the state"; senators and representatives elected under the new constitution would then be "entitled to appear" in Congress. If on the other hand, the convention refused to adopt a constitution in accordance with the stipulations, the state would remain under the provisional military government and be subject to congressional legislation until the people were willing to form a government in conformity with the act. In such an eventuality, reconstruction would be initiated by the President, who would order another election whenever he was satisfied that the loyal electors numbered 10 per cent of the voting population of 1860.[21]

In comparing Ashley's bill with the executive plan, it is necessary to observe, first, that Lincoln's proclamation set forth minimum conditions, much in the way of an outline of a policy, while Ashley's proposal prescribed specific steps to be followed in reorganizing state governments. Necessarily, therefore, the latter dealt with matters not touched on by the President. Aside from this difference, which reflected Lincoln's desire to avoid a commitment to any rigid scheme and which to contemporaries signified, not opposition, but rather a complementary relationship, Ashley's bill differed substantially in certain other respects.

The most important difference was Ashley's answer to the question which Lincoln posed as basic to the entire problem: "Who constitutes the State?"[22] Ashley's radical tendencies were most apparent in his conspicuous omission of any racial

[21] *Ibid.*, secs. 6, 7, 8.   [22] John Hay, *Lincoln and the Civil War*, 135.

qualification for participation in reconstruction. Lincoln's plan allowed only those qualified under existing state election laws —in other words, white men—to form a new government; Ashley's bill ordered the enrollment of "all loyal male citizens of the age of 21 years," and stated that "every male citizen of the United States" of proper age, with the exception of rebels, "shall be entitled to vote" in the convention election. This last was of course a provision for Negro suffrage, one of the earliest of such proposals made in Congress, and an indication of the new issues that were emerging among antislavery men, now that it was clear, as it was after the President's proclamation of December, that emancipation was assured. Ashley's bill was more rigorous, furthermore, in excluding former rebels. Whereas Lincoln ruled out civil or diplomatic officers and military and naval officers above the rank of colonel or lieutenant, Ashley excluded the mass of southern fighting men; his bill barred from voting in the convention election "persons who have voluntarily borne arms against the United States, or held any office civil or military" under the rebel authority. And as for political rights after the formation of a new government, Ashley's bill excluded civil or military officers not pardoned by the state legislature, in contrast to Lincoln's proclamation, which did not specifically consider this phase of the subject, but by implication extended its ban to fewer officers.

In other important respects, however, Ashley's reconstruction measure adhered to the presidential plan. First, it followed the executive policy of appointing provisional military governors to rule over occupied states. The possibility that southern Unionists might organize state governments on their own initiative had long since disappeared, which meant that whether under the supervision of Congress or the President, reconstruction would involve a great assertion of federal power. In Ashley's congressional plan this assertion of national power was to be no less extensive—and no more radical—than in Lincoln's. Ashley's bill, furthermore, employed the oath of the amnesty proclamation and, like the presidential plan, required the oath of all persons, irrespective of their past loyalty. The bill also embodied Lincoln's idea that the loyal 10 per cent of the population could form a state government, though Ashley's inclusion of freedmen in the body of loyal citizens drastically altered this provision. Based as it was on the clause guaranteeing republican government to the states, Ashley's bill regarded the rebel states as still in the Union. Like the President's plan, too, it provided for the enforcement of existing laws in the states, except measures relating to slavery. With respect to the initiation of reconstruction, Ashley and the President were not far apart. Lincoln's proclamation seemed to leave the first steps to the inhabitants of the state, though operationally, as the next few weeks showed, the President actually took the initiative himself, acting through his military commanders. Ashley's plan asserted greater federal initiative and control from the start, though—at least in theory —it, too, recognized southern initiative, for according to the bill, reconstruction was to begin when the people of a district or state signified their desire to form a new government; how this wish was to be expressed Ashley did not say. Finally, the bill in its broadest implications demanded, as the basis of reconstruction, new constitutions prohibiting slavery. Such a constitution had been Lincoln's objective in Louisiana in 1863, and although the amnesty proclamation had not specified constitutional conventions, there was nothing in it to suggest that these had ceased to be elements of executive reconstruction policy.

In the transitional situation that existed in December 1863, with important changes in Lincoln's Louisiana policy yet to develop and with the amnesty proclamation regarded as the outline of a policy that remained to be worked out in detail,[23] Ashley's bill seemed to implement the President's plan. Lincoln had, after all, just made clear his fundamental agreement with his party—and

[23] Whitelaw Reid, a correspondent for the Cincinnati *Gazette*, wrote, for example, "The President has presented his plan, or rather the framework on which the details of a plan may be elaborated" (Dec. 19, 1863).

its radical wing—on the basic issue that had been debated for six months: emancipation as the minimum condition of reconstruction. Now Ashley's proposal, incorporating the 10-per-cent concept, requiring the loyalty oath of the amnesty proclamation, and providing for state governments based on new constitutions prohibiting slavery, seemed to move in the direction already taken by the President.

This was the conclusion of most contemporary commentators on Ashley's bill.[24] Benjamin Perley Poore, of the Boston *Journal*, noted on December 17 that Ashley would introduce a bill providing, in accordance with the suggestions of the President's message and proclamation, for the establishment of a provisional military government over the districts of country in rebellion. The New York *Post*, after describing Ashley's proposal, stated editorially, "This bill, it will be seen, fully carries out the programme indicated in the President's proclamation of amnesty." Predicting that conservatives would find the bill "too sweeping with regard to slavery," the New York *Tribune* declared that Ashley's bill "is very radical and thorough, and provides very effectually for the ends in view." Stressing the importance of keeping the reorganized governments in loyal hands, the *Tribune* concluded, "The test proposed by President Lincoln, and here applied by Mr. Ashley, is a very searching one; but no other could be relied on." [25]

[24] The provision for Negro suffrage, which obviously departed radically from Lincoln's conception and which strikes the modern student as a most significant part of the bill, strangely enough received no criticism and not even any comment from observers who in other respects reviewed carefully the contents of the proposed measure. Although some extreme antislavery men were beginning to raise the question, suffrage for the freedmen was not yet an issue in the debate over reconstruction; this was a transitional period, and people were not yet thinking of reconstruction in terms of this new concern. Perhaps this as much as anything else explains the failure to call attention to the radical suffrage provision of Ashley's bill.

[25] Boston *Journal*, Dec. 17, 1863; New York *Post*, Dec. 26, 1863; New York *Tribune*, Dec. 28, 1863.

Even those who criticized the bill believed that it carried out Lincoln's plan of reconstruction. A New York *Times* correspondent pointed out that the provisions of the bill respecting qualifications of voters, especially the exclusion of all who had borne arms voluntarily, were a departure from the executive plan. But these weaknesses could be corrected, and on balance he considered Ashley's proposal an "important bill for recognition of the rebel States . . . [which] seems to be based mainly on the President's amnesty proclamation and in most respects seems to be well conceived." Orestes Brownson, who had supported Ashley's bill of 1862, criticized the new measure, which he said aimed at "organizing the rebellious states under military governors, and providing for their reorganization as states, on the basis of the scheme set forth in the president's proclamation." The main difficulty of Lincoln's plan—and with Ashley's bill— was the 10-per-cent feature, which Brownson called unjust and unfair to the loyal states. Furthermore, Ashley's proposal, like the President's plan, sought to use military power to perform an essentially civil function. Brownson thought that Ashley was seeking a compromise between radical and moderate views. "It is all very well to get over difficulties by way of compromise when one can," he remarked, "but here is a question of law, and an unconstitutional mode of proceeding even by congress may vitiate the whole." Alexander C. Twining, a professor of law at Yale, also criticized the 10-per-cent proviso of Ashley's bill, holding that "neither the President nor Congress can, constitutionally, under a fiction that such governments cover the entire insurgent population, recognize them in Congress with representatives ten times disproportioned in fact—or even at all disproportioned—to the constituted basis for just representation." Yet Twining thought, "So far as the bill prepared by Mr. Ashley . . . provides for carrying into effect the President's plan for loyal governments in the insurgent States, its proposed enactments carry a look of thoroughness in details as well as of soundness in principle." He said that the main difference between the plans was that Ashley's bill seriously offered the prospect of a rapid return of the states to the Union, which, because it was based on the loyalty of 10 per cent, he considered unsafe, while Lincoln was concerned mainly to regenerate the states, leaving the question of their admission to Congress.[26]

There were other indications besides Ashley's bill of congressional and executive cooperation on reconstruction. One was the likelihood that Congress would approve reconstruction efforts already under way in some of the seceded states. The New York *Tribune* predicted in December that Tennessee, Louisiana, and Arkansas would be reorganized and restored to the Union on the basis of the President's proclamation, a view shared by other Republican journals in the following weeks. Surveying the situation in January, the New York *Times* reported that Lincoln's policy toward the rebel states was acceptable generally, and that "neither those on the Democratic side, or on the Republican side dare commit themselves to any positive plans of reconstruction essentially different from his." Less than half of the Democrats would support the proposal of George Yeaman,[27] argued the *Times*, and "if a proposition were made . . . to receive the rebel States back only as territories, it would not secure a quarter of the Republican vote." Adam Gurowski, the refugee Polish nobleman who was in close touch with Sumner and other radicals, wrote in his diary on January 10, 1864, "Reconstruction is the order of the day. . . . Lincoln is very sanguine for his one-

[26] New York *Times,* Jan. 21, 1864; Orestes Brownson, "The President's Message and Proclamation," *Brownson's Quarterly Review,* Nat. Ser., I (Jan. 1864), 103–111; New York *Times,* Jan. 19, 1864. Twining sent a copy of his analysis of Ashley's bill to Lincoln, along with an editorial from the New York *Times* (January 21, 1864), advising that readmission of rebel states be permitted only when a majority of the people in a state had pledged loyalty to the Union. Twining marked this part of the editorial and wrote: "But Mr. Ashley's Bill does not secure this, nor even profess to require it" (Alexander C. Twining to Lincoln, Jan. 21, 1864, nos. 29711, 29765, 29766, Robert Todd Lincoln Collection, Library of Congress).

[27] See above, n. 12.

tenth idea, . . . [which] gives presidential votes." According to
Gurowski, "The stern and earnest patriots in both Houses, men
such as Wade, Fessenden, etc., wish to keep this whole question
in suspense, rather than see it pressed and thus bring it to an
issue between Congress and Mr. Lincoln." [28]

The accord between Lincoln and the Republican majority
over reconstruction that followed the proclamation of amnesty
proved to be short-lived. As Gurowski implied in describing the
situation in January, conflict seemed to lie below the surface.
Indeed, shortly after the promulgation of Lincoln's proclamation, some Republicans began to have second thoughts about it.
According to Whitelaw Reid of the Cincinnati *Gazette*, although their first reaction to the President's message was favorable, "as they began to scan it more closely the radical wing of
the Administration party became more cautious in their praise."
Reid said that the "intense radicals" felt that the message and
proclamation were popular because Lincoln had avoided issues
about which he knew that anything he might say "would arouse
differences among his supporters." Some antislavery men found
a good deal to criticize, however, in what Lincoln did say about
reconstruction. Ben Butler, for example, wrote to Wendell Phillips, "The Administration has put the negro, his liberty, his
future, into the hands of the Supreme Court. God help him if he
has no other refuge!" Illustrating the emergence of new issues
that went beyond emancipation, Phillips in reply pointed out
that Lincoln's plan "leaves the large landed proprietors of the
South still to domineer over its politics, and make the negro's
freedom a mere sham." Speaking at Cooper Institute in New
York a few days later, Phillips declared, "This nation owes to
the negro, not merely freedom, but land and education." The
President's proclamation "frees the slave and ignores the negro,"
he concluded. After initially applauding the proclamation, the

[28] New York *Tribune*, Dec. 10, 1863; Cincinnati *Gazette*, Dec. 25,
1863; New York *Post*, Jan. 20, 1864; Boston *Journal*, Jan. 27, 1864; New
York *Times*, Jan. 28, 1864; Adam Gurowski, *Diary* (3 vols., Boston, New
York, Washington, 1862–1866), III, 68–69.

Boston *Commonwealth* protested that the executive plan left former slave owners in control of nine-tenths of the land of the South. The proclamation "as a staging for reconstruction . . . is very well as far as it goes," the *Commonwealth* asserted, "but it is still perilously one-sided." Besides policy toward the emancipated slaves, some Republicans criticized what they considered undue leniency toward the rebels, especially in Lincoln's failure to set a time limit on the offer of amnesty. Remarked William Pitt Fessenden on this score, "I think Abraham's proclamation . . . was a silly performance, but he is lucky, and I hope it may work well. Think of telling the rebels they may fight as long as they can, and take a pardon when they have had enough of it." A strongly worded criticism from an anonymous Unionist which appeared in the New York *Tribune* captured the sense of disenchantment that was beginning to be felt in antislavery circles: "Time and events will prove that Southern society must be reorganized, and Peace and Freedom must be secured by some very different process from that propounded by the President." [29]

Thus some criticism of Lincoln's reconstruction proclamation began to develop shortly after its pronouncement. But the protest was isolated and weak.[30] It was only when Lincoln made major changes in his Louisiana policy that significant opposition

[29] Cincinnati *Gazette*, Dec. 10, 1863; Benjamin F. Butler to Wendell Phillips, Dec. 11, 1863, in *Correspondence of Benjamin F. Butler*, III, 204; Wendell Phillips to Benjamin F. Butler, Dec. 13, 1863, in *ibid.*, 206; New York *Tribune*, Dec. 23, 1863; Boston *Commonwealth*, Dec. 25, 1863, Jan. 1, 1864; New York *Herald*, Dec. 22, 1863; William Pitt Fessenden to his wife, Dec. 19, 1863, in Francis Fessenden, *The Life and Public Services of William Pitt Fessenden* (2 vols.; Boston, 1907), I, 266–267; New York *Tribune*, Dec. 11, 1863.

[30] In their correspondence, both Butler and Phillips remarked that few others seemed to share their negative view of Lincoln's proclamation. "I was beginning to ask whether I mistook or exaggerated the danger when your note came," Phillips wrote to Butler, who himself had complained, "No one seems to see the point, at least so far as I can see from the newspapers," and who had been led to ask, "Will Congress arouse to the question?" (Phillips to Butler, Dec. 13, 1863, Butler to Phillips, Dec. 11, 1863, in *Correspondence of Benjamin F. Butler*, III, 206, 204).

to executive reconstruction emerged and found expression in Congress.

Throughout 1862 and 1863, as we have seen, Lincoln relied on the Free State General Committee to reorganize a loyal government and supported its plans for a new state constitution prohibiting slavery. In December 1863, however, he concluded that closer administration control over reconstruction was necessary and hence gave the exclusive direction of Louisiana affairs to General Nathaniel Banks, the commander of the Department of the Gulf. Leaving no doubt as to the locus of authority in this new policy or its urgency, Lincoln told Banks that he was to be "master of all" and was to "give us a free-state re-organization of Louisiana, in the shortest possible time." Banks promptly rejected the plan of the Free State General Committee for a constitutional convention and ordered an election of state officers on the basis of the old constitution. Of course this constitution recognized slavery, but Banks solved that problem by issuing military decrees nullifying the proslavery sections of the document.[31] He told Lincoln that he wished to avoid confronting the people of the state with a direct vote on slavery, so that "their self-respect, their *amour propre* will be appeased."

[31] Banks, in working out the constitutional theory of his action, conceded the validity of the contention which for Republicans such as Davis and Ashley fo med the basis of congressional reconstruction: the rebel state constitutions and governments had been overthrown or abrogated. Banks wrote concerning reorganization in Louisiana: "This proceeding does not recognize *as existing* the constitution and laws of Louisiana: It revives and adopts them for purposes of convenience by the military authority, until a convention is held for the reform or reconstruction of the organic Law. The military authority has the right to adopt a part of such constitution and laws for the purposes of the election, and to establish a government, and to exclude a part. . . . It proceeds upon the fact that the government having absolute power under martial law surrenders so much to the People as may be consistent with their interest and its . . . safety." This statement, incidentally, confirmed the radicals' criticism that Banks regarded martial law as the fundamental law of the state, susperseding all civil authority (undated note, Banks Papers, container 57, Library of Congress).

Though he promised a constitutional convention after a new government was formed, such a gesture was irrelevant, for the first and essential step, according to the radical view, was to frame a new constitution for the state, and this was no longer the goal of federal policy.[32]

Lincoln's new policy in Louisiana aroused strong opposition among the members of the Free State party in New Orleans and eventually among their supporters in Congress. The former, who would now be superseded as the controlling force in Louisiana reconstruction and would thus lose the inside track they had held in the contest for political offices and patronage, felt that they had been betrayed by the President. They translated their grievance into the charge that the policy recognized the old state constitution and gave unlimited and exclusive power to the military, in derogation of the principles of republican government, and also that it might allow conservatives to get elected who might continue to recognize slavery, inasmuch as New Orleans and the surrounding parishes had been excepted from the Emancipation Proclamation. Pointing out that they had "never meddled with the military authorities," Benjamin F. Flanders wrote to Lincoln, "The Free State men are bitterly disappointed by the course of Gen. Banks in ordering an election

[32] Lincoln to Nathaniel Banks, Dec. 24, 29, 1863, Jan. 13, 1864, in *Collected Works of Lincoln*, VII, 89–90, 95, 123–124. On political developments in Louisiana generally see Willie M. Caskey, *Secession and Restoration of Louisiana*, ch. v, and Gerald M. Capers, *Occupied City: New Orleans under the Federals, 1862–1865* (Lexington, Ky., 1965), ch. vi. A similar tightening of administration control took place in Arkansas, where in January 1864 a convention was held under military auspices which amended the state constitution by prohibiting slavery and which formed a loyal government. In Tennessee and Florida, Lincoln sought unsuccessfully to organize loyal governments. See Thomas S. Staples, *Reconstruction in Arkansas, 1862–1874* (New York, 1923); James W. Patton, *Unionism and Reconstruction in Tennessee, 1860–1869* (Chapel Hill, N.C., 1934); and George Winston Smith, "Carpetbag Imperialism in Florida, 1862–1868," *Florida Historical Quarterly*, XXVII (Oct. 1948, Jan. 1949), 99–130, 260–299.

for State officers and in his not ordering an election for a Convention." Flanders warned that the proslavery faction might "bring back slavery and fasten it upon us for years," and accordingly urged Lincoln to direct Banks to hold an election for a constitutional convention as the first step in reorganization.[33]

Lincoln refused to alter the policy Banks had set in motion, elections were held for seven state executive officers on February 22, 1864, and Free State radicals, who had participated in the elections, continued their protest. Thomas J. Durant, the president of the Free State General Committee, in a letter to Henry L. Dawes, the chairman of the elections committee which would be involved in deciding the claims of representatives elected under Banks's authority, explained that differences among Louisiana Unionists as to whether or not the old constitution was still in effect had been resolved by agreeing to form a new constitution; but now Banks, in ordering elections, "was recognizing the Constitution of the State to be in force, and solving, erroneously, a legal question by a military order." To Henry Winter Davis, the chairman of the select committee on reconstruction, Durant condemned Banks for announcing "the absurd and despotic doctrine that 'the fundamental law of the State is martial law,' i.e. the caprice of a military officer." And to the President himself Durant said that the Free State party was "deeply mortified" when Lincoln, "without assigning any cause, took the whole question of civil reorganization out of our hands, and gave it to the exclusive control of the military." Protesting that there had been irregularities in procedure, Durant argued that Banks's action was inconsistent with the Proclamation of Amnesty and Reconstruction because authority for it had been established by military force and "not by votes"; the election had "no value as an expression of the opinion of civilians, by reason of the overshadowing influence of the military," Durant reasoned. "What sort of a State is this, which we have reestab-

[33] Benjamin F. Flanders to Lincoln, Jan. 16, 1864, no. 29524, Robert Todd Lincoln Collection, Library of Congress.

lished," he asked the President, "where one man, not a citizen of the State, and having none but military power, is entire master of its civil destiny, calling its convention at his will to modify or abolish its governments?" Besides the Free State General Committee's dislike of military rule, another reason for its opposing Lincoln's altered Louisiana policy was Banks's conservative response to questions concerning the freedmen. A labor system which drew hostile criticism in antislavery circles was Banks's main achievement with regard to the freedmen, and with Negro rights and protection becoming an issue and with a large number of Louisiana Negroes demanding the right to vote, it was not likely that he would sympathize with the radical answer to such questions. A related consideration was the restriction that would be imposed on the Free State party if the residence requirements of the old constitution were enforced. Many northerners had gone to Louisiana as hangers-on of the army and in connection with treasury department operations, and the Free State party feared that without their support its proposals on issues such as immediate emancipation might not command majority approval.[34]

As events unfolded in Louisiana, reaction against presidential reconstruction became more pronounced. On January 11, 1864, for example, Thaddeus Stevens introduced a bill which differed greatly from Ashley's December proposal patterned on the executive plan. Based on the theory that the rebel states were alien enemies, Stevens' bill stated that certain states had declared their independence of the Union and had formed a separate government, which, as a "belligerent power," was waging war against the government of the United States. By such acts, said

[34] Thomas J. Durant to Henry L. Dawes, Feb. 8, 1864, Dawes Papers, Library of Congress; Durant to Henry Winter Davis, March 31, 1864, in New York *Tribune*, April 23, 1864; Durant to Lincoln, Feb. 26, 28, 1864, nos. 30985, 31072, Robert Todd Lincoln Collection, Library of Congress; Caskey, *Secession and Restoration of Louisiana*, 87–89, 141; Capers, *Occupied City*, 224–226; Springfield *Weekly Republican*, Jan. 30, 1863.

Stevens, the Confederate States had, "so far as they are concerned, abrogated and destroyed all municipal obligations, compacts, constitutions, and laws which were formerly binding on said belligerents"; they had become subject only to the laws of war and the law of nations. Stevens' bill provided that within Confederate territory held by Union arms "all laws and parts of laws which permit slavery shall be and are hereby abolished; and slavery shall never again be established within said territory." Not concerned with reorganizing loyal state governments, Stevens sought only to make clear the conditions on which the seceded states might re-enter the Union. His one specific reference to reconstruction stated, "No portion of said territory shall be admitted into the Union as a State, or be represented in its Congress . . . until the people within the territory forming such State, shall, by its organic law, forever prohibit slavery therein." [35]

In late January and February 1864, as the changes in the administration's Louisiana policy became fully understood, a growing number of Republicans in Congress came to share the main assumption of Stevens' proposal: the rebel states ought to be kept waiting for an indefinite period, instead of having their early readmission considered, as Lincoln's plan and Ashley's bill seemed to propose. Election cases from Louisiana and Arkansas provided an opportunity to investigate the whole question of reconstruction and pointed to a contest between the President and Congress. The Washington correspondent of *The Independent*, the abolitionist weekly, wrote on January 25: "The question of 'reconstruction' cannot much longer be postponed in Congress. . . . The House must soon decide the great constitutional points raised by the appearance of . . . [representatives] from 'rebellious States.' If Gen. Banks' course is approved by Congress, it follows that no bill providing . . . governments for the people of the rebel states will ever pass." [36]

[35] 38 Cong., H.R. 118, Jan. 11, 1864, Preamble, sec. 1.
[36] *The Independent*, Jan. 28, 1864.

Since the Louisiana members seeking admission were representatives of the conservative planter faction, it was a foregone conclusion that the House would reject their bid, as indeed it did. Nevertheless, the case attracted attention because it opened the door to a review of recent developments in Louisiana. In what was an obvious attack on the Banks regime, Henry Winter Davis offered a resolution declaring, "There is no legal authority to hold any election in the State of Louisiana; . . . [and] any attempt to hold an election by any body of persons is a usurpation of sovereign authority against the authority of the United States." Though it was ruled out of order, Davis' proposition reflected the increasing congressional dissatisfaction with presidential reconstruction. According to Whitelaw Reid of the Cincinnati *Gazette*, Davis had prepared other resolutions, which he did not introduce, maintaining that no system of reconstruction could be instituted without the sanction of Congress.[37]

The Louisiana case, which did not involve representatives chosen according to Banks's new plan, was followed by a situation in Arkansas which offered a better test of congressional reaction to Lincoln's reconstruction policy. The question in the Arkansas case was not whether the House would admit to a seat a representative of the free state government organized under executive authority in January 1864, but merely whether it would receive his credentials. Though the House many times during the war had received credentials from representatives from occupied rebel states, Winter Davis objected to it now on the ground that it was "not a mere question of election law . . . but a question of the recognition or refusal to recognize the organization of a State government in Arkansas." When a Republican colleague suggested that the loyal citizens of Arkansas had formed a government based on a free-state constitution, Davis replied, "Let us have proofs of those facts, and let there be a direct vote of the House of Representatives as to whether they

[37] *Cong. Globe*, 38 Cong., 1 sess., 412 (Jan. 29, 1864); Cincinnati *Gaeztte*, Jan. 28, 1864.

will recognize as a government this thing organized without any
authority of law, without the supervision of any official authority, organized merely under the dictation of a military commander." The chairman of the reconstruction committee made it
clear that Lincoln's Louisiana policy was the source of his opposition. He objected to receiving the Arkansas credentials, he said,
"because the President has called on General Banks to organize
another hermaphrodite government, half military, half republican, representing the alligators and the frogs of Louisiana, and
to place that upon the footing of a government of a State of the
United States." [38]

Though the House rejected Davis' advice and received the
credentials from Arkansas, the vote revealed growing dissatisfaction with Lincoln's policy. Davis' proposal to table the matter
was defeated, 53 to 104, but 41 Republicans supported the
Maryland radical and 46 opposed him. Noting that a large
number of administration men, "including nearly all the Radicals," opposed referring the problem to the Committee on Elections, Whitelaw Reid commented, "The debate and vote are
among the most significant of the session." According to the
correspondent of the New York *Herald*, the Arkansas case
"developed the fact that both sides of the House are greatly
divided in regard to the status of the rebellious States in the
Union." Editorially the *Herald* warned, "Let President Lincoln
prepare to take in his sails accordingly; for all dispassionate,
thoughtful men agree in opinion upon this business with Winter
Davis." [39]

While opposition to presidential reconstruction was emerging
in the House, the Senate was concerned with the "iron-clad"
oath. The specific issue was whether James Bayard of Delaware,
the only senator who had not done so, ought to be made to
swear the retrospective oath, in accordance with the act of June
1862 which required the oath of all federal officers. In late

[38] *Cong. Globe*, 38 Cong., 1 sess., 681–682 (Feb. 16, 1864).
[39] Cincinnati *Gazette*, Feb. 17, 1864; New York *Herald*, Feb. 18, 1864.

January the vote finally went against Bayard, who took the oath and then resigned his seat.[40] The debate was relevant to reconstruction, for it revealed that many Republicans believed that an oath stronger than the prospective one in Lincoln's amnesty proclamation was needed for readmitting rebel states. Furthermore, remarked Whitelaw Reid, "The matter here is constantly connected with the 'reconstruction' movement initiated in Louisiana, and the one in preparation in Arkansas." Skepticism prevailed concerning the existence of sufficient loyal men to warrant organizing a state government, he said, and "from more than one quarter there comes the inquiry, why all this haste in giving up the power we now have over these States?"[41]

Thus by the middle of February 1864 conflict between the President and Congress over reconstruction appeared imminent. Adam Gurowski, who in early January had observed a tendency in Congress to avoid a clash with the administration on this issue, wrote on February 19, "The struggle is going on. What law, what basis or principle is to be laid down for the eventual reconstruction and reorganization of the rebel States?"[42] Four days earlier Henry Winter Davis had introduced a measure which provided the congressional answer to this question: the Wade-Davis Bill of 1864.

---

[40] *Cong. Globe*, 38 Cong., 1 sess., 331 (Jan. 25, 1864). The case is described in detail in Harold M. Hyman's *Era of the Oath* (Philadelphia, 1954), 26–32.

[41] Cincinnati *Gazette*, Feb. 2, 1864.   [42] Gurowski, *Diary*, III, 113.

VIII

The Wade-Davis Bill

THE Wade-Davis Bill of 1864 reflected the congressional involvement in reconstruction from the beginning of the war and the opposition to executive reconstruction that had developed in Louisiana and Arkansas since December 1863. Introduced in the midst of the debate over Arkansas representation by Henry Winter Davis of the Select Committee on the Rebellious States, the bill was in many respects similar to James Ashley's December proposal. The theoretical framework and constitutional basis were the same, and the purpose was identical—to provide for the reorganization of loyal state governments based on new constitutions prohibiting slavery. Yet because of changes both in Lincoln's reconstruction policy in Louisiana and in the general political situation, Davis' February bill served, not to implement executive policy, but to challenge it.

In December 1863 the Republican party was united on reconstruction, after Lincoln's commitment to emancipation as a fundamental condition for readmission to the Union, the crucial issue of several months' debate. Accordingly, Ashley's reconstruction bill, which though it embodied much of Lincoln's plan differed from it in important respects, could appear as an implementation of the more general executive policy. By February

1864, however, Republican unity was breaking down. Lincoln's decision to turn Louisiana reconstruction over to General Banks, who reorganized a government based on the old state constitution, represented to many Republicans the unwarranted intrusion of military power into an area of policy where civil—especially legislative—authority ought to prevail. Concern for guarantees—both against a resurgence of political activity among former rebels and in behalf of freed Negroes—also led many Republicans to oppose Lincoln's reconstruction policy, which seemed deficient on both counts. Political considerations related to the election of 1864 were also involved in giving the Davis reconstruction bill its antiadministration character. Since as early as December 1863 dissident elements within the Republican party had been hoping to replace Lincoln as the nominee in 1864; by February their efforts had taken the form of a definite campaign to make Secretary of the Treasury Salmon P. Chase the party standard-bearer. This movement profited from criticism directed at the administration's reconstruction policy. In part, for example, Henry Winter Davis' opposition to executive reconstruction rested on political considerations. Davis' first public protest, in late January, against Louisiana reconstruction coincided with his bitter resentment against Lincoln for refusing to aid him in his struggle against the Blair faction in Maryland politics. Complaining that "Lincoln is thoroughly Blairized," Davis said that he was breaking off political relations with the President and declared that he "would be responsible for Lincoln's not getting the electoral vote in Md." A few weeks later Lincoln, observing that "Mr. Davis had become very cool towards him," expressed his belief that he "was now an active friend of the Secretary of the Treasury." [1] Under these circumstances Davis' reconstruction bill signfied, not only his adherence to the principle of congressional control of reconstruction, but

[1] Henry Winter Davis to S. F. Du Pont, Jan. 28, 1864, S. F. Du Pont Papers, Eleutherian Mills Historical Library; Riddle, *Recollections of War Times*, 276.

also the rejection of Lincoln's policy in Louisiana and Arkansas and opposition, in some circles at least, to his renomination.

Though broadly similar to Ashley's bill, the measure introduced by Davis from the House committee on reconstruction incorporated important changes which made it at once more radical and more conservative than the earlier proposal.[2] The first part of the bill, dealing with methods of controlling occupied areas, was somewhat more conservative, in consequence of a greater emphasis on pre-existing state forms and on the temporary, provisional nature of the governments to be created. Providing for the appointment of a civil rather than a military governor, the bill charged this officer, not only with "the civil administration of such State until a State government therein shall be recognized," but also with enforcing "the laws of the State in force when the State government was overthrown by the rebellion." As if to emphasize continuity with preexisting state governments, the Davis bill authorized the President to appoint "such officers provided for by the laws of the State when its government was overthrown as he may find necessary to the civil administration of the State." Also included was a provision which required that until a state government was recognized, the provisional governor should collect taxes according to state laws that were in effect before the war. Tax proceeds would be applied to the expenses of administration, subject to the direction of the President, and any surplus was to be deposited in the federal treasury "to the credit of such State, to be paid to the State . . . when a republican form of government shall be recognized therein by the United States."[3] None of these provisions was present in Ashley's bill.[4]

[2] In the changed political situation of 1864 "radical" was equated with stronger guarantees against former rebels and in defense of freedmen's liberties. In addition it meant a belief in the further expansion of federal power and in the eclipse of state rights, a meaning it had always had. "Conservative" referred to the opposite of each tendency.

[3] 38 Cong., H.R. 244, Feb. 15, 1864, secs. 1, 10, 11.

[4] Ashley's bill provided for the administration "of such District" in

Although the antislavery provisions of the two bills were the same, the Davis bill in some respects went further in guaranteeing the freedom of former slaves. Like Ashley's bill, it declared that all persons held to involuntary servitude or labor in the rebellious states "are hereby emancipated and discharged therefrom, and they and their posterity shall be forever free." It went on to provide that emancipated slaves deprived of their liberty under any claim to service or labor should be freed by federal courts on writs of habeas corpus, a protection not included in Ashley's proposal. Essentially the same as one in the earlier bill was a further provision that "no law or usage whereby any person was heretofore held in involuntary servitude shall be recognized or enforced by any court or officer in such State," and that the laws for the trial and punishment of white persons should extend to all persons.[5]

The Davis bill introduced one major conservative change concerning the status of the freedmen, however, which was related to the reorganization process. This was the addition of a racial qualification for suffrage. The reorganization of a state government would begin when military resistance to the Union had been suppressed and the people in a given state, in the judgment of the provisional governor, had "sufficiently returned to their obedience to the Constitution and the laws of the United States." Then would follow an enrollment of "all white male citizens of the United States resident in the State in their respective counties," each of whom would be required to subscribe an oath to support the Constitution. If those taking the oath numbered one-tenth of the persons enrolled, the governor would order the election of delegates to a constitutional convention which would create a new frame of state government.[6] The most significant change from the procedure prescribed by Ashley was the limiting of enrollment to white citizens only. This

which a provisional government was formed. The Davis bill substituted the word "State" for "District" in this instance.

[5] H.R. 244, secs. 10, 12.   [6] *Ibid.*, sec. 2.

provision was decidedly conservative and brought the Davis bill
into line with Lincoln's policy on the all-important question of
Negro suffrage. It more than outweighed the judicial guarantees
extended to the freedmen in the form of the privilege of habeas
corpus. Another change from Ashley's bill which was in accord
with executive policy was the addition of residence requirements
for suffrage. To the extent that these would confine reconstruction to southern whites and exclude northern hangers-on of the
army, they, too, were conservative in tendency.

Though more conservative than Ashley's plan on the question
of who constituted the state, the Davis bill was more radical in
the requirements it imposed on the white minority who would
be entrusted with organizing loyal state governments. The most
important change in the constitution-forming process was the
inclusion of the provision that all who would vote for or be
members of the constitutional convention must swear the "iron-
clad" oath. This contrasted sharply with Ashley's bill, which,
though excluding those who had borne arms voluntarily,
required only the prospective oath of Lincoln's amnesty proclamation in order to vote in the convention election. The "iron-
clad" oath looked to past loyalty and required a person to swear
that he had never borne arms voluntarily against the United
States or aided the rebellion. The oath had recently been under
discussion in the Senate and its substitution for the simple prospective oath of the amnesty proclamation reflected the view,
shared by an increasing number of Republicans, that assuring
security during reconstruction demanded such a test of past
conduct. The Davis bill also barred from United States citizenship "every person who shall hereafter hold or exercise any
office, civil or military, in the rebel service, State or Confederate." Ashley's plan had contained no such radical proposal. And
a feature of Ashley's bill which the Davis committee omitted
from its plan was a provision that persons disqualified from participating in reconstruction might be pardoned by the state legislature. Thus, to the degree that Negroes were excluded from

participation, more stringent guarantees were to be imposed on southern whites.[7]

The new state constitutions envisioned in the Davis bill were similar to those projected in Ashley's measure. The key provisions were that no person who had held office, civil or military, state or Confederate, could vote for or be a member of the legislature or a governor; that slavery was prohibited and the freedom of all persons guaranteed in the rebel states; and that no debt, state or Confederate, was to be recognized or paid by the rebel states. If the voters of a state approved the new constitution, the President, "after obtaining the assent of Congress," was to recognize the new government as the constitutional government of the state. Thereafter senators, representatives, and electors for President and Vice-president could be elected. Should the convention refuse to adopt a constitution along the lines specified, it would be dissolved, and reconstruction would then depend on the President, who, whenever he believed there were enough eligible voters willing to form a government—in number equal to at least 10 per cent of the voters in the presidential election of 1860—could order another election for a convention.[8] This provision placed the initiative for reconstruction, which previously rested with the provisional governor, squarely in the hands of the President. It expressed more emphatically the idea of federal control over state reorganization.

Constitutionally the Davis bill rested on the same basis as Ashley's December bill. Not the theory of territorialization, but the clause guaranteeing to each state a republican form of government provided the constitutional foundation for congressional reconstruction. According to the title, the purpose of Davis' bill was "to guarantee to certain States whose governments have been usurped or overthrown, a republican form of government." In debate Davis elaborated on this idea, trying to show that the bill stayed within constitutional limits. "It purports . . . not to exercise a revolutionary authority," he explained, "but

[7] *Ibid.*, secs. 3–5, 7, 14.   [8] *Ibid.*, secs. 8–9.

to be an execution of the Constitution of the United States, of the fourth section of the fourth article . . . which not merely confers the power upon Congress, but imposes upon Congress the duty of guarantying to every State in this Union a republican form of government." [9] Because the guarantee applied only to states, the Davis bill, furthermore, regarded the rebellious states as still in the Union; in this connection, the reliance upon pre-existing state forms and the provisional governor's charge to enforce the laws and conduct the civil administration of the state were significant. Such provisions conveyed the idea of the continued existence of the states, as Henry Dawes showed when he pointed out that the bill was based "not on the old theory of a colonial government, . . . nor indeed on that later and more modern policy of treating each State in the condition of a Territory." Rather, said Dawes, "the bill proceeds upon the supposition . . . that there are States still existing." [10]

Though Davis and the reconstruction committee were prepared to regard the states in some sense as still in the Union, they could not let the matter rest there. For to do so would have been to overlook the origins of the war and the fact that secession and insurrection had produced changes too great to be disregarded by Union men. Obvious changes in the actual condition of the southern states—they were now joined together as a nation engaged in war and had been recognized as belligerents by the United States—somehow had to be translated into law; public law affecting the southern states could not be allowed to continue on the assumption that they were still members of the Union standing in perfect equality with the loyal states. Accordingly, the Select Committee on the Rebellious States stated in its reconstruction bill that the governments of states declared in rebellion had been "usurped or overthrown" and that the way to revive state governments was to hold constitutional conventions. These assertions satisfied the more earnest patriots who

[9] *Cong. Globe,* 38 Cong., 1 sess., App., 82 (Mar. 22, 1864).
[10] *Ibid.,* 38 Cong., 2 sess., 934 (Feb. 20, 1865).

felt that the rebellion had interrupted the political and constitutional life of the states, making necessary the renewal of republican government by a constituent act of the people, and were also acceptable to Union men of less radical views who believed that the states were merely out of their proper relationship to the Union—a circumstance that could be rectified by a new constitution. Conservatives were fond of describing the states as in a condition of suspended animation, saying metaphorically what the committee on reconstruction said in concrete political, constitutional terms. In either case the remedy was a constitutional convention.

On the constitutional status of the rebel states the Davis bill thus occupied a middle position, recognizing the continued existence of the states yet taking into account their changed condition. Of these two ideas, the first received greater emphasis among supporters of congressional reconstruction, who were trying to eliminate the destructive connotations of earlier legislation designed to territorialize the South. Moreover, despite the growth of federal power, northerners were unwilling to give up state-rights concepts altogether. Reconstruction, to be successful, had to take this into consideration, as even the most radical antislavery men recognized. Wendell Phillips, for example, in a speech in which he criticized Lincoln's plan of reconstruction, said of the state-suicide theory: "Mr. Sumner's theory has one exceedingly bad feature. The strongest cord in the heart next to love of the Union is State pride." Taking Mississippi as an example, Phillips said he would "save the State alive" for its "speechless Unionists," so that they could "bring it back in their own method and their own time." In Congress, Nathaniel Smithers, a member of the reconstruction committee, argued against the notion that the states had been destroyed: "I do not agree . . . with those who hold that the suspension or subversion of an existing government necessarily destroys the State." Legitimate constitutional governments in the states had been overthrown, making it necessary for the United States "to guaranty to each

State a republican form of government." The people of the seceded states "have the right to demand that this guarantee shall
be fully and faithfully executed," he continued. "It is a public
right, and the obligation to its performance does not depend on
the presence of a government in the State." That the Davis bill
occupied a middle ground constitutionally was evident in Thaddeus Stevens' criticism that it "does not . . . meet the evil. It
partially acknowledges the rebel States to have rights under the
Constitution." Echoing the same sentiment, William D. Kelley
of Pennsylvania objected that the bill was "drawn too largely
from the President's plan" and asserted: "We have a simple and a
better mode of governing Territories. We give them a territorial
government." [11]

Although the Davis bill to some extent respected state-rights
beliefs, at the same time its sweeping assertion of federal power
directly repudiated them. On this constitutional issue—the scope
of national, especially congressional, power—the bill was as far-
reaching as any proposal based on the territorial theory. Just as
the conduct of the war necessitated an increase in national
power, so too would reconstruction in any form acceptable to
northern opinion involve the exercise of federal power to an
unprecedented degree and its intrusion into spheres of policy
hitherto reserved to the states. In this respect both the congressional and executive plans of reconstruction were constitutionally radical, for Lincoln's policy, especially as it was taking shape
in Louisiana and Arkansas, was an effective denial of state rights.

To support their assertion of congressional power under the
guarantee clause, the framers of the Davis bill relied on the opinion of the Supreme Court in the famous Rhode Island case of
1849, Luther versus Borden. Concerning the guarantee clause
Chief Justice Taney had written:

Under this article . . . it rests with Congress to decide what government is the established one in a State. For as the United States guar-

[11] New York *Tribune*, Dec. 23, 1863; *Cong. Globe*, 38 Cong., 1 sess.,
1741 (Apr. 19, 1864); 2041 (May 2, 1864); 2080 (May 3, 1864).

antee to each State a republican government, Congress must necessarily decide what government is established in a State before it can determine whether it is republican or not.[12]

According to Henry Winter Davis, this ruling meant "that it is the exclusive prerogative of Congress—of Congress, and not of the President—to determine what is and what is not the established government of the State." Another member of the reconstruction committee, Republican Daniel Gooch of Massachusetts, concluded from Taney's opinion, "The question of the recognition of a government in one of the revolted States . . . is a political one, and is to be decided by Congress, not by the Executive or the judiciary." Although the Constitution simply charged "the United States" to guarantee republican government to the states, leaders of congressional reconstruction were able, on the basis of the Supreme Court's opinion, to posit an exclusive power in the federal legislature to decide on the legitimacy of state governments. The final decision of Congress would be made in pursuit of its power to judge the elections and qualifications of its own members, but to Republican theorists this had to be understood in relation to a more important power of Congress to guarantee republican governments. At the same time, by reason of its connection with the guarantee clause, the specific power to judge elections and qualifications assumed a broader significance; it extended beyond the evaluation of merely technical aspects of the election of representatives.[13]

Having established that power under the guarantee clause resided in Congress, supporters of the Davis bill took an expansive view of the nature and scope of that power. The clause guaranteeing republican government, asserted Davis, "vests in the Congress of the United States a plenary, supreme, unlimited political jurisdiction, . . . subject only to the judgment of the people of the United States, embracing within its scope every legislative

[12] 7 Howard 42 (1849).
[13] *Cong. Globe*, 38 Cong., 1 sess., App., 83 (Mar. 22, 1864); 2071 (May 3, 1864).

measure necessary and proper to make it effectual." The duty of guaranteeing a republican government, he argued, "means the duty to accomplish the result. It means that republican government shall exist . . . [and] places in the hands of Congress the right to say what is and what is not, with all the light of experience and all the lessons of the past, inconsistent, in its judgment, with the permanent continuance of republican government." Nathaniel Smithers reasoned, "as the exigencies requiring the exercise of the power [conferred through the guarantee clause] are undefinable, the authority conferred is equally incapable of limitation, and rests in the sound discretion of Congress applying its own will and employing its own judgment in the enforcement of its own guarantee." Interpreted in this way, the clause guaranteeing republican government was the source of as much national power as was the theory of territorialization. Referring to his position in 1862, James Ashley noted that he had insisted "that until such time as the loyal citizens, in each of the rebellious States, are numerous enough to maintain a State government . . . they ought to be treated and governed as citizens of the United States residing within the national jurisdiction, on national territory, without State governments." Ashley concluded about the reconstruction committee's proposal, "Practically, this idea pervades the entire bill." [14]

Democratic opponents of the congressional plan of reconstruction advocated the return of the rebel states without conditions. Typical of Democratic opinion was Aaron Harding of Kentucky, who insisted, "When the rebellion is suppressed by force of the Federal arms, or by the voluntary submission of the people of those States . . . , then that State is thereby restored to all its rights and privileges under the Constitution, may send Representatives to Congress, and do all other acts which any other State in the Union can do." Congressional Democrats held that the southern states should resume their prewar standing,

[14] *Ibid.*, App., 83 (Mar. 22, 1864); 1740 (Apr. 19, 1864); 1354 (Mar. 30, 1864).

except for changes that might be agreed upon between or among the states. In a statement on reconstruction issued in July 1864 they declared that neither the President by proclamation nor Congress by statute "can alter, add, or diminish the conditions of Union between the States." Accordingly, Democrats viewed the Davis reconstruction bill as a violation of the Constitution. George Yeaman of Kentucky delivered a representative judgment when he said that he was "unable to see our power to legislate away the laws and institutions of States, though the people of such States be in rebellion." Francis Kernan of New York argued that the Davis bill "is at war with the principles upon which the Federal Government rests, and is subversive of the State governments and the reserved rights of the people of each State to change and administer them." [15]

Responding to their opponents' emphasis on the need for republican governments in the South, Democrats agreed that such governments ought to be the criterion for readmission but insisted that the rebel states met this requirement. Whereas Republicans defined republican government in terms of a state's acceptance of the Constitution and the Union and of its hostility toward slavery, Democrats defined it as self-government. Thus James C. Allen of Illinois pointed out that the constitutions and laws of the southern states "are such as have always been recognized by the Federal Government as republican in form and consonant with the principles of our Constitution." Furthermore, according to Democratic understanding, Congress under the guarantee clause could only protect the states in the enjoyment of pre-existing institutions; Congress could not, argued Allen, initiate new governments or directly intervene in the affairs of the states, as the reconstruction bill proposed. Aaron Harding of Kentucky, who had vigorously opposed Ashley's

[15] *Ibid.*, 2029 (May 2, 1864); 2006 (Apr. 30, 1864); 2068 (May 3, 1864); *Congressional Address, by Members of the 38th Congress, Politically Opposed to the Present Federal Administration* . . . (Washington, 1864), 24–25.

territorial reconstruction bill in 1862, continued to point out the vast and fundamental difference between Republican and Democratic conceptions of what was happening in the war. Trying to stave off the Davis bill, Harding told the House at the close of the debate on the measure: "The very idea of reconstruction is an absurd and revolutionary idea, because it admits the dissolution of the Union. There can be no reconstruction of a State government that is still in existence." [16]

On May 4, 1864, at the end of six weeks of debate, Henry Winter Davis reported from the reconstruction committee two amendments which changed the bill in important respects. The first amendment made 50 per cent of the enrolled population, rather than 10 per cent, the minimum required for reconstruction. In other words, before the provisional governor could order an election for a constitutional convention, a majority of the enrolled citizens of a state had to subscribe a prospective oath to support the Constitution. This was a major change in the direction of greater control and security at the outset of the reconstruction process envisioned by the bill. What it meant practically was that reconstruction would be put off until after the war. As long as the bill contained the 10-per-cent provision, it offered the prospect, as Ashley's and the President's plan did, of inaugurating state governments while the war still continued. But by setting the minimum popular basis at 50 per cent, the reconstruction committee foreclosed this possibility. From the start of the debate some supporters of the bill had reservations about the 10-per-cent principle but were willing to go along with it. Ashley, for example, said on March 30, "I believe the democratic idea the better one, that the *majority* and not the *minority* ought to be invested with the organization and government of a State." He added, however, "Under the circumstances, . . . it is the best we can get. . . . If it is deemed safe to intrust ten per cent of the number of the electors in each State

[16] *Cong. Globe*, 38 Cong., 1 sess., 2006 (Apr. 30, 1864); 1738–1739 (Apr. 19, 1864); 2030 (May 2, 1864).

in 1860 with this power and responsibility, so be it." But within the next few weeks the select committee on reconstruction changed its mind. On April 19, Nathaniel Smithers informed the House of the committee's intention "to change the provisions authorizing a State government to be re-established by one tenth and to require the assent of a majority of those who may be controlled." Republicans as well as Democrats were thoroughly critical of the 10-per-cent feature of executive reconstruction by this time, having seen its fruits in Louisiana, and approved the change recommended by the committee.[17]

Having stiffened the requirements for starting reconstruction, the committee in its second amendment proposed to liberalize provisions for the final stages of the process by easing the ban on political privileges for former rebels. In contrast to the original bill, which affected all Confederate and rebel state officers, Davis' second amendment would exclude from voting for or being a member of the state legislature only civil officers of ministerial rank and military officers with at least the rank of colonel. Also, only these officers would be deprived of United States citizenship. Explaining the proposed change, Davis said it "softens the operations of the clause excluding officers of the State and confederate rebel governments, . . . so that the exclusion merely operates on persons of dangerous political influence." Since the whole thrust of the bill had been altered by its provision for maximum security in the earliest stages of reconstruction, the liberalizing feature was acceptable to Republicans concerned with guarantees, and the House approved the amendment by voice vote.[18]

After securing the desired amendments, Davis gave Republican critics of the bill an opportunity to write their theory of reconstruction into the measure by offering a preamble drawn from a substitute proposal of Thaddeus Stevens. Stevens' substi-

[17] *Ibid.*, 2107 (May 4, 1864); 1356 (Mar. 30, 1864); 1740 (Apr. 19, 1864).
[18] *Ibid.*, 2107 (May 4, 1864).

tute, which is additional evidence that the committee bill was too moderate for some Republicans, stated that whenever a rebellious state came under federal control, "the same shall be deemed and held to be a territory of the United States, subject to the same conditions as other territories; and Congress shall make all needful rules and regulations respecting said territories." Stevens' bill also declared that none of the rebel states "can be considered and treated as within the Union." The preamble drawn from this proposal described the rebel states as "a public enemy, waging an unjust war," and declared, "None of the States which, by a regularly recorded majority of its citizens, have joined the southern confederacy can be considered and treated as entitled to be represented in Congress, or to take any part in the political government of the Union." Although crucial references to the states' having seceded and put themselves out of the Union were omitted, Stevens' proposition was substantially more radical than the bill itself on the constitutional status of the states. Accordingly, seventeen Republicans joined with the Democrats to defeat the preamble by a vote of 76 to 57.[19]

The same Republicans, however, together with five others who had abstained on the preamble, voted to pass the reconstruction bill itself. They joined with the Republican majority to give the bill an overall 73 to 59 vote. Together the two ballots provided a clear test of radicalism and showed that the Davis bill was not an extremist measure. The situation was similar to that in March 1862 when Ashley's territorial bill was before the House. But whereas the moderate Republicans had voted with the Democrats to defeat Ashley's bill, they supported the Davis bill, enabling it to pass. The chief difference was that the congressional reconstruction plan of 1864 was moderate by contrast with the plan of 1862. Important also was this difference: in 1862, Lincoln had just begun to put into effect a plan of reconstruction based on military power, while in 1864 this plan had

[19] H.R. 244, amendment by Stevens, Apr. 29, 1864; *Cong. Globe,* 38 Cong., 1 sess., 2107–2108 (May 4, 1864).

evolved into an operational policy unsatisfactory to most members of Congress. Comparison of the votes on the two plans for reconstruction suggests that Republican opinion had become more moderate. Of Republican representatives who voted on both occasions, nineteen supported Ashley's radical bill of 1862 and the radical Stevens preamble of 1864. But five Republicans who had supported the earlier radical proposal voted against the Stevens preamble, though they voted in favor of the main bill. This shift in opinion, limited though it was in quantitative terms, reflected the greater shift, manifest in the Davis bill itself, from the radicalism of territorialization to the idea of guaranteeing republican governments to states in the Union.[20]

Following House passage, the reconstruction bill went to the Senate where, over the objection of Doolittle of Wisconsin, who wanted it to go to the judiciary committee, it was referred to the Committee on Territories, under Ben Wade. Wade reported the bill with amendments on May 27, but thereafter let the matter rest until the end of June. Meanwhile two developments closely related to reconstruction were taking place: the Republican party convention at Baltimore in early June and the attempt in Congress to pass a constitutional amendment prohibiting slavery throughout the United States. While these events were unfolding, Wade adopted a wait-and-see attitude.

Although it had seemed that reconstruction would be an important issue at the Republican convention, administration supporters were fearful of its divisive effect and succeeded in keeping it out of the party platform altogether. Concerning the central purpose of the convention, meanwhile, there was never any

[20] *Cong. Globe*, 38 Cong., 1 sess., 2107–2108 (May 4, 1864). Republicans who opposed the preamble but voted for the bill were Isaac Arnold, J. A. J. Creswell, Henry Blow, John Farnsworth, Reuben Fenton, Orlando Kellogg, James Marvin, Calvin Hulburd, Theodore Pomeroy, Walter McIndoe, Alexander Rice, Glenni Scofield, M. Russell Thayer, Nathaniel Smithers, James Wilson, Justin Morrill, and William Windom. Henry Dawes, Henry Deming, Nathan Dixon, and Samuel Miller abstained on the preamble but voted for the bill. Only five Republicans voted against the bill, and three of them were border-state men.

doubt: Lincoln was renominated by acclamation, which meant that if the party went into the campaign with a definite policy on reconstruction, it would—in the absence of a specific platform plank dealing with the question—be identified with the President's plan. The convention also in effect endorsed the administration's reconstruction policy by giving the vice-presidential nomination to Andrew Johnson of Tennessee and by admitting delegates from rebel states to seats and to voting rights. The choice of Johnson, who as Lincoln's military governor in Tennessee effectively symbolized the executive outlook on reconstruction, repudiated the theory that the seceded states were out of the Union. Montgomery Blair revealed the significance that this action had for conservative Union men when he wrote to Lincoln in December, "Andrew Johnson was associated with you on the ticket . . . as a practical comment to go to the country in condemnation of the doctrine of State suicide." The admission of delegates from southern states conveyed the same implication. According to James G. Blaine, "It involved the effect of the rebellion upon the relation of rebelling States to the Union. Could they have a voice in public affairs without specific measures of restoration, or were the acts of secession a nullity without influence upon their legal status?" Radicals such as Stevens opposed the admission of southern delegates, insisting that to seat them would be a partial recognition of the rights of the rebel states and would give those which were going through the process of presidential reconstruction the right to be represented in the electoral college. The convention, safely in the hands of administration men, rejected his counsel, however, and admitted delegates from Florida, Virginia, Louisiana, Arkansas, and Tennessee, granting voting privileges to the last three states.[21]

[21] Montgomery Blair to Lincoln, Dec. 6, 1864, no. 39066, Robert Todd Lincoln Collection, Library of Congress; Blaine, *Twenty Years in Congress*, I, 519; Washington *Chronicle*, June 8, 1864; New York *Herald*, June 8, 1864.

This decision was plainly at odds with congressional reconstruction plans in their present state of development. Commented the Boston *Commonwealth:* "We must notice the extraordinary admission of delegates from the 'debatable lands' of Tennessee, Arkansas, Louisiana, Virginia, [and] Florida. . . . With as much consistency might delegates have been admitted from Canada." What the convention had done with respect to reconstruction, however, could largely be undone by the passing of the Davis bill: the congressional, not the executive, plan would then stand as the party statement on reconstruction. Passage of the reconstruction bill would, furthermore, settle the question of the electoral college by excluding rebel states until they had formed governments in accordance with the act, and it would underscore the principle that the southern states, though in some sense members of the Union, could not simply be readmitted to a role in national affairs without some prior action by Congress, as the convention's actions implied they could.[22]

The second issue that had a bearing on the reconstruction bill in the interim between House approval and Senate action was the antislavery amendment that was being considered in Congress. Starting in December 1863, Republicans introduced eight separate measures that either carried into effect the Emancipation Proclamation or proposed to abolish slavery by constitutional amendment. Although some antislavery men thought that Congress already possessed the power to destroy slavery in the states, the overwhelming majority believed that it could achieve this end only by amending the Constitution. Consequently the Republican party proposed an amendment declaring, "Neither slavery nor involuntary servitude, except as a punishment for crime, whereof the party shall have been duly convicted, shall exist within the United States, or any place subject to their jurisdiction." The Senate approved this resolution in April, 38 to 6, but Republicans in the House could not muster the necessary two-thirds majority when the amendment came to a vote on

22 Boston *Commonwealth*, June 17, 1864.

June 15. Hence it failed to pass, though the poll was 93 to 65.[23]

The failure of the amendment meant that the Davis reconstruction bill was the sole significant antislavery measure that had a chance of passing in the short time remaining before Congress adjourned. The Republican convention had gone on record in favor of an amendment abolishing slavery, and though the reconstruction bill would be limited in its effect, since it pertained only to the rebel states, it was a vehicle for the kind of antislavery action that many Republican members of Congress considered politically necessary. It was in this context that Davis on June 21 wrote to Ben Wade, in whose committee the bill had lain for several weeks, "Can you not do something practical towards emancipation this session by getting a vote on H. Bill 244 relative to the Rebel States which you have reported?" As though to remind Wade of the significance the bill now had, Davis explained that in addition to providing governments for the seceded states "till fit to govern themselves," it proposed "to emancipate all slaves, to give them & their paternity the writ of habeas corpus in the United States courts wherenow if free they could seek protection." Observing that the "constitutional amendment is dead—as I always knew & said it was," he emphasized that "the Bill before you is the *only* practical measure of emancipation *proposed* in this Congress." It was all the more necessary because the Emancipation Proclamation "if valid . . . exempts large regions in the rebel States." Davis concluded: "Surely the strong Senate will not allow the session to close without a vote on . . . [the bill]. No one ought to delay or endanger it by debate on our side. . . . It will be a beautiful crown to our session." [24]

[23] *Cong. Globe*, 38 Cong., 1 sess., 553 (Feb. 10, 1864); 1490 (Apr. 8, 1864); 2995, (June 15, 1864).

[24] Henry Winter Davis to Benjamin F. Wade, June 21, 1864, Wade Papers, Library of Congress. Davis and Wade later charged that Senate conservatives, especially James Doolittle of Wisconsin, a Republican,

Despite Davis' urging, Wade did not bring the bill up for over a week. Finally, on July 1, after two unsuccessful attempts, he got the Senate to consider it.[25] The Committee on Territories, in the amendments it reported in late May, had made one major change in the bill—the removal of distinctions based on race. The amended bill thus allowed Negroes to vote and to participate in the reconstruction of loyal governments. By July 1, however, with only a few days remaining in the session, Wade favored eliminating the provision for Negro political equality, because he thought it would arouse opposition that would prevent the bill from passing. He explained, "Although I agreed to this amendment in committee I would rather it should not be adopted, because, in my judgment, it will sacrifice the bill." Under these circumstances the Senate rejected the amendment by a vote of 5 to 24.[26]

At this point, B. Gratz Brown of Missouri offered a substitute which, by confining itself to the question of representation of the rebel states in the electoral college, practically emasculated the Wade-Davis Bill. Originally proposed by Jacob Collamer, a Republican of Vermont, but now introduced by Brown, a radical in Missouri politics, the substitute amendment provided that the inhabitants of the seceded states "shall be . . . declared to be, incapable of casting any vote for electors of President or

---

deliberately prevented the reconstruction bill from being taken up until a time too late in the session to require the President to veto it in order to defeat it. But Wade did not try to bring the bill before the Senate until June 29, which was already too close to adjournment to allow Congress to reconsider any bill the President might veto. Wade's tardiness in pressing the bill underlines its relationship to the antislavery amendment (Henry Winter Davis, *Speeches and Addresses,* 453; *Cong. Globe,* 38 Cong., 2 sess., 658 [Feb. 8, 1864]).

[25] On June 29 the Senate rejected a motion by Wade to consider the reconstruction bill rather than continue with the question of representation from Arkansas. The vote was 28 to 5. On June 30, Wade lost another vote on the reconstruction bill, 17 to 11 (*Cong. Globe,* 38 Cong., 1 sess., 3365 [June 29, 1864]; 3407 [June 30, 1864]).

[26] *Ibid.,* 3449 (July 1, 1864).

Vice President of the United States, or of electing Senators or
Representatives in Congress." This political disability would
continue in effect until the rebellion was over and the return of
the people to obedience to the United States had been "declared
by proclamation of the President, issued by virtue of an act of
Congress, hereafter to be passed, authorizing the same." [27]

Brown wanted definite action on what many considered the
most critical present aspect of the reconstruction problem, and
he had doubts about the wisdom of the Wade-Davis Bill. An
answer to the question of the rebel states and the electoral college was "the necessity of the hour," argued Brown, whose substitute measure accordingly offered a solution unencumbered
with any other legislative propositions. Perhaps as important, he
thought a fully articulated and detailed reconstruction bill
would be premature. "I do not think, furthermore, that the attitude of the country to which this bill is proposed to apply is
sufficiently distinct and sufficiently developed to justify us at this
hour in passing upon the work of reconstruction," he explained.
He recommended leaving reconstruction "to a later day when
events shall have perhaps altered some of the relations in which
these districts now stand to us." [28]

Suddenly placed on the defensive by Brown's substitute bill,
Wade replied that reconstruction was too important to be put
off; political expediency demanded that it be dealt with at once.
Wade asserted, "The question will be asked of every man who
goes out to canvass during the coming election, 'What do you
propose to do with these seceded States in regard to their coming back?'" Unless a positive program was set forth, Democrats
would make political capital of the charge that, although Republicans refused to accept states organized by executive power on
the basis of free state constitutions, they refused to say on what
principle the states could gain readmission.[29] Taking up the

27 *Ibid.*   28 *Ibid.*

29 By this time the House had rejected representatives from Louisiana
and taken no action on the request of claimants from Arkansas. The
Senate a few days earlier had rejected senators-elect from Arkansas.

constitutional aspect, Wade defended the principle on which the reconstruction bill rested. The bill did not territorialize the states. "I utterly deny," said Wade, "that the States may lose their organization, may lose their rights as States, may lose their corporate capacity by rebellion. I hold that once a State of this Union, always a State." Constitutional governments in the rebel states had been overthrown, and it was the duty of the federal government to guarantee a republican government to them. In Wade's opinion, the substitute proposal of Brown was a "miserable dodge" and "a mere negation . . . [which] settles no principle." It asserted that the reconstruction of the rebel states would depend on congressional action but failed to state "any principle on which their organization shall take place." [30]

Acting as a committee of the whole, the Senate unexpectedly approved Brown's substitute bill by a vote of 17 to 16. Six Republicans joined with eleven Democrats to pass the amendment against the opposition of fifteen Republicans and one Democrat.[31] The vote was a test of radicalism, since the substitute was obviously more moderate than the Wade-Davis Bill. As in the House, therefore, a split occurred between radical and moderate Republicans, but with the difference that the radical and moderate positions were both now closer to the conservative pole. A movement to the right had occurred, which was reflected in the desire of a minority of regular Republicans, who held the balance of power, to postpone reconstruction. Despite the Senate's recent rejection of the Arkansas government reorganized under executive direction, the vote for the Brown amendment and against the Wade-Davis Bill in effect meant further acquiescence to Lincoln's plan of reconstruction.

On Saturday, July 2, the amended—really, emasculated—

---

[30] *Cong. Globe*, 38 Cong., 1 sess., 3449–3450; 3460 (July 1, 1864).

[31] *Ibid.*, 3460 (July 1, 1864). The six Republicans who crossed over to vote with the Democrats were Edgar Cowan, James Doolittle, James Grimes, Henry Lane, Lyman Trumbull, and Brown. In the vote in the Senate proper—not in the committee of the whole—Republicans James Harlan, Samuel Pomeroy, and William Sprague switched from opposition to support of the Brown version, giving it a vote of 20 to 13.

reconstruction bill went back to the House, where it seemed to
have a chance of acceptance. Imminent adjournment, scheduled
for Monday, was one reason why the House might go along
with the Senate. As an independent proposition, too, the Brown
amendment was no doubt acceptable to most Republicans, even
if it was not far-reaching enough, and might appeal to sentiment
that appeared to be emerging in favor of postponing a decision
on reconstruction.[32]

Under Winter Davis' leadership, however, the House rejected
the Senate amendment of the reconstruction bill, though for a
moment the result appeared in doubt. When Davis brought up
the bill and immediately moved that the House not agree to the
amendment, Thaddeus Stevens interjected: "I think we had better concur. It is one good thing to get, if we cannot get anything
else." Davis replied that it would be for a committee of conference to see if something better could be got and promptly
moved for consideration of the previous question. In a vote that

[32] On June 22, Henry Dawes of the Committee on Elections, reporting
on the claim of representatives-elect from Arkansas, proposed a recon-
struction-investigating commission, to be appointed by the President.
Dawes recommended that during the recess of Congress a three-man
commission visit states undergoing reconstruction and attempt to answer
three questions: whether loyal government had been restored, to what
extent the loyal people supported it, and whether the people could
defend themselves against domestic violence. Dawes's resolution declared
further that Congress would not admit representatives from any rebel
state until it was satisfied that a republican government had been established that prohibited slavery and was able to defend itself. At the urging
of Winter Davis, who saw it as interfering with his efforts on behalf of
the original Wade-Davis Bill, the House on June 29 voted, 80 to 46, to
table the whole Arkansas question, including Dawes's proposal for an
investigating commission. Nevertheless, 32 Republicans voted against
tabling, some of whom, it appeared, might support the Brown amendment, which had the similar effect of postponing consideration of the
problem. According to one Washington correspondent, many Republicans supported the Dawes resolution because it avoided the question of
the actual political status of the rebel states, putting it off until the next
session of Congress (*Cong. Globe*, 38 Cong., 1 sess., 3178 [June 22, 1864];
3389–3394 [June 29, 1864]; New York *Post*, June 23, 1864).

followed strict party lines, the House defeated a Democratic motion to table the bill, then by voice vote of 63 to 42 rejected the Senate amendment. Davis, James Ashley, and John Dawson, a Democrat from Pennsylvania, were named managers to represent the House in a conference committee.[33]

With Congress thus deadlocked and only one day left in the session, the bill went back to the upper chamber, where a startling development took place: the Senate voted to recede from its amendment—thereby adopting the House version of the bill. Late in the afternoon of July 2, the day the House insisted on disagreeing, Wade moved that the Senate take up the reconstruction bill. At once Hendricks of Missouri, a Democrat, proposed a recess until the evening, hoping to round up opposition to Wade's bill. Wade quickly objected and, after getting the measure to the floor, moved that the Senate withdraw its amendment. Democrats, trying to secure a recess, protested, but Republicans—especially Lane of Kansas and Sumner—shouted them down and outvoted them on a motion to recess, 16 to 14. The question recurred on Wade's motion, and the Senate voted, 18 to 14, to recede from the Brown amendment. Thus it passed the Wade-Davis Bill.[34]

An analysis of Senate voting reveals three basic positions. Consistently opposed to the Wade-Davis Bill were nine Democrats, who rejected the idea of imposing conditions on the rebel states, and five Republicans—James Doolittle, John Ten Eyck, Lyman Trumbull, Henry Lane, and John Henderson—who favored Lincoln's plan of reconstruction. At the opposite pole, solid in their support of the congressional plan, were ten Republicans—Zachariah Chandler, Daniel Clark, James Lane, Edwin D. Morgan, Charles Sumner, Henry Wilson, Alexander Ramsey, Morton Wilkinson, Ben Wade, and John Sherman—and one Democrat, John Conness of California. In the center were ten

[33] *Cong. Globe*, 38 Cong., 1 sess., 3518 (July 2, 1864); *Journal of the House of Representatives*, 38 Cong., 1 sess., 1000–1001.
[34] *Cong. Globe*, 38 Cong., 1 sess., 3491 (July 2, 1864).

Republicans and two Democrats who were tentative and uncertain in their support but who on balance approved the bill or were willing to let it pass. Included in this number were Republicans Henry Anthony, Timothy Howe, Solomon Foot, and Ira Harris, who abstained on July 1 but voted for the Wade-Davis Bill on July 2; Republicans William Sprague, Samuel Pomeroy, and James Harlan, who alternately supported and opposed, but then voted for, the bill after the House refused to accept the Senate version; and finally Democrats Reverdy Johnson and William Richardson, and Republicans Edgar Cowan, James Grimes, and—most conspicuous—B. Gratz Brown, who opposed the House bill on July 1 but were absent on July 2.

No evidence has turned up to explain why five senators, who by maintaining their earlier opposition could have defeated the Wade-Davis Bill, were absent, or what pressures were exerted on those who had previously been absent but were there to vote for the bill on July 2. The final disposition of the measure went almost unnoticed as the newspapers gave full attention to the resignation of Salmon P. Chase as Secretary of the Treasury and to Confederate raids near Washington. Despite the paucity of information on behind-the-scenes maneuvering, however, certain points seem clear. First, much credit for the passage of the bill must go to Wade, who skillfully seized the initiative late in the afternoon of July 2. As the sympathetic correspondent of the Cincinnati *Gazette* put it, "The most signal triumph of radical principles this session, the country owes to Ben Wade for forcing through the Senate Winter Davis' great reconstruction bill." But not only Wade was responsible: equally important were the senators who were not present to vote against the Wade-Davis Bill. If Wade "forced" the bill through the Senate, it was also true, as a few newspaper correspondents noted, that the victory of the bill "was wrought by absenteeism." Was this absenteeism fortuitous, or did it have political meaning? Under the circumstances it seemed to signify, not positive support or strong endorsement of the bill, but at least a willingness to accept it and see it tried out. Considering how close the vote was the day before, it is reasonable to think that those who strongly supported the Brown amendment instead of the original bill would have been present to vote for it again if necessary. On the other hand, if Brown's proposal seemed merely preferable, there would have been a tendency to let the original Wade-Davis Bill pass. And this feeling could have been expressed by staying away. With the House having insisted on its version of the bill, and with very little time for a compromise to be worked out, the choice seemed to be between the Wade-Davis Bill and no bill at all dealing with reconstruction, the electoral college, and emancipation. Facing these alternatives, senators who had previously voted for the Brown amendment, as well as others who had not voted, now assented to the Wade-Davis Bill by abstaining or remaining absent.[35]

Congress passed the Wade-Davis Bill on July 2, 1864, and sent it to the President.[36] Although Lincoln could defeat the mea-

[35] Cincinnati *Gazette*, July 4, 1864; Boston *Evening Transcript*, July 5, 1864; Cincinnati *Daily Commercial*, July 4, 1864; Chicago *Tribune*, July 6, 1864. Some historians have, incorrectly I think, interpreted failure to vote on the Wade-Davis Bill as implying opposition to it. Charles A. Jellison, for example, in his biography of Senator William P. Fessenden, says that Fessenden did not support the bill, but since he was "reluctant because of party considerations to oppose the . . . measure outright, . . . on the day of the Senate vote on the bill [July 2] he absented himself from the roll call. In this he was joined by sixteen of his moderate colleagues" (*Fessenden of Maine, Civil War Senator* [Syracuse, N.Y., 1962], 174–175). Jellison fails to consider that the vote on July 2 was not on the bill itself but on whether the substitute ought to be retained, that the retention of the substitute was an alternative which permitted avoidance of outright opposition to the bill, and that the effect of abstention was to enable the bill to pass.

[36] This is an appropriate place to note the careless manner in which some historians have written about the congressional plan of reconstruction of 1864. They do not even have the date correct. An example is the well-known biography of Lincoln by James G. Randall, which was completed by Richard Current. Concerning the Wade-Davis Bill Current wrote, "The Senate finally passed the bill on July 4, 1864, within an hour of the *sine die* adjournment of the session." He stated further that Wade

sure without a formal veto simply by holding it until the adjournment of Congress prevented its reconsideration, it seemed highly unlikely that he would do this. The pocket veto, while not a new or untried instrument of executive power, had been used infrequently by previous presidents and was not a well-established or routine element of constitutional custom.[37] Lincoln had not tried to influence members of the House when they debated the Wade-Davis Bill in May, and no one expected

tried to strike the word "white" from the bill and that "other Senators succeeded in attaching amendments, none of them drastic, and the minor differences between the House and Senate versions had to be reconciled by a conference committee" (Randall and Current, *Lincoln the President*, IV, 190 ff). Taking up these points in reverse order: a conference committee, though appointed by the House, did not prove necessary because the Senate receded from the amendment it had adopted on July 1; the amendment attached by B. Gratz Brown and approved by the Senate *was* drastic, proposing to do nothing less than postpone consideration of the entire question of reconstruction, except for the electoral college; Ben Wade was in favor of *retaining* the word "white" when the bill came up for consideration on July 1; and the Senate finally adopted the bill on July 2, not July 4.

[37] According to the Constitution, if a bill approved by Congress is not returned by the President within ten days, it becomes a law, unless Congress by its adjournment prevents its return, in which case it fails to become law and the President is exonerated of the responsibility of sending Congress a formal veto. Up to 1861 there were 18 pocket vetoes, 15 of them by Democratic presidents, starting with Andrew Jackson. The power was not utilized on a large scale, however, until after the Civil War; Grant, for example, pocket-vetoed 48 bills, while Grover Cleveland and Benjamin Harrison disposed of 110 and 25 bills respectively in this way. Before the Wade-Davis Bill, Lincoln had used the pocket veto once, to defeat an insignificant bill concerning naval officers. Opposition to executive veto had been an important principle of the Whig party which many Republicans endorsed during the war—especially as executive power expanded. Concerning the pocket veto, see "Report on the Pocket Veto," 70 Cong., 2 sess., *House Doc.*, no. 493; Lindsay Rogers, "The Power of the President to Sign Bills after Congress Has Adjourned," *Yale Law Journal*, XXX (Nov. 1920), 1–22; John D. Long, "The Use and Abuse of the Veto Power," *The Forum*, IV (Nov. 1887), 253–267; Joseph Kane, *Facts about the Presidents* (New York, 1959), 320; and Carlton Jackson, *Presidential Vetoes, 1792–1945* (Athens, Ga., 1967).

that he would kill the measure now. The surprise and disbelief of congressmen were great, therefore, when rumor spread that Lincoln would not approve the bill. James Garfield, a first-term representative from Ohio, related that when one such report reached the House on the morning of July 4, "Norton of Ills. the special friend of the Presidents [*sic*] said it was impossible and would be fatal." Noah Brooks, one of the best war-time correspondents, recalled that despite Winter Davis' opposition to administration policies, "nobody seemed to think that this extraordinary scheme [the Wade-Davis Bill] would be disapproved by the President." [38]

Yet a pocket veto was exactly what Lincoln had decided upon. It was a move which stunned Congress. Garfield, when convinced of the President's purpose, urged Norton to go to Lincoln and argue against it. Norton did so, only to return with the report that the President would not sign the bill. It was a "great mistake," Norton said, but there was "no use trying to prevent it." This unexpected turn filled the final moments of the session with unusual tension and excitement. According to Noah Brooks, "As the hands of the clock drew near the fateful hour of adjournment, it was suddenly whispered about the House that the President had so far failed to sign the Wade-Davis Reconstruction Bill." Brooks said, "Now for the first time men who had not seriously opposed the passage of . . . the bill began to wish that it had never gone to the President; but all was uncertainty." [39]

Meanwhile, a committee from the House was confirming the rumors about the Wade-Davis Bill. Elihu Washburne, Thaddeus Stevens, and John Dawson called on Lincoln, at work in his room in the Capitol, to inform him that the House was ready to

[38] Nicolay and Hay, *Abraham Lincoln*, IX, 119; Chase, *Inside Lincoln's Cabinet*, 232–233; Noah Brooks, *Washington in Lincoln's Time* (New York, 1895), 164.

[39] Chase, *Inside Lincoln's Cabinet*, 233; Brooks, *Washington in Lincoln's Time*, 167.

adjourn if he had no further communications for it. Lincoln rose to greet them, gave them "a pump handle shake," then sat down and went on writing. Stevens gave his message, but Lincoln continued at work without saying a word. The committee waited for a reply; getting none after a few moments, it left. Returning to the House chamber, Dawson, a Democrat, complained to Stevens that the President showed little grace and not much courtesy, and added that he "looked . . . as if he was ashamed of himself—out of place—like a tom boy at a feast." "Damned like—I think," Stevens replied.[40]

Shortly before noon the committee reported that the President had no further communication for Congress: the reconstruction bill was dead. Lincoln had unceremoniously killed it without a formal veto or so much as an explanatory remark. Realization of what had happened produced general commotion in the House. And Henry Winter Davis, who had been most closely involved and had the most at stake—"Blair & Doolittle, etc. could not abide my carrying what every body said was impossible & no body else would undertake except a few energetic friends," he wrote at the time—was especially upset. Standing "at his desk, pale with wrath, his bushy hair tousled, and wildly brandishing his arms," Davis, as Noah Brooks recalled the scene, "denounced the President in good set terms." Other members of Congress bitterly criticized Lincoln, including Samuel Pomeroy of Kansas, who went about saying, "I told you so." But some were not disappointed. B. Gratz Brown, for example, reflecting the ambiguity evident in his own voting record, said he was well satisfied with the result.[41]

Lincoln vetoed the Wade-Davis Bill in part because it seemed to be unconstitutional, but mainly because it contradicted his reconstruction policy in Louisiana and Arkansas. The anti-slavery sections of the bill he questioned on constitutional

[40] Henry Winter Davis to S. F. Du Pont, July 7 or 8, 1864, S. F. Du Pont Papers, Eleutherian Mills Historical Library. Dawson related the incident to Davis.

[41] *Ibid.*; Brooks, *Washington in Lincoln's Time*, 167–168.

grounds. When Senator Chandler, trying to persuade him to approve the measure, argued that the prohibition of slavery would be of great importance for Republicans in the November elections, Lincoln answered, "That is the point on which I doubt the authority of Congress to act." A few days after Congress adjourned, Lincoln gave additional—and more compelling— reasons for letting the Wade-Davis Bill lapse. In a highly unorthodox maneuver, he issued a proclamation stating that the congressional plan was one satisfactory solution to the problem of reconstruction which he would put into effect if the people of any seceded state desired to adopt it. He had pocket-vetoed the bill, however, he explained, because he was "unprepared, by a formal approval of this Bill, to be inflexibly committed to any single plan of restoration." More to the point, he was "unprepared to declare, that the free-state constitutions and governments, already adopted and installed in Arkansas and Louisiana, shall be set aside and held for nought, thereby repelling and discouraging the loyal citizens who have set up the same, as to further effort." Nevertheless, Lincoln reiterated that he was "fully satisfied with the system for restoration contained in the Bill, as one very proper plan for the loyal people of any State choosing to adopt it." Should such a desire become manifest, he would appoint military governors "with directions to proceed according to the Bill." [42]

Perhaps fearing that reconstruction would be a significant issue in the election, Lincoln issued this proclamation in an attempt to maintain party harmony. In it he made concessions to the congressional view, but instead of appeasing the leaders of congressional reconstruction, he only exacerbated their resentment. Thaddeus Stevens wrote: "What an infamous proclamation! . . . The idea of pocketing a bill and then issuing a proclamation as to how far he will conform to it, is matched only by signing a bill and then sending in a veto. . . . But what are we

[42] Nicolay and Hay, *Abraham Lincoln*, IX, 120–121; Proclamation concerning Reconstruction, July 8, 1864, in *Collected Works of Lincoln*, VII, 433–434.

to do? Condemn privately and applaud publicly?" Charles
Sumner and Samuel Pomeroy told Salmon P. Chase about intense
indignation against Lincoln, and James G. Blaine thought that if
Congress had been in session, "a very rancorous hostility would
have been developed against the President." But of course Congress, the natural forum for criticism of the administration, had
adjourned, and the proclamation had its effect. Some observers
now professed to see a rapprochement between President and
Congress. The correspondent of the New York *Tribune* reported that Lincoln's state paper practically approved the congressional bill and accepted the spirit of the plan, while the New
York *Times* stated editorially that the proclamation "dispels all
fears of any such variance" with Congress as was suggested by
his failure to sign the reconstruction bill.[43]

The apparent harmony did not last long. On August 5, 1864,
Henry Winter Davis and Ben Wade issued the famous Wade-
Davis Manifesto, a bitter indictment of Lincoln charging him
with obstructing the congressional plan of reconstruction. In a
sense the protest was unrelated to the struggle between the President and Congress over reconstruction, for the specific purpose
of its framers was to unseat Lincoln as the Union candidate.[44]
Despite its political origins and purpose, however, the manifesto
gave an accurate summary of the congressional position on
reconstruction in 1864.

[43] Thaddeus Stevens to Edward McPherson, July 10, 1864, Stevens
Papers, Library of Congress; Chase, *Inside Lincoln's Cabinet*, 230–232;
Blaine, *Twenty Years in Congress*, II, 43; New York *Tribune*, July 11,
1864; New York *Times*, July 11, 1864.
[44] Republican dissidents, some of whom disagreed with Lincoln on
reconstruction while others did not, hoped to get War Democrats to split
from the Democratic party and join them in support of a candidate who
would replace Lincoln as the Union standard-bearer. The Wade-Davis
Manifesto was to be the initial step in a public campaign that, it was
hoped, would produce results before the Democrats held their convention at Chicago in late August. General Benjamin F. Butler was mentioned as a possible candidate (J. Shaffer to B. F. Butler, July 23, 1864,
J. K. Herbert to Butler, Aug. 6, 1864, in *Correspondence of Benjamin F.*

Written by Davis, the manifesto offered substantive criticism of Lincoln's Louisiana policy and went on to a broad-gauged argument asserting congressional authority over reconstruction. The governments of Louisiana and Arkansas, declared Wade and Davis, rested on no substantial popular base; they were "mere oligarchies, imposed on the people by military orders under the form of election, at which generals, provost marshals, soldiers and camp-followers were the chief actors, assisted by a handful of resident citizens, and urged on to premature action by private letters from the President." The protest charged that Lincoln, by letting the bill lapse in order to protect these new governments, was disregarding the judgment Congress had made in rejecting their senators and representatives. The President's refusal to be bound to any single plan meant, further, that he "held for naught" the will of Congress on the crucial issues of slavery, the rebel debt, and the political status of former rebels. In other words, said Wade and Davis, "the President is resolved that people shall not *by law* take *any* securities from the rebel States against a renewal of the rebellion, before restoring their power to govern us." Even more ironic, by proposing to adopt the congressional plan if the people of a rebel state wanted it, the President was in effect saying that the people of the United States were not to be allowed to protect themselves unless their enemies agreed to it. Calling Lincoln's action "a . . . studied outrage on the legislative authority," Wade and Davis warned that if Lincoln wished the support of friends of the administration, "he must confine himself to his Executive duties—to obey and execute, not make the laws—to suppress by arms armed rebellion, and leave political reorganization to Congress." [45]

Butler, IV, 513, V, 8; Cuthbert Bullitt to John Hay, Aug. 20, 1864, no. 42991, Robert Todd Lincoln Collection, Library of Congress; Henry Winter Davis to S. F. Du Pont, Aug. 18, 1864, S. F. Du Pont Papers, Eleutherian Mills Historical Library; Henry Winter Davis to Ben Wade, Aug. 3, 1864, Wade Papers, Library of Congress).

[45] New York *Tribune*, Aug. 5, 1864.

Although they might have won Republican approval on the specific constitutional issues involved, Wade and Davis seriously misjudged the political situation.[46] So far from hurting Lincoln, the protest actually seemed to help him. As Blaine put it, the "very strength of the paper was . . . its special weakness. It was so powerful an arraignment of the President that of neces-

[46] Albert G. Riddle said that despite the intemperate nature of the protest, "At the Capital, thinking Union men were quite unanimous in sustaining Mr. Wade and Mr. Davis, as was a majority of both Houses of Congress." Riddle himself, a critic of territorialization in the Thirty-seventh Congress, considered the creation and admission of loyal governments to be within the jurisdiction of Congress and said that it was difficult to support the President's position. Even Gideon Welles, a dedicated opponent of congressional reconstruction, seemed to agree that the Wade-Davis Manifesto was partially correct. Welles wrote concerning Lincoln's reaction to the protest: "From what has been said of it, he had no desire to [read it, and] could himself take no part in such a controversy as they seemed to wish to provoke. Perhaps he is right, provided he has some judicious friend to state to him what there is really substantial in the protest entitled to consideration without the vituperative asperity." In Republican constitutional theory the only justification for a pocket veto was lack of time to examine the contents of a bill; accordingly Wade and Davis were at pains to show that Lincoln had had ample opportunity to learn of what their bill consisted. To use the pocket veto for other reasons—for example, because of a policy disagreement—was to deprive Congress of its constitutional prerogative of reconsidering legislation not approved by the executive. Some Republican members of Congress were so jealous of executive power that they opposed, not only presidential veto, but also presidential *approval* of legislation after the adjournment of Congress. In June 1864 the House judiciary committee unanimously reported that a bill which Lincoln had signed eight days after the adjournment of Congress in March 1863 was "not in force." The committee held that "the spirit of the Constitution evidently requires the performance of every act necessary to the enactment and approval of laws to be perfect before the adjournment of Congress." Otherwise, reasoned the committee, the executive could hold bills for long periods of time and thus "render the laws of the country too uncertain" (Riddle, *Recollections of War Times*, 304–305; Welles, *Diary*, ed. Beale, II, 98–99; John D. Long, "The Use and Abuse of the Veto Power," *The Forum*, IV, [Nov. 1887], 261; *Cong. Globe*, 38 Cong., 1 sess., 2290 [May 16, 1864]; 2880 [June 11, 1864]; *House Reports*, 38 Cong., 1 sess., no. 108).

sity it rallied his friends to his support." Abolitionists such as Gerrit Smith went on record against the attack because they felt that despite his faults Lincoln offered the best hope for Union men, and the *National Anti-Slavery Standard*, though opposed to Lincoln's 10-per-cent plan, criticized the narrow political purpose of the manifesto. Seeing the lack of favorable public response, Davis complained that the New York *Tribune* was hedging and that Charles Sumner "sends me two speeches on the Arkansas Senator—but not a word about the Protest!!" Two weeks after the manifesto was published, Davis bitterly concluded: "Wilkes' Spirit of the Times is the only decided paper now! All the rest are trimming—None heartily for Lincoln—all afraid to speak. . . . None *attack* our Protest but the [New York] *Times*—none venture to controvert or approve it." [47]

The attempt to unseat Lincoln was still-born, and the Union conquest of Atlanta in early September 1864 consolidated his position all the more. By mid-September the campaign in which the Wade-Davis Manifesto was the opening volley had failed utterly. In the next few months reconstruction was an issue in the election only in a general sense, to the extent that Democrats and Republicans were sure to adopt different attitudes toward and proposals for the return of the rebellious states. But there was little inclination to discuss details of specific plans, especially among Republicans. This was not because division within the party on this question had been transcended, but because, in the words of Blaine, "the pending struggle for the Presidency demanded harmony, and by common consent agitation on the issue was abandoned." [48]

In summary, two questions are significant for an analysis of

[47] Blaine, *Twenty Years in Congress*, II, 43–44; Washington *Chronicle*, Aug. 17, 1864; *National Anti-Slavery Standard*, quoted in *New York Times*, Aug. 13, 1864; New York *Tribune*, Aug. 5, 1864; *New York Times*, Aug. 9, 1864; Henry Winter Davis to S. F. Du Pont, Aug. 10, 18, 1864, S. F. Du Pont Papers, Eleutherian Mills Historical Library.

[48] Blaine, *Twenty Years in Congress*, II, 44; W. F. Zornow, *Lincoln and the Party Divided*, 165–167.

reconstruction in 1864: First, what was the basis of the conflict between Lincoln and Congress concerning reconstruction? Second, how different were the executive and congressional plans for political reorganization of the South?

Congress would probably have acted on reconstruction regardless of what Lincoln did, and as Ashley's bill of December 1863 showed, its action need not have been an antiadministration measure. The Wade-Davis Bill, however, was definitely antiadministration, representing both political opposition to Lincoln and disagreement with his policy of reconstruction. The key to this development was Louisiana, where the general plan outlined in the reconstruction proclamation of December 1863 was being put into operation. As new issues—in particular the rights of Negroes and the political position of former rebels—emerged, Lincoln turned away from the policy he had followed in 1863 of aligning himself with local radical Unionists in Louisiana. Instead he placed General Banks in control of Louisiana reconstruction. In a letter written to Lincoln shortly before his assassination in April 1865, Salmon P. Chase probed into the origin of the split within the Republican party over reconstruction and concluded that the turning point came in Louisiana. Chase reminded Lincoln that the order to Military Governor Shepley in 1863 directing an enrollment of loyal citizens had not been limited to white men only; in view of Attorney General Bates's opinion that Negroes could be citizens, it applied to loyal Negroes as well as to whites. The Proclamation of Amnesty and Reconstruction restricted political privileges to white men only, but, Chase added, "As I understood you not to be wedded to any particular plan of reconstruction, I hoped & believed that reflection & observation would probably satisfy you that the restriction should not be adhered to." The executive plan did not seem the best possible, but Chase supported it, expecting that General Banks would cooperate with the Free State party in Louisiana. That was why Chase, in advising Lincoln in November 1863 as to whether the President's reconstruction proclamation ought to discuss the question of legislation on behalf of Negroes, had recommended "leaving the whole subject to the judgment of those immediately concerned." But then Banks took over effective political control from the Free State General Committee, which had supported Negro representation in the party convention and a qualified Negro suffrage. "This created the impression," said Chase, "that the advocates of general suffrage were to be treated with disfavor by the representatives of the Government. Discouragement & disinterest were the natural consequences." [49]

The reaction against Lincoln's Louisiana policy in Congress took the form of the Wade-Davis Bill, which though broadly similar to Ashley's December bill, was charged with an antiadministration political purpose. In the debate on the bill in the House, it was significant that Republicans did not object to Lincoln's Proclamation of Amnesty and Reconstruction. George Boutwell, for example, said, "The President has initiated steps for the organization of civil authority, and in the absence of legislative action here I hold it to have been his duty to take steps in that direction." Fernando Beaman, a consistent supporter of congressional reconstruction, declared: "This is the first distinct act of any branch of the Government looking to a solution of the difficulty [of reconstruction]. . . . I hail the proclamation with gladness as a step in the right direction." But Lincoln's Louisiana policy came under sharp attack. According to James Ashley, the actions of General Banks constituted an "unwarrantable and indefensible assumption of civil authority." John Longyear of Michigan argued that some kind of government was necessary as the southern country was recovered, and that "if civil government is not provided for it must be a military government—a thing inimical to the spirit of our institutions." Events in Louisiana pointed up the need, said Longyear, for a

[49] Salmon P. Chase to Lincoln, Apr. 12, 1865, in *Collected Works of Lincoln*, VIII, 400; Chase to Lincoln, Nov. 25, 1863, no. 28217, Robert Todd Lincoln Collection, Library of Congress.

reconstruction bill that would "afford a rallying-point for the Union sentiment remaining there . . . [and] prevent perplexing and complicated irregularities and diversities of action." [50]

Congressional reconstruction policy also sought to prevent reorganized governments from participating in the presidential election. This was the exclusive purpose of B. Gratz Brown's substitute amendment to the Wade-Davis Bill, and many Union men regarded it as the central feature of the bill itself. Reviewing legislative achievements at the end of the session, the New York *Tribune*, without mentioning the bill by name, emphasized that "Congress has decided that none of the States which have been formally declared in insurrection shall vote for President till readmitted into the Union." Congressional leaders, moreover, addressed themselves specifically to this subject after Lincoln's pocket veto of the reconstruction bill. Referring to what he termed Lincoln's "infamous" proclamation of July 8, Thaddeus Stevens said, "The Prest. is determined to have the electoral votes of the seceded States, at least of Tenn., Ark., Lou. & Flor. —Perhaps also of S. Car." Henry Winter Davis held that "the Bill to govern the rebel States was more important *now* than hereafter—for it forbade electoral votes from those states for President." Davis believed that "the chief motive for the pocket-veto was to keep open the field to supply by sham states any deficiencies in the votes of the real states." The Wade-Davis Manifesto repeated the charge: "The President, by preventing this bill from becoming a law, holds the electoral votes of the Rebel states at the dictation of his personal ambition." Although Congress would count the electoral votes, it was possible that a victory for Lincoln in November might persuade a majority of congressmen to accept the votes of Louisiana, Arkansas, and perhaps other southern states. In July 1864 some congressional leaders such as Davis may have thought it possible to deny Lincoln the election by keeping the reorganized governments out of

[50] *Cong. Globe*, 38 Cong., 1 sess., 2102 (May 4, 1864); 1245 (Mar. 22, 1864); 1358 (Mar. 30, 1864); 2012 (Apr. 30, 1864).

the electoral process. More likely, however, they wanted to exclude these states as a sign of congressional rejection of the President's reconstruction policy.[51]

Policy differences threw into sharp relief, and intensified, the fundamental jurisdictional conflict between the President and Congress over reconstruction. It is impossible to say how much weight should be given to this issue in comparison with disagreement over specific policy issues, but certainly it formed an essential basis of the Wade-Davis Bill. Congressmen who did not agree with all the ideas of Wade, Davis, Ashley, and other acknowledged radicals nevertheless supported Davis' bill because they considered reconstruction a subject of legislative action and because they objected to the application of military power to a problem that was essentially political. Isaac Arnold, for example, a close friend of Lincoln, held that "whatever it is necessary to do, to execute . . . this constitutional guarantee [of republican government], Congress and the President may rightfully do. The right to crush armed resistance to the Constitution and laws, and for Congress to make and the President to execute such laws as will result in the establishment of a republican government, is . . . clear." Seeing the issue in this way, Arnold voted for the Davis reconstruction bill, though he opposed the radical preamble of Thaddeus Stevens. Arnold still supported the measure after the Senate had substituted Gratz Brown's proposal and voted against the Senate amendment on July 2. Henry Dawes, another moderate Republican who voted for the Wade-Davis Bill, later wrote, "[Congress] insisted that this whole question of reconstruction was one belonging to the legislature and not to the Executive. . . . They therefore undertook by legislation to take the matter out of the hands of the President, and prescribe

[51] New York *Tribune*, July 4, 1864; Thaddeus Stevens to Edward McPherson, July 10, 1864, Stevens Papers, Library of Congress; Henry Winter Davis to S. F. Du Pont, July 7, 1864, S. F. Du Pont Papers, Eleutherian Mills Historical Library; Wade-Davis Manifesto, New York *Tribune*, Aug. 5, 1864.

by law the terms of reconstruction and rehabilitation, in a fixed formula, applicable to all the States whose people had been in rebellion." James G. Blaine pointed to the same conclusion in stating that the Wade-Davis Bill "was commonly regarded as a rebuke to the course of the President in proceeding with the grave and momentous task of reconstruction without waiting the action or invoking the counsel of Congress." [52]

It is clear that Lincoln, on the other hand, saw reconstruction as an executive responsibility and wanted, in order to prevent radical change as well as weaken the rebellion, to reorganize loyal state governments as soon as possible. This did not mean that he thought no other plan feasible, but that he did not wish to be restricted in his approach to the problem, as he said in his proclamation on reconstruction in July. Gideon Welles indirectly described Lincoln's attitude toward reconstruction when he wrote in August 1864, "I think the President would have done well to advise with his whole Cabinet in the measures he has adopted, not only as to reconstruction or re-establishing the Union, but as to this particular bill, and the proclamation he has issued in regard to it." According to Senator Henry Wilson, a Republican of Massachusetts, Lincoln believed that "there were certain official responsibilities resting upon him that he must discharge according to his own ideas of what was right and best." The President saw reconstruction in this light, Wilson said, and two things were uppermost in his mind with regard to it: "first, . . . the great importance of making a beginning; and, secondly, . . . the impolicy . . . of fixing upon any single plan to which all must conform." [53]

Given these conflicts in the interpretation of constitutional

---

[52] *Cong. Globe*, 38 Cong., 1 sess., 115 (Jan. 6, 1864); Dawes, "Reconstruction and Rehabilitation," MS, 19–20, Dawes Papers, Library of Congress; Blaine, *Twenty Years in Congress*, II, 42.

[53] Welles, *Diary*, ed. Beale, II, 98–99; Henry Wilson, *History of the Rise and Fall of the Slave Power in America* (3 vols.; Boston, 1872–1877), III, 527–529.

power between the executive and legislative branches, disagreement on specific plans was perhaps in some degree inevitable. Henry Dawes felt that the constitutional conflict "naturally drew [Congress] toward the other extreme from the position occupied by [Lincoln], and led to the incorporation into all their measures, of much more stringent provisions, designed to be enactments that would by law bar restoration in any other manner." [54] Whether or not one agrees with Dawes's view, it is clear that by July 1864 the President and Congress were divided on the problem of reconstruction. The final question is, How great were the differences between them?

In this connection it is relevant to recall that although usually considered a thoroughly radical measure, the Wade-Davis Bill was considerably less radical than the reconstruction proposals of Ashley and other Republicans in the Thirty-seventh Congress. It did not provide for confiscation and Negro suffrage, and it eschewed territorialization as a basis of reconstruction but was in favor of the clause guaranteeing republican government. By the terms of the bill the rebel states were in a sense still in the Union, though they lacked constitutional governments which the United States could recognize. The bill was thus a compromise that those who considered the states still in the Union could support, as well as those who held that the rebellion had changed the condition of the states.[55] James Ash-

---

[54] Dawes, "Reconstruction and Rehabilitation," 20.

[55] Joel Prentiss Bishop, a writer on law who became involved in the constitutional issues of the war, illustrated the significance which the shift from the territorial principle to the principle of republican government could have for Union men who regarded themselves as conservatives. Describing the reaction to Sumner's state-suicide resolutions of February 1862, Bishop wrote: "But lo, what a storm! The sound and conservative men . . . *condemned the resolutions as amounting to a proposed infringement of the Constitution of the United States. We all deemed, that it would violate the provisions of this instrument to deprive the seceded States of their condition as States, and compel them to assume the lower status of territories.*" The guarantee clause was a different matter, however, which provided a proper basis for reconstruc-

ley, speaking as a member of the Select Committee on the Rebellious States, explained the compromise nature of the Wade-Davis Bill on this issue: "The committee have sought to avoid the adoption of any especial theory in the bill which they have presented. Whether the rebel usurpation has destroyed the constitutional governments of the seceded States, or whether those State governments are simply suspended or in abeyance by reason of the abdication of their officers, or whether by the acts of treason and rebellion on the part of their citizens and constituted authorities, the States thus in rebellion have committed State suicide, the committee have thought best to leave to the determination of each member for himself." [56]

Placing the Wade-Davis Bill in this perspective better enables one to see the similarities between it and the President's plan. First, the congressional plan of reconstruction followed the executive practice of appointing a federal officer to carry on the civil administration of a state and enforce existing state laws, except those relating to slavery, until a loyal government was formed and recognized. Lincoln would appoint military governors, but Congress would create provisional civil governors; both officers, however, had the same function, and both represented a vast extension of federal power into areas of policy that were hitherto exclusively within state jurisdiction. In the constitutional sense one plan was as radical as the other. The President

tion. Bishop explained, "All of us of the conservative class were distinct in this one voice, that . . . the Constitution . . . bound the United States to establish in the seceded States, not loyal territorial governments, but loyal State governments." Equally important, Bishop roundly criticized Lincoln's plan of reconstruction, especially its 10-per-cent feature, as disregarding the Constitution and being too concerned with the "work of being politic." He proposed for consideration by Congress a bill based on the guarantee clause, for the purpose of establishing loyal state governments and extending the suffrage to Negroes (*Secession and Slavery: Or the Effect of Secession on the Relation of the United States to the Seceded States and to Slavery* [Boston, 1864], 40–41, 109–112). Bishop's conservatism was evidently of the constitutional variety.

[56] *Cong. Globe*, 38 Cong., 1 sess., 1354 (Mar. 30, 1864).

and Congress also agreed on the slavery question: both were committed to emancipation as a minimum condition of reconstruction. And even on the Negro question, which was otherwise a source of conflict, there was an important area of agreement in a negative sense, for both Lincoln and Congress would deny the right of suffrage to the freedmen. It was probably this agreement which George Julian had in mind when he said that the Wade-Davis Bill was "somewhat incongruous" and "would probably have proved a stumbling-block in the way of the more radical measures which afterward prevailed." [57] Furthermore, compared to the reconstruction acts of 1867, the congressional plan of 1864 allowed the President a considerable role in the process.[58] Thinking no doubt of these several features, James Ashley later wrote apologetically that the Wade-Davis Bill "was the best, and in fact all the bill we could get that Committee [the Select Committee on the Rebellious States] to report." [59]

To notice these areas of agreement is to be reminded that Lincoln and Congress were advancing in the same direction on the central issues of national power and the destruction of slavery. Within this framework, however, there were important differences between the reconstruction plans of President and Congress. And in the context of the situation in 1864 it was these differences which stood out.

The related issues of the political status of former rebels and

[57] George W. Julian, *Political Recollections, 1840–1872* (Chicago, 1884), 247.

[58] In the reconstruction acts of 1867 the President was involved only in the appointment of military officers to command the five districts into which the South was divided. Thereafter reconstruction would proceed under the supervision of Congress, which was practically in control of the army. According to the Wade-Davis Bill, the President would appoint not only the provisional governor, but also, as he found necessary, officers provided for by state laws. The application of taxes to state expenditures was subject to the direction of the President, and if the state convention refused to comply with the act, the President would take over and decide when the process should begin again.

[59] Ashley, *Orations and Speeches*, 362.

the guarantee of freedmen's rights were sources of disagreement. In Lincoln's plan the test for participation in reconstruction was the amnesty oath, which meant that, with certain exceptions, all former rebels who swore to support the Constitution and abide by laws and proclamations concerning slavery could vote and hold office in the reorganized state government. Only 10 per cent of the prewar voting population needed to participate in order to form a legitimate government. The congressional plan, in contrast, permitted only those who could pass the test of the "iron-clad" oath—a test of *past* loyalty—to rebuild a state government. Thus a majority of the enrolled population must first swear to support the Constitution, subscribing an oath similar to that in the executive plan; then those who could take the "iron-clad" oath would elect a constitutional convention and draw up a new organic state law. This procedure was clearly more restrictive, providing greater guarantees against rebel political influence, than Lincoln's policy. The congressional plan was also more rigorous in excluding former rebels from politics once the process of reconstruction was completed. Lincoln excluded from amnesty, and by implication from subsequent political activity, several categories of rebels, of which the most significant were civil or diplomatic officers of the Confederate government, and Confederate military officers of the rank of colonel or above. Congress would exclude both Confederate and rebel-state officers above ministerial rank and military officers of the rank of colonel and above. And it would also permanently bar from United States citizenship every person who, after the passage of the Wade-Davis Bill, should hold military or civil office at these ranks in either the state or Confederate service—an extreme form of punishment that exceeded anything in the executive plan and that Congress never thereafter accepted, even in the military reconstruction policy of 1867.

Though they agreed on the slavery question, Lincoln and Congress disagreed on the Negro question. In his proclamation of December 1863, Lincoln emphasized the necessity of educating and of guaranteeing the freedom of the former slaves, but he would allow the states to determine policy for achieving these goals. General Banks's coercive labor policy in Louisiana and the refusal of the state convention, called under Banks's authority, to guarantee the rights of Negroes showed what the administration policy could lead to. Congress, on the other hand, proposed to support by legislation the Emancipation Proclamation and make it apply to those parts of the rebel states exempted from the President's original edict. Congress would go further, however, and ensure that Negroes would be tried under the same rules as white men, extend the privilege of the writ of habeas corpus to freedmen deprived of their liberty, and impose heavy penalties on persons convicted of kidnapping Negroes. Thus a central purpose of the congressional plan, as Winter Davis put it in October 1864, was "to consolidate the legal freedom of the slaves of the rebel States, and give them judicial guarantees." [60]

Of course many Republicans wanted to punish the South, and in part this spirit informed the Wade-Davis Bill. The exclusion of top Confederates from citizenship, for example, unquestionably went beyond the demands of security. It was true, therefore, that the executive plan was more lenient than the congressional plan. But there was a more fundamental difference between the two plans: Lincoln's was intended to be used during the war, while the Wade-Davis Bill was intended to be used after the war. Lincoln desired the speedy reconstruction of loyal state governments in order to press the rebel borders still farther back and resume national authority, as he said in his proclamation of December 1863, and also because the sooner reorganization was effected, the less would be the chance of radical social dislocation and change. For these reasons Lincoln would allow a mere tenth of the prewar voters in a state to form a new government. Congress, in contrast, did not want reconstruction to begin until after the war. Increasingly concerned with "guaran-

---

[60] Henry Winter Davis, *Speeches and Addresses*, 453.

tees" in support of freedmen's rights and against former rebels, it wished to deal with reconstruction systematically and uniformly, unimpeded by the complications of war, and it sought to provide a maximum degree of security at the outset of the process. The decision to take this approach was signified by the change in the reconstruction bill in April 1864 from the 10-percent to the 50-per-cent requirement as the minimum popular base for a new government. The reason for this change, said Winter Davis, was that "there is no rebel State held now by the United States enough of whose population adheres to the Union to be intrusted with the government of the State. In my judgment it is not safe to confide the vast authority of State governments to the doubtful loyalty of the rebel States until armed rebellion shall have been trampled into the dust." [61] Closely related to this was the fact, plain for all to see, that the 10-per-cent plan could not be reconciled with the principle of majority rule, any more than military control of reconstruction, as in Louisiana, could be squared with the principle of civilian control of political and constitutional change. To halt the process of executive reorganization, therefore, and at the same time establish a method of reconstruction that was more reliable and more in accord with basic principles of the American polity, Congress enacted the Wade-Davis Bill.

Though Lincoln and Congress agreed on the overarching issues of slavery and the assertion of national power, on the specific issues that were beginning to dominate reconstruction they clashed. The Wade-Davis Manifesto accurately summarized:

Mark the contrast! The bill requires a majority, the proclamation is satisfied with one-tenth; the bill requires one oath, the proclamation another; . . . the bill governs the rebel States *by law*, equalizing all before it, the proclamation commits them to the lawless discretion of Military Governors and Provost Marshals; . . . the bill exacted exclusion of dangerous enemies from power and the relief of the nation from the rebel debt, and the prohibition of slavery for-

[61] *Cong. Globe*, 38 Cong., 1 sess., App. 84 (Mar. 22, 1864).

ever. . . . [The proclamation] is silent respecting the rebel debt and the political exclusion of rebel leaders; leaving slavery exactly where it was by law at the outbreak of the rebellion, and adds no guaranty even of the freedom of the slaves he undertook to manumit.[62]

In the contemporary setting these differences far outweighed the points of agreement between Lincoln and Congress. Whether the differences would cause a final rupture depended on the course each would take after the November elections.

[62] Wade-Davis Manifesto, New York *Tribune*, Aug. 5, 1864.

IX

Compromise Attempted

THOUGH the Wade-Davis Manifesto indicated that there were real differences between the President and Congress, it did not mark a final parting of the ways between them nor preclude an attempt to compromise on reconstruction policy after Lincoln's re-election in November 1864. Perhaps the most important influence on Lincoln and Republican congressional leaders at this time was the unity created within the party by the struggle against McClellan and the Democrats. During the campaign, intraparty feuding ceased, and the result was evident in the changed political atmosphere in which Congress met in December. Henry Dawes, the chairman of the important elections committee, wrote after arriving in Washington for the start of the session: "There are indications of more harmony and good feeling among our friends here than I have seen for a long time, which is a good omen. There has been great lack of it and much paralyzing of well meant effort in consequence of it." [1]

The antislavery amendment, the welfare of the freedmen, and the readmission of rebel states were the central issues as the second session of the Thirty-eighth Congress opened. On the

[1] Henry L. Dawes to Electa Dawes, Dec. 6, 1864, Dawes Papers, Library of Congress.

first of these questions Lincoln and Congress were, of course, in agreement. The Republican party platform had endorsed the amendment prohibiting slavery, and Congress went on to approve it by the necessary two-thirds majority on January 30, 1865. No one could deny the significance of this action, the culmination of more than thirty years of antislavery protest. Yet, inevitably, as the destruction of slavery became certain, other issues assumed greater significance. The welfare of the freedmen was one of them, raising a variety of problems connected with homes, jobs, conditions of labor, education, legal advice and assistance, and the treatment of the freed Negro in general. Though Lincoln in his amnesty proclamation had proposed leaving the question to the southern states, a short while later he referred it to Congress. The House and Senate passed different bills for a freedmen's bureau in 1864 and finally agreed on a measure creating a special agency in the War Department, which Lincoln signed on March 3, 1865. Because the problem had to be dealt with by either the War or the Treasury Department, both of which were under the executive, and because it did not involve Negro political rights, which would have concerned the states and raised a federal question, Lincoln and Congress were able to avoid the kind of conflict that had developed in late 1864 on the third major issue, reconstruction.[2]

Though muted as a campaign issue, reconstruction loomed as an increasingly important problem as Union armies, following Sherman's march through Georgia, began a strategic convergence on Richmond aimed at bringing down the Confederacy within a matter of months. In contrast to the establishment of the Freedmen's Bureau, which could be treated as an administrative problem, reconstruction raised fundamental constitutional issues, such as the nature of a state's political organization

[2] Message to the Senate and House of Representatives, Dec. 17, 1863, in *Collected Works of Lincoln*, VII, 76–77; George R. Bentley, *The Freedmen's Bureau* (Philadelphia, 1955), *passim*; J. M. McPherson, *The Struggle for Equality*, 178–191.

and the political rights of its citizens—issues which could hardly
be avoided and over which jurisdiction was unclear, having been
given neither to the President nor to Congress outright. These
circumstances made cooperation on reconstruction seem unlikely in the winter of 1864–1865, especially in view of the
recent struggle over the Wade-Davis Bill. Yet there were forces
driving both Congress and the President in the direction of a
compromise on this momentous question.

For several reasons Lincoln was in a strong position in relation
to Congress and his Republican critics on reconstruction. First,
his re-election would make opposition to administration policies
more difficult than it was in 1864, when his political stock was
much lower. Furthermore, to the extent that reconstruction was
indirectly an issue in the election, having been bound up with
Lincoln's over-all performance, the result indicated approval of
his policy toward the rebel states. In the President's favor also
were the loyal governments in Louisiana and Arkansas, which
had been operating for almost a year: the longer they lasted,
even within the limited scope allowed them by the military situation, the more pressure there was on Congress to recognize
them. And if they should be recognized, as one Republican
organ put it, it "will establish a precedent that will be likely to
influence strongly, if not control, the action of Congress in all
other cases of the same kind." [3]

If these facts strengthened Lincoln in his relations with Congress, others influenced him to seek an accommodation with the
legislative branch. There was of course the ever present demand
for party unity, evidence of which had already appeared in September when Lincoln removed Montgomery Blair from the
Cabinet. This change was generally understood to be a concession to radical critics of the administration, as were the subsequent appointments of Salmon P. Chase as Chief Justice and
William Dennison as Postmaster General; both men had close

[3] Worcester *Daily Spy*, Dec. 16, 1864.

ties with the radical wing of the party. Lincoln realized, furthermore, the necessity of securing cooperation on reconstruction.
He may have considered the restoration of loyal governments in
the South to be basically his own responsibility, but he knew
also that Congress was a necessary partner in the process and
that if the executive enjoyed the exercise of the initiative in
organizing state governments, Congress must finally approve or
reject them. The pocket veto of the Wade-Davis Bill did not
mean that Congress must take no part in reconstruction, but that
it ought not to undo what had been done in Louisiana in restoring loyal government. It was apparent, too, that while advances
had been made in renewing local government, in other respects
little progress had been made. Although the presidential policy
had been in operation a full year, the number of southerners
taking the amnesty oath was small, and if 10-per-cent governments existed in two states, they were frail structures dependent
on the military.[4] Both facts might suggest a reconsideration and
possible alteration of executive policy. The President's critics, at
any rate, felt the situation propitious for influencing the administration. According to Henry Winter Davis, they believed that
"much has been accomplished by forcing him [Lincoln] on," and
they were "ready to look to Congress for a guarantee of Lincoln's good behavior." [5]

Less than a fortnight after Lincoln's election victory, one correspondent wrote that the necessity of adopting a fixed policy
concerning the reconstruction of the seceded states was being
vigorously pressed on the administration. In particular, the position of the freedmen now commanded more attention in discussions of the states' return. Montgomery Blair, for example,
asserting that James Ashley and Winter Davis were seeking to
disfranchise the white race and make Negroes its masters, advised Lincoln that the states must, above all, retain exclusive

[4] Dorris, *Pardon and Amnesty under Lincoln and Johnson*, 71–72.
[5] Henry Winter Davis to S. F. Du Pont, Sept. 23, 25, 1864, S. F. Du
Pont Papers, Eleutherian Mills Historical Library.

power over voting rights. "If the States resume their places in the Union under your proclamation," Blair wrote, "they may assert the political sovereignty as it stood of yore. This would enable the State Government to exclude the classes from suffrage which from time immemorial the policy of governments everywhere has for the most part retained in pupilage as well for the good of these feebler classes as the greater good of the commonwealth." From the opposite end of the political spectrum Charles Sumner, in order "to secure that harmony and unity in our public counsels, which will render the government irresistible," urged Lincoln to consider "whether the whole subject of 'terms' & of 'reconstruction' does not properly belong to Congress." Advising, not Negro suffrage, but guarantees against former rebels, Sumner said, *"Next to Rebellion itself I most dread a premature State Government in a rebel State,* placing at hazard, as it must, those two things which we so much desire, Peace & Liberty." *The Liberator,* pointing out that Lincoln's amnesty proclamation did not assume to be "absolute or final as against the action of Congress," urged Congress to act independently yet "aim to preserve as much unity of action as possible with the Executive." Like Sumner, the abolitionist journal insisted that the administration take "special care to guard the ballot-box, so that those who may still be treasonable in spirit and design shall not find access to it; and so that the truly loyal and the emancipated may not come under the State rule of their blood-thirsty enemies." [6]

Responding to the postelection situation, Lincoln in his annual message to Congress suggested possible changes in reconstruction policy of a kind that might anticipate a rapprochement with Congress. While not neglecting the theme of peace and reconciliation, the President emphasized that a more stringent policy toward the South might be necessary. Reviewing events since

[6] New York *Herald,* Nov. 17, 1864; Montgomery Blair to Lincoln, Dec. 6, 1864, Charles Sumner to Lincoln, Nov. 20, 1864, nos. 39066, 38535, Robert Todd Lincoln Collection, Library of Congress; *The Liberator,* Dec. 2, 1864.

the offer of amnesty was first made, he observed, "Thus, practically, the door has been, for a full year, open to all, except such as were not in condition to make free choice—that is, such as were in custody or under constraint." The situation was likely to change, however. The door of amnesty "is still so open to all," Lincoln continued, "but the time may come—probably will come—when public duty shall demand that it be closed; and that, in lieu, more rigorous measures than heretofore shall be adopted." Indirectly recognizing the power of Congress over reconstruction, he said, furthermore, "The Executive power itself would be greatly diminished by the cessation of actual war." Though pardons would still be within presidential control, "some certain, and other possible, questions are, and would be, beyond the Executive power to adjust; as, for instance, the admission of members into Congress." These statements reiterated what *The Liberator* a few days earlier had pointed to as a significant feature of Lincoln's proclamation on reconstruction: his recognition "that whether members sent to Congress from any State shall be admitted to seats, *constitutionally rests exclusively* with the respective Houses, AND NOT TO ANY EXTENT WITH THE EXECUTIVE." [7]

Lincoln's appointment of a commission to investigate army administration in Louisiana and Arkansas may also have indicated a tendency to reconsider the government's reconstruction policy. On December 10, 1864, Lincoln named Major General William F. Smith and Henry Stanbery "special commissioners to investigate and report . . . upon the civil and military administration in the military division bordering upon and west of the Mississippi." While the origins of this decision are not very clear, it seems to have resulted from a conflict between civil and military officers in New Orleans.[8] The commission, which began its

[7] Annual Message to Congress, Dec. 6, 1864, in *Collected Works of Lincoln*, VIII, 151–152; *The Liberator*, Dec. 2, 1864.

[8] Lincoln to Stephen A. Hurlbut, Nov. 14, 1864, Lincoln to Edward R. S. Canby, Dec. 12, 1864, in *Collected Works of Lincoln*, VIII, 106–108, 164.

work in January 1865, for the most part reviewed the administration of trade, finances, abandoned lands, and the like. But it
also investigated the origins of the Louisiana civil government, as
well as policies with respect to Negro labor. Whether or not
Lincoln would have agreed with the highly critical evaluation of
the Louisiana government contained in the final report of September 1865, the scope of the commission's inquiries, which
were undertaken in part while Lincoln was still living, suggests
dissatisfaction with Louisiana reconstruction.[9]

In Congress, meanwhile, there were signs of a willingness to
compromise with the President. One indication that opinion on
reconstruction had changed was the unwillingness, even of
Republicans, to refer matters to Winter Davis' Select Committee
on the Rebellious States. Twice in the first week of the session
measures dealing with reconstruction were sent instead to the
judiciary committee, headed by Republican James Wilson of
Iowa. On one proposal concerning Louisiana, introduced by
Thomas D. Eliot of Massachusetts, sixty-two Republicans voted
against referral to the reconstruction committee.[10] More significant still was the substance of Eliot's resolution. Eliot, who
had been a radical in the voting on the Wade-Davis Bill in 1864,
now proposed to recognize the executive-inspired government

[9] Order Appointing Commissioners, Dec. 10, 1864, in *ibid.*, 161–162;
Smith-Brady Commission Report, pp. 1–13, MS, entry 737, RG 94, National Archives. James Brady, a New York lawyer, replaced Stanbery,
who declined the appointment. Harold Hyman and Benjamin P. Thomas,
in their biography of Stanton, state that Lincoln launched the investigation in order to forestall a congressional inquiry and because he "was
beginning to doubt whether his was the best way toward reconstruction
in practice" (*Stanton: The Life and Times of Lincoln's Secretary of
War* [New York, 1962], 346–347, 460–462).

[10] *Cong. Globe*, 38 Cong., 2 sess., 12 (Dec. 8, 1864); 26 (Dec. 13, 1864).
Eliot's resolution was referred to the judiciary committee, but on motion
of Allen of Illinois, a Democrat, the vote was reconsidered and the
resolution was sent to the reconstruction committee. Speaker Schuyler
Colfax broke a 66 to 66 tie to decide the issue. Only 17 Republicans,
including Ashley and Davis, voted to refer to the Select Committee on
the Rebellious States.

of Louisiana as the legitimate government of the state. He explained that the rebellion had been so far suppressed in Louisiana that the laws of the United States could again be enforced, and that the loyal citizens had "ordained a constitution for said State which will secure to the inhabitants thereof a republican form of government." Eliot therefore proposed that Congress declare that the "State of Louisiana may resume its political relations with the government of the United States upon the terms and under the provisions of [the United States] constitution; and that senators and representatives from said State duly elected and chosen . . . shall be duly received."[11] Coming from a consistent supporter of congressional reconstruction, who had earlier advocated territorialization, this was a most significant concession to the administration. And the fact that three-fourths of the Republican members wanted to keep the Louisiana question away from Davis, who could hardly be thought sympathetic to the resolution, suggested that a majority of them agreed with Eliot's recommendation.

It soon became apparent that the pressure to reach an accommodation with the President was affecting even the select committee on reconstruction. On December 15, James Ashley, a member of the committee, reported a bill offering a compromise: recognition by Congress of Lincoln's 10-per-cent government in Louisiana, in return for Lincoln's acceptance of Negro political equality. The measure was actually the Wade-Davis Bill revised in two all-important particulars: it provided for the enrollment of "all male citizens of the United States resident in the State in their respective counties," and it stated that delegates to the state convention "shall be elected by the loyal male citizens of the United States . . . enrolled as aforesaid or absent in the military service of the United States."[12] Here of course was a proposal for Negro suffrage, which was becoming the objective of

[11] 38 Cong., H.R. Joint Res. 125, Dec. 13, 1864, MS, National Archives, RG 233, 37A-B1.
[12] 38 Cong., H.R. 602, Dec. 15, 1864, secs. 8, 10.

an increasing number of Republicans.[13] In return for this concession to radicalism, Congress would "recognize the government of the people of the State of Louisiana, inaugurated under and by the convention of the people of Louisiana, . . . and declare the same to be entitled to the guarantee and all other rights of a State government under the Constitution of the United States." [14]

This compromise proposal emerged from a conference between Lincoln and congressional leaders which resulted in the understanding that executive approval of the reconstruction bill depended upon the readmission of Louisiana.[15] When the bill was reported, Lincoln took a definite interest in it—the Robert Todd Lincoln Collection contains a printed copy of the measure with marginal annotation of the contents in Lincoln's hand—and was generally in favor of it, provided that it would be modified in certain respects.[16]

Lincoln expressed his views on the bill to General Nathaniel Banks and Montgomery Blair on December 18. According to John Hay, "The President had been reading it [the reconstruction bill] carefully, & said that he liked it with the exception of one or two things which he thought rather calculated to conceal a feature which might be objectionable to some." One was that

[13] Boston *Commonwealth*, Jan. 21, 1865; New York *Tribune*, Dec. 28, 1864, speech of Wendell Phillips; Springfield *Weekly Republican*, Jan. 14, 1865. Ithmar Sloan of Wisconsin, for example, on December 7 introduced a resolution proposing a constitutional amendment by which representatives in Congress would be apportioned according to the number of qualified electors in a state. This indirect method of trying to extend suffrage to the freedmen eventually found its way into the Fourteenth Amendment (*Cong. Globe*, 38 Cong., 2 sess., 6 [Dec. 7, 1864]).

[14] H.R. 602, sec. 7.

[15] New York *Tribune*, Dec. 17, 1864; Boston *Commonwealth*, Dec. 24, 1864; New York *Herald*, Dec. 27, 1864; New York *Times*, Dec. 19, 1864; Boston *Journal*, Dec. 19, 1864; Worcester *Daily Spy*, Dec. 19, 1864; Charles Sumner to Francis Lieber, Dec. 27, 1864, in Pierce, *Memoir and Letters of Charles Sumner*, IV, 205.

[16] H.R. 602, Dec. 15, 1864, no. 39293, Robert Todd Lincoln Collection, Library of Congress.

Negroes were to be made jurors and voters. Banks agreed that this provision constituted "a fatal objection," since it would "simply throw the Government into the hands of the blacks, as the white people under that arrangement would refuse to vote." He said, however, that the provision was to be dropped and the racial qualification of the Wade-Davis Bill, allowing political rights to white citizens only, restored. Banks, who was in Washington lobbying on behalf of the Louisiana government and who was having an aide do research showing that Congress had on two occasions rejected proposals for limited Negro suffrage, was in touch with Republican members and may have spoken with some authority. Lincoln's second reservation concerned the emancipation section of the bill. Though he had previously said that this provision was unconstitutional because Congress had no power to legislate concerning slavery in the states, he now took a different view. Noting the argument that this was "not a prohibition of slavery by Congress but a mere assurance of freedom to persons actually there in accordance with the Proclamation of Emancipation," Lincoln said that it was "not objectionable" according to that point of view, though he thought "it would have been preferable to so express it." [17]

Except for these qualifications, Hay recorded, "the President and General Banks spoke very favorably . . . of Ashley's bill." The readmission of Louisiana would constitute a precedent of sufficient weight to more than counterbalance the enactment of a congressional plan of reconstruction. At least that was Lincoln's idea, for even if such an act were passed, Congress could still control the return of the seceded states by its power to determine its own membership. According to Hay, Banks "does not regard it, nor does the President, as laying down any castiron policy in the matter." Hay explained that if Louisiana were admitted and the bill passed, the President would not be stopped by it from recognizing, and urging Congress to recog-

[17] J. M. Barclay to Nathaniel Banks, Dec. 30, 1864, Banks Papers, Library of Congress; Hay, *Lincoln and the Civil War*, 244–246.

nize, another state coming in with a different constitution and under different conditions. Banks thought that the objective of Congress was "merely to assert their conviction that they have a right to pass such a law, in concurrence with the executive action. They want a hand in reconstruction." Nor did this seem unreasonable to him. "It is unquestionably the prerogative of Congress to decide as to qualifications of its own members," Hay pointed out; "that branch of the subject is exclusively their own." The feeling was, Hay observed, that "it does not seem wise therefore to make a fight upon a question purely immaterial, that is, whether this bill is a necessary one or not, and thereby lose the positive gain of this endorsement of the President's policy in the admission of Louisiana." [18]

On December 20, two days after Lincoln criticized the reconstruction bill to Banks, Ashley reported it back from committee with amendments obviously made in accordance with the President's views. Whether Banks acted as liaison or whether members of the reconstruction committee consulted with Lincoln is not clear, but the compromise was being carried a step farther. The first change clarified the connection between the bill and the Emancipation Proclamation. The amendment stated, "All persons held to involuntary servitude or labor in the States or parts of States in which such persons have been declared free by any proclamation of the President, are hereby emancipated." Not only did this, unlike the Wade-Davis Bill, recognize Lincoln's proclamation as a source of authority, but it also restricted the emancipating effect of the act to the limits set by the edict of 1863—in contrast to the Wade-Davis Bill, which declared slaves free in parts of states exempted by the President. The second change reported by Ashley on December 20 restored in substantial degree the racial qualifications of the Wade-Davis Bill. Only white male citizens could be enrolled and counted for the purpose of calling a convention election, "together with the citizens

[18] Hay, *Lincoln and the Civil War*, 245–246.

of the United States from such State in the military or naval service of the United States." Similarly, voting should be by "loyal male citizens . . . enrolled as aforesaid, or absent in the military or naval service of the United States." [19] Thus, only white persons and Negroes in the army or navy could participate in reconstruction. Here was at least a step toward Negro political equality, though it fell far short of what the most ardent champions of the freedmen demanded.[20] In addition to these further concessions to the administration, the bill provided, of course, for the recognition of Louisiana.

Ashley reported the revised bill on December 20 with the hope of having it passed. In view of the importance of the measure, however, and of the imminent adjournment of Congress for the Christmas holiday, several members from both parties urged postponement until January. Delay would also give time for a further harmonizing of opinions, and Ashley, who did not regard postponement as a threat to the bill, agreed to put it off until after the recess.[21]

In the next few weeks the proposed compromise on reconstruction provoked much comment. Opinion ranged from endorsement by regular Republicans and some leading antislavery men, to opposition by other prominent antislavery spokesmen and Democrats. The correspondent of the Republican Boston *Journal*, Benjamin Perley Poore, wrote with evident approval, "The reconstruction bill has been so amended as to meet the views of every Administration Senator and Representative, and it will not only be passed by Congress, but will receive the signature of the President." Louisiana would be admitted, Poore thought, and "the happy adjustment of differences of opinion on this question will secure a harmonious ses-

---

[19] H.R. 602, amendments by Ashley, Dec. 20, 1864, secs. 4, 8, 10.
[20] Cf. *The Equality of All Men before the Law Claimed and Defended* . . . (Boston, 1865); McPherson, *The Struggle for Equality*, 308–309.
[21] Boston *Journal*, Dec. 20, 1864; *Cong. Globe*, 38 Cong., 2 sess., 81 (Dec. 20, 1864); Chicago *Tribune*, Dec. 21, 1864.

sion." Leading antislavery senators Charles Sumner and B. Gratz
Brown also agreed to the compromise. Sumner wrote to Francis
Lieber on December 27: "I have presented to the President the
duty of harmony between Congress and the Executive. He is
agreed. It is proposed to admit Louisiana (which ought not to be
done), and at the same time pass the reconstruction bill for all
the other States, giving the electoral franchise to 'all citizens'
without distinction of color." Sumner was either too sanguine as
to the specific suffrage provision or simply in error, but on the
basic terms of the bargain he was right. A few days later he
explained that Lincoln was "exerting every force to bring Congress to receive Louisiana under the Banks government."
Though not regarding Louisiana as "strong enough in loyalty
for an independent State," Sumner said: "I will hold my peace if
I can secure a rule for the other States, so that we may be saved
from daily anxiety with regard to their condition." B. Gratz
Brown, who had refused to vote for the Wade-Davis Bill in
July, supported the revised bill as a step toward freedom and the
franchise for the emancipated slaves. Praising the provision in
the new Louisiana constitution permitting the enfranchisement
of Negroes, and crediting Lincoln with promoting that development in his letter to Governor Hahn of March 1864 suggesting
that certain classes of Negroes be given the suffrage, Brown
wrote to his Missouri constituents: "In Congress opinion is still
more advanced, and the act restoring Louisiana to her federal
relations will, if it shall become a law, contain a direct clause
giving the franchise at once to those freed blacks who have
served as soldiers of the republic, and opening an avenue to all
others who may choose to qualify in a like manner." Even Henry
Winter Davis grudgingly supported the compromise. He wrote
to Admiral Samuel Francis Du Pont, "Banks has been pressing
his Louisiana govt. All Mass. took his part & the Prest. joined."
Davis explained, "It was plainly a combination not to be resisted
so I had to let La. in under Banks' govt in condition of it going
in the *Bill* defeated by the Prest. last year." "Sumner & Ashley

say Lincoln will sign it!!'" Davis added, but, perhaps because of his belief that the President was "being *manipulated* by persons hostile to [Davis] into a very ugly frame of mind," he doubted that Lincoln would.[22]

Other antislavery men rejected the proposed compromise between President and Congress. The Boston *Commonwealth* pointed out that supporters of the plan thought it would check the creation of "fictitious and mischievous organizations" such as the Louisiana government. But "if Congress allows the President to determine the conditions on which Louisiana shall return to the Union," the *Commonwealth* asked, "what resistance can it make when he brings Florida and Alabama along? We regard . . . the seventh section of this bill [recognizing Louisiana] as practically the whole bill, and the rest of it as likely to be a dead letter." Wendell Phillips told the Massachusetts Anti-Slavery Society in January 1865 that he opposed the compromise because of his belief that any state that was readmitted would necessarily be a model for every other rebel state. "When, therefore, Congress submits—as even Mr. Sumner is understood to say they must submit, however reluctantly, in this single objectionable instance, to the wishes of the President—" said Phillips, "it establishes the principle underlying Louisiana as the guide for future reconstruction." And the essence of that principle was "a brutal, domineering, infamous overseer spirit." Emphasizing the near "impossibility, even with the Constitution on our side, of attacking a State," Phillips warned that "the white men of the reconstructed States can keep inside the Constitution, be free from any legal criticism, and yet put the negro where no Abolitionist would be willing to see him." At the opposite pole, the

[22] Boston *Journal*, Dec. 19, 1864; New York *Times*, Dec. 19, 1864; Charles Sumner to Francis Lieber, Dec. 27, 1864, Sumner to John Bright, Jan. 1, 1865, in Pierce, *Memoir and Letters of Charles Sumner*, IV, 205, 221; B. Gratz Brown to the editor of the *Missouri Democrat*, Dec. 22, 1864, in Boston *Commonwealth*, Jan. 21, 1865; Henry Winter Davis to S. F. Du Pont, Dec. 20, 1864, S. F. Du Pont Papers, Eleutherian Mills Historical Library.

correspondent of the Democratic New York *Herald* described the proposed compromise as one in which "one side yields a little, and the other almost everything." The radical faction of Sumner, Wade, Stevens, Davis, and others was to consent to the admission of Louisiana, while the President and his supporters would agree to a policy of restoring the other states only through an organic act, as though the nation was admitting original territories as new states. The *Herald* correspondent said that conservatives opposed the compromise because they opposed any bill which recognized the right of secession and which in effect treated the seceded states as no more than foreign territory. But there was no reason to doubt that the compromise would carry, he wrote, "now that Mr. Lincoln has gone over to the radicals." [23]

Perhaps influenced by abolitionist criticism, but probably because they were more confident that Lincoln and his supporters in Congress would come around to their point of view, the Select Committee on the Rebellious States upped its demands when Congress convened in January. According to "W. R." in the Boston *Commonwealth*, many radicals who had agreed to admit Louisiana in the hope of checking similar experiments in other states had concluded that it was "a poor way to prevent wrong-doing, and a poor record to make for the future." Suggestions of radical strength, arising probably from radicals' own estimate of the situation, were evident in speculation that the reconstruction bill would fail if it included recognition of Louisiana.[24] In any event, Ashley on January 7 submitted two amendments that drastically altered the compromise. One provided that every new constitution in a southern state should guarantee "equality of civil rights before the law . . . to all persons in said State." Although protection of the civil rights of

[23] Boston *Commonwealth*, Dec. 24, 1864, Feb. 18, 1865; *The Equality of All Men before the Law*, 29–34; New York *Herald*, Dec. 27, 1864.

[24] Boston *Commonwealth*, Jan. 14, 1865; Boston *Journal*, Jan. 12, 1865; Cincinnati *Daily Gazette*, Jan. 7, 1865.

freedmen had been included in earlier legislation, this was a sweeping provision which dramatically illustrated the direction of advanced Republican thinking on the Negro question. Whether or not it would have been acceptable to the President and his congressional supporters at this time is doubtful, though a judgment cannot be conclusive, because of the general nature of the injunction and because attitudes on this score were changing.[25] It was Ashley's second amendment that decisively altered the situation by bringing Louisiana and Arkansas under the act. Congress would recognize the governments of both states, the amended bill stated, provided that they submitted to the enrollment process and wrote into their constitutions the three conditions prescribed for the other rebel states: the exclusion of rebel officeholders from political privileges, the prohibition of slavery and guarantee of equal civil rights for all persons, and the repudiation of Confederate debts. Until these steps were taken, the states would be subject to the act.[26] Although it was provisional recognition of Louisiana and Arkansas, this amendment in substance denied the very basis of the compromise between the administration and Congress and called into question the existence of the loyal governments in those states. To require Louisiana and Arkansas to go through the enrollment phase of the process was to require a majority of the enrolled citizens to swear loyalty to the United States, and if a majority could not be obtained, as it almost certainly could not in wartime, the 10-per-cent governments would be deprived of legitimacy. This was precisely the one-sided compromise that conservatives com-

[25] The Boston *Journal*, for example, a proadministration Republican paper, held that events were "tending" toward Negro suffrage and that there would be no peace until the principles of the Declaration of Independence were recognized in all the states. "The only question," said the *Journal* in an editorial on reconstruction, "is, whether we shall make the political equality of the blacks the sine qua non of readmission, or whether we shall wait the gradual change in public opinion at the South which will accomplish it in time" (Mar. 3, 1865).

[26] H.R. 602, amendment by Ashley, Jan. 7, 1865, secs. 12, 15.

plained about, in which the President gave almost all, while the radicals on the reconstruction committee gave almost nothing.

Republicans who had supported previous reconstruction proposals now withdrew support from the Select Committee on the Rebellious States. Believing that the committee was overreaching itself and destroying an opportunity to fix congressional authority over reconstruction, James Wilson and Thomas D. Eliot, prominent House Republicans, introduced substitute amendments which retreated from the high ground of Ashley's most recent version of the bill. Wilson and Eliot rejected the idea of imposing a single plan on all the rebel states yet insisted on congressional supervision of reconstruction. Wilson's substitute excluded representatives from any rebellious state "until by an act or joint resolution of Congress, approved by the President or passed notwithstanding his objections, such State shall have been first declared to have organized a just local government, republican in form, and to be entitled to representation in the respective Houses of Congress." Eliot proposed that seceded states "shall not be permitted to resume their political relations with the Government of the United States until by action of the loyal citizens within such States respectively a State Constitution shall be ordained and established republican in form." Eliot also continued to seek a compromise by proposing to readmit Louisiana and by requiring that new state constitutions, in addition to prohibiting slavery, guarantee "to all persons freedom and equality of rights before the law." [27]

The split among House Republicans indicated by these substitute amendments was openly revealed on January 16, 1865, when the reconstruction bill came to the floor and was criticized from two directions. Though the committee bill demanded that Louisiana and Arkansas submit to congressional reconstruction, it did not go far enough on the Negro question to please the antislavery vanguard. Accordingly, William D. Kelley of Penn-

[27] H.R. 602, amendment by Wilson, Jan. 7, 1865, amendment by Eliot, Jan. 12, 1865, secs. 1, 2.

sylvania proposed to include in the enrollment process, in addition to white male citizens, "all other male citizens of the United States who may be able to read the Constitution thereof." Although not a proposal for universal suffrage, and actually a compromise in that respect, Kelley's amendment went beyond the reconstruction committee's recommendation for ensuring Negro political equality.[28] In support of it he made a long speech in favor of impartial manhood suffrage which abolitionists hailed as "the most advanced and thorough speech" of the session.[29] The next day Eliot moved his substitute amendment and delivered a strong attack on the bill. Critical of certain provisions on policy grounds, he objected mainly to forcing every seceded state into the same rigid pattern of reorganization. Even Louisiana, he explained, would go through the process and be treated as though the loyal citizens there had done nothing to re-establish a state government. Eliot asked, "Can we undertake in one bill to state what shall be applicable in detail in all these rebel States? Why is it not more wise to take the States as they shall present themselves for admission?" Congress ought to establish the basic principles on which reconstruction should proceed and then leave the work of reorganization to the people in the states. "Let them establish their constitution; let it prohibit slavery; let them grant freedom and equality of rights, and we need nothing else," Eliot concluded. "No matter . . . how a State shall have brought itself before us, so only that it comes with a constitution that we can recognize." [30]

[28] Benjamin Perley Poore described the origin of this proposal when he wrote on January 9: "At present the great question is as to whether the right of suffrage shall be extended to all or only white male inhabitants of States to be reconstructed. It has been suggested that a compromise can be effected by adopting the Massachusetts proviso permitting all to vote who can read and write. This . . . will restrict the freedmen from voting until they have been somewhat educated" (Boston *Journal*, Jan. 10, 1865).

[29] *Cong. Globe*, 38 Cong., 2 sess., 281 (Jan. 16, 1865); *The Independent*, Mar. 16, 1865.

[30] *Cong. Globe*, 38 Cong., 2 sess., 300 (Jan. 17, 1865).

Although the reconstruction bill of January 1865 was essentially similar to the Wade-Davis Bill, which had received the support of almost all Republicans, in the new political situation following Lincoln's re-election it was too radical for most Republicans. The measure fell short of what radicals such as Kelley and Sumner wanted, but the decisive difference between it and the plan of 1864 was that it failed to meet the requirements of moderate Republicans because it would interfere with, if not undermine, Lincoln's 10-per-cent governments in Arkansas and Louisiana. Following Eliot's powerful dissent from the reconstruction committee's report on January 17, James Wilson, also an opponent of the bill, moved to postpone it for two weeks. Henry Winter Davis vigorously protested, arguing that a "vote to postpone is equivalent to a vote to kill the bill." But Davis now commanded little support. In a decisive test on the merits the House voted, 103 to 34, against the reconstruction bill and postponed it. In a striking shift from the previous session, 58 Republicans opposed the bill and only 25 supported it.[31]

The action of the House clearly seemed to spell defeat for the bill. Pleased by the result, the New York *Times* remarked that it was "glad to see indications that the schemes of 'reconstruction' now before Congress are likely to be abandoned or to fail." The Springfield *Republican* stated that Congress was showing "a more catholic and practical spirit" and that the contest with the President over reconstruction was not likely to be renewed. The revised Wade-Davis Bill, "imposing an iron and almost impossible plan of reconstruction upon all the rebellious states alike, . . . has been abandoned now by some of its former prominent friends," the *Republican* pointed out. "The general and growing feeling," it added, "is to lay down no system of fixed rules for the restoration of a state." Partisans of the reconstruction committee's plan gloomily drew the same conclusion. Whitelaw Reid, a correspondent of the radical Cincinnati *Gazette*, wrote that the reconstruction bill had received a setback which its friends feared would prove fatal, while the Boston *Common-*

[31] *Ibid.*, 301 (Jan. 17, 1865).

wealth noted that the chances of passing any reconstruction legislation appeared to be very doubtful. The Worcester *Daily Spy* observed a strong disinclination on the part of Republicans to act on reconstruction and said that it was "hardly probable that any law of the kind proposed will be passed at this session." [32]

Although it was highly improbable that the bill could pass without a section admitting Louisiana, the Select Committee on the Rebellious States persisted in revising it, hoping perhaps to get it through, but probably with the main purpose of asserting what it considered to be correct principles of reconstruction. Thus, on February 18, Ashley brought in yet another version of the bill, this time aiming at full political equality for the freedmen. Of its several amendments, the most important removed the racial qualification for enrollment, thereby opening the franchise to Negroes. Other changes, which were concessions to the administration, included a provisional recognition of Tennessee in addition to Louisiana and Arkansas, if the minimum conditions of the act were incorporated into the state constitution by May 1, 1865, and the removal of the enrollment requirement in the last two states. Thus Louisiana and Arkansas could be recognized if they wrote into their organic law the terms prescribed by the act; they would not be governed by the rule that a majority of the enrolled citizens had to swear an oath of loyalty to the United States before reconstruction could begin. In other words, the 10-per-cent principle was thus permitted to stand in these three states. Ashley also reported several amendments made specifically in accordance with Eliot's criticisms of the bill.[33] A final change of great significance was a proposal to recognize the rebel governments as the legitimate governments

[32] *New York Times,* Jan. 19, 1865; Springfield *Weekly Republican,* Feb. 18, 1865; Cincinnati *Daily Gazette,* Jan. 18, 1865; Boston *Commonwealth,* Jan. 21, 1865; Worcester *Daily Spy,* Jan. 19, 1865.

[33] For example, the committee deleted sections dealing with the collection of state taxes, the enforcement of existing state laws, the appointment of state officers, and the permanent exclusion of former rebels from citizenship, all of which Eliot had attacked.

in the southern states if they would give up the rebellion. The bill stated that if the governor and legislature of any seceded state should submit to the United States, swear an oath to the Constitution, repudiate the rebel debt, and ratify the antislavery amendment, the President might "recognize the said Governor and Legislature as the lawful State government . . . and . . . certify the fact to Congress for its recognition." [34] While this provision looked to the unconditional surrender of the Confederacy, it was a startling and ironic proposal nonetheless, for it would have legitimized rebel authority for the purpose of making peace—precisely what Lincoln eighteen months earlier had said must at all costs be avoided. [35]

In this amended form Ashley brought the reconstruction bill before the House once more, on February 20. The changes had no effect on Republican opinion, however, as became clear when Henry L. Dawes, definitely taking sides on reconstruction as he did on few other occasions, delivered a set speech in which, like Eliot, he protested forcing a single method of reorganization on every southern state. The bill assumed, Dawes said, "that there is no power in these people except what we give them by the legislation of the Federal Government here to establish a State government there." Denying the truth of this assumption, Dawes advised letting loyal citizens form state governments according to their own methods, subject only to the condition that they be "republican in form." [36]

Dawes's speech, which some observers credited with accomplishing the defeat of the bill, was another demonstration of the split within the Republican party on reconstruction. "Some dis-

[34] H.R. 602, amendment by Ashley, Feb. 18, 1865, secs. 3, 5, 12, 13.

[35] Advising Andrew Johnson on reconstruction in September 1863, Lincoln wrote: "The re-inauguration [of a state government] must not be such as to give control of the State, and it's [*sic*] representation in Congress, to the enemies of the Union, driving it's friends there into political exile. The whole struggle for Tennessee will have been profitless to both State and Nation, if it so ends that Gov. Johnson is put down, and [rebel] Gov. Harris is put up" (*Collected Works of Lincoln*, VI, 440).

[36] *Cong. Globe*, 38 Cong., 2 sess., 936 (Feb. 20, 1865).

like and some like it, about half and half," Dawes wrote to his
wife. "We killed the Bill dead—and Fernando Wood killed me
dead by complimenting me."[37] Following Dawes's attack,
James Ashley, conceding that "no bill providing for the reorganization of loyal State government in the rebel States can pass
this Congress," withdrew the most recent version of the congressional plan and substituted a measure that restored the
"white only" qualification, but with an extension of the suffrage
to Negro soldiers. It contained no recognition of Arkansas,
Louisiana, or Tennessee, and on February 21 the House voted,
91 to 64, to table it.[38] The issue was decided by 21 Republicans
who joined 70 Democrats and border-state Unionists to defeat
the bill, voting against 63 Republicans who opposed tabling.
Most Republicans thus opposed the move, but this did not necessarily mean that they supported the reconstruction committee's
bill. The amendments of Eliot and Wilson were covered by the
motion, so members who favored these proposals would have
voted against tabling—as indeed Wilson and Eliot, opponents of
the committee bill, did. Probably 38 Republicans opposed the
motion to table for the same reason.[39]

Thus Republicans were split three ways on reconstruction: 21
opposed any congressional action, taking the conservative position; 25 supported the revised Wade-Davis Bill, taking the radical position; and 38 favored a broad-gauged assertion of con-

[37] Boston *Evening Courier*, Feb. 24, 1865; Springfield *Weekly Republican*, Mar. 4, 1865; Henry L. Dawes to Electa Dawes, Feb. 22, 1865,
Dawes Papers, Library of Congress. Fernando Wood was a leading
Democrat from New York.
[38] H.R. 602, amendment by Ashley, Feb. 21, 1865; *Cong. Globe*, 38
Cong., 2 sess., 967–971 (Feb. 21, 1865).
[39] The vote on January 17 was a clearer test of the strength of the
reconstruction committee's bill. At that time the substitute amendments
were included in the motion to postpone, but Wilson and Eliot voted for
it. Subtracting the 25 Republicans who opposed postponement on January 17 from the 63 who voted against tabling on February 21, one can
conclude that 38 Republicans opposed the reconstruction bill of the
select committee, but favored some kind of more moderate substitute.

gressional authority such as Wilson's or Eliot's, which would
have allowed for variation in the several states and been reconcilable with the executive plan—this was the moderate position
in February 1865. The alignment revealed how the political situation had altered since the previous summer. Then almost all
Republicans had supported the Wade-Davis Bill, including
moderates who rejected the Stevens-inspired preamble; there
was no conservative Republican opposition to speak of in the
House; and only a small element in the Senate opposed congressional action of any sort. In 1865, however, essentially the same
plan of reconstruction received the backing of only about a
quarter of the Republicans in the House. With a provision for
limited Negro suffrage, it was more radical than the Wade-Davis
Bill, but even without this it could not have passed. To make
every state conform to a carefully detailed plan, to force each
into a Procrustean bed, as Lincoln often put it, now seemed too
radical for the majority of Republicans. Accordingly, many of
them shifted their position: nine who had voted for the Wade-
Davis Bill now opposed any congressional action, and thirty-five
others who had supported the plan in 1864 voted against the
revised version, favoring instead a more moderate form of congressional supervision. What is more, twenty-five of the latter
had voted for the radical Stevens preamble in 1864. Thus, as
Lincoln's political strength increased after his election to a
second term, and as the end of the war approached, most Republicans drew back to more modest reconstruction plans.

The action of February 21 was repeated the next day when
James Wilson made a final effort to secure reconstruction legislation. Wilson introduced his amendment to the reconstruction
committee's bill as a separate proposal prohibiting the election of
senators and representatives from any seceded state until the
President had declared an end to armed hostility and until the
state had adopted a "constitution of government republican in
form . . . [which] shall have been submitted to and approved
by Congress." This amendment fared no better than the other
propositions on reconstruction as both Democrats and conserva-

tive Republicans attacked it. Ashley then brought matters back to where they had started from by offering as a substitute for Wilson's bill the measure which had been tabled the day before. Ashley especially wanted a vote on Negro suffrage and, unable to get the Select Committee on the Rebellious States to report a bill without racial qualifications, arranged for Kelley of Pennsylvania to move an amendment striking out the word "white." A Democratic motion to table both the bill and the amendments upset this strategy, however, as the House voted, 80 to 65, to shelve the whole problem. A coalition of 19 Republicans and 61 Democrats again defeated congressional reconstruction. The Springfield *Republican* expressed the sense of relief felt by conservative Republicans: "Thus the president's reconstruction policy stands, and the readmission of the recovered states will be obstructed by no inflexible rule, but each case can be determined according to circumstances existing when it comes up. This is the right solution of the matter." [40]

The outcome of the other part of the reconstruction question in early 1865—the proposed readmission of Louisiana—demonstrated the need for compromise if a viable federal policy was to be established. From the moment that the congressional reconstruction plan appeared headed for defeat, a struggle on this issue took shape. Applauding the anticipated defeat of the reconstruction bill, the Springfield *Republican* advised Congress not to adjourn "without so far recognizing the new and loyal governments, established or in process of organization, in [Louisiana, Arkansas, and Tennessee], as to give them early settlement, and allow them before the year is over to undertake all the responsibilities of states." But the radicals, thwarted in their plans for reconstruction, were anxious for revenge. "We hope now to defeat the proposed admission of Louisiana and Arkansas," Ashley wrote to the editor of the Boston *Commonwealth*, "and if so the whole question will go over to the next Congress.

[40] 38 Cong., H.R. 740, Feb. 4, 1865; *Cong. Globe*, 38 Cong., 2 sess., 997–1002 (Feb. 22, 1865); James Ashley to the editor, Boston *Commonwealth*, Mar. 4, 1865; Springfield *Weekly Republican*, Feb. 25, 1865.

In the meantime I hope the nation may be educated up to our demand for universal suffrage." [41]

For several reasons the admission of Louisiana seemed likely in February 1865. Most Republicans, it was clear from the disposition of the reconstruction bill, were convinced that it would be better to let Lincoln's 10-per-cent governments in rather than keep them out. Of course the point of arguments against imposing a single plan on all the states was that adherence to an inflexible scheme would threaten the loyal government in Louisiana, which the President was known to favor. Indeed, Lincoln gave up his usual passive role toward Congress and tried to influence it on this issue. He kept General Banks in Washington all winter lobbying for Louisiana, caused the reconstruction bill to be modified to allow for the recognition of the 10-per-cent government, and told Lyman Trumbull, the chairman of the Senate judiciary committee, that the admission of Louisiana senators was the best way to bring the state into "proper practical relations with the Union." And since Louisiana had already adopted a free-state constitution, her admission would also provide support for the constitutional amendment prohibiting slavery. [42]

Even without the compromise projected in the reconstruction bill, which by mid-January seemed to have failed, it appeared that the administration would win on the Louisiana question. The situation looked all the more promising when the elections committee voted on January 17 to seat two members-elect from New Orleans. [43] A few days later, however, the Field-

[41] Springfield *Weekly Republican*, Feb. 18, 1865; Boston *Commonwealth*, Mar. 4, 1865.

[42] Lincoln to Nathaniel Banks, Dec. 2, 1864, Lincoln to Lyman Trumbull, Jan. 9, 1865, in *Collected Works of Lincoln*, VIII, 131, 206–207; Hay, *Lincoln and the Civil War*, 246; A. P. Field *et al.* to Nathaniel Banks, Dec. 12, 1864, Banks Papers, Library of Congress; *Cong. Globe*, 38 Cong., 2 sess., 1064 (Feb. 24, 1865), remarks of Sen. James Doolittle.

[43] *The Independent*, Jan. 19, 1865; Philadelphia *Press*, Jan. 10, 1865; Detroit *Free Press*, Jan. 24, 1865; Minutes of the Committee on Elections, House of Representatives, 38 Cong., 2 sess., Jan. 17, 1865, MS, National Archives, RG 233, 34A–D6.9.

Kelley incident occurred, creating ill feeling against the Louisiana bid for recognition.[44] And early in February, Lincoln's 10-per-cent government received another setback when Congress rejected Louisiana's vote in the electoral college, a move which many people considered a decision on the entire question of the validity of the reorganized loyal government. In actuality, this disposition of the issue was not so far-reaching, for before the final vote Lyman Trumbull, the chairman of the judiciary committee, caused the joint resolution on the electoral college to be amended so as to remove the implication that the state was still in insurrection. Trumbull said his purpose was to avoid a decision by Congress on "whether Louisiana is in the Union or out of the Union, whether she is a State or not a State." [45]

Administration supporters chose the Senate rather than the House for their test of Louisiana reconstruction, probably because the admission of senators directly involved the state government and because at least one of the senatorial terms would

[44] The incident involved A. P. Field of Louisiana, who was seeking admission to the House, and William D. Kelley of Pennsylvania. It began when Field, in the company of several Republicans at the Willard Hotel on the evening of January 22, raised the question of Louisiana recognition and specifically accused Kelley of being afraid to face the issue squarely. A heated argument ensued, which ended when Field attacked the Pennsylvania radical with a knife. Opponents of Louisiana reconstruction of course seized on the incident to point up the folly of admitting the reorganized state. Salmon P. Chase wrote to Kelley that the assault "was prompted by the very spirit which, if the blacks are not secured in the right of suffrage, will prompt the most cruel legislation against them, and probably produce a renewal of bloody civil strife" (*Cong. Globe*, 38 Cong., 2 sess., 971 [Feb. 21, 1865]; New York *Tribune*, Jan. 23, 1865; Salmon P. Chase, to William D. Kelley, Jan. 22, 1865, in Warden, *Private Life and Public Services of Salmon P. Chase*, 633).

[45] Washington *Chronicle*, Feb. 8, 1865; Toledo *Blade*, Feb. 9, 1865. Instead of stating that Louisiana and the other rebel states "have continued in a state of armed rebellion for more than three years," the resolution declared that the states "were in such a state of rebellion on the 8th day of November 1864, that no valid election for President and Vice-President of the United States . . . was held therein" (*Cong. Globe*, 38 Cong., 2 sess., 535 [Feb. 1, 1865]).

not expire at the end of the Thirty-eighth Congress. The Senate judiciary committee which considered the matter, had opposed the seating of Arkansas senators in June 1864. Now, however, it advocated the admission of the senators from Louisiana. In doing so, the committee, under Lyman Trumbull's direction, adopted a middle position in the jurisdictional conflict between Congress and the executive. It concluded that the Louisiana government "fairly represents a majority of the loyal voters of the State," thereby vindicating Lincoln's policy, but at the same time it asserted congressional authority over reconstruction by holding that, because Louisiana had been declared to be in a condition of insurrection by act of Congress in 1861, her senators could not be admitted until Congress recognized the reorganized state government. The committee therefore proposed that "the United States do hereby recognize the government of the State of Louisiana inaugurated under and by the convention which assembled on the 6th day of April, A.D. 1864, . . . as the legitimate government of the said State, entitled to the guarantees and all other rights of a State government under the Constitution of the United States." According to Maryland Democrat Reverdy Johnson, "The committee were of opinion that it was not in the power of the Executive under the circumstances to bring the State back. . . . They were of opinion, however, that it was competent for Congress to do so." [46]

Although a majority of the senators favored recognizing Louisiana, a handful of radicals—Sumner, Wade, Zachariah Chandler, Jacob Howard, and B. Gratz Brown—vigorously opposed it. Protesting against executive reconstruction generally as a usurpation of congressional authority, they specifically objected to the failure of the Louisiana constitution to extend voting rights to Negroes; only in doing this, they believed, lay security for the future. Accordingly, Sumner proposed that the

[46] *Senate Reports*, 38 Cong., 2 sess., no. 127, Charles Smith and R. King Cutler, 2–3; 38 Cong., S. Joint Res. 117, Feb. 17, 1865; *Cong. Globe*, 38 Cong., 2 sess., 1096 (Feb. 25, 1865).

resolution admitting Louisiana not take effect "except upon the fundamental condition that within the State there shall be no denial of the electoral franchise, or of any other rights on account of color or race, but all persons shall be equal before the law." [47]

It soon became clear that the opponents of Louisiana would filibuster to prevent a final vote on the resolution reported by the judiciary committee. A climax was reached on Saturday evening, February 25, when Lyman Trumbull attempted to get a final vote and the radicals persisted in blocking it. Tempers flared as Trumbull decried "a determination to browbeat the Senate on the part of a minority," and Sumner accused Trumbull of trying "to cram his resolution down the throats of the Senate," in a manner reminiscent, he said, of Stephen Douglas trying to force the Kansas-Nebraska Bill upon the Senate. Sumner vowed to use "all the instruments . . . in the arsenal of parliamentary warfare" to defeat what he called a "dangerous" measure. By midnight, as one onlooker described the scene, "the majority were losing their temper . . . [and] Mr. Trumbull was becoming demoralized fast." The radicals, with the support of a few conservatives such as Garrett Davis of Kentucky, who opposed the admission of Louisiana with equal ardor because it would help bring about the ratification of the antislavery amendment, had achieved their goal. The Senate adjourned without a final vote on the Louisiana resolution. On Monday, February 27, the radicals sealed their triumph, this time with the help of John Sherman of Ohio. Sherman, the chairman of the Senate finance committee, argued that appropriation bills essential to the operation of the government would be lost if Trumbull insisted on pressing the Louisiana question. Accordingly, though he favored readmitting Louisiana, Sherman moved to put the matter off until December. Seventeen Republicans who had either supported the resolution or been absent during pre-

[47] *Cong. Globe*, 38 Cong., 2 sess., 1099 (Feb. 25, 1865); Boston *Journal*, Mar. 1, 1865, Washington correspondence.

vious votes joined the coalition of radicals and conservatives to postpone the measure, 34 to 12.[48]

Even more ironic than the alignment which brought radicals and conservatives together was the final constitutional position of the former. Persistent critics of executive control of reconstruction, they ended up defending this power against the judiciary committee's assertion of congressional authority. Jacob Howard, for example, in contrast to the judiciary committee, held that it was "for the President . . . to announce to Congress and to the world that the state of insurrection . . . has ceased; and that therefore the rights of the people . . . to be represented in Congress as a loyal people have recurred; . . . We cannot ascertain the fact." So, too, Charles Sumner argued that no rebel state could elect members of Congress "until the President, by proclamation, shall have declared that armed hostility to the Government of the United States within such State has ceased." On behalf of moderates who were trying to maintain the power of Congress while meeting the policy demands of the administration, Lyman Trumbull replied critically that Sumner "would put it in the power of the President to keep out a State forever by refusing to issue his proclamation." Declared Trumbull, "I do not believe in placing any such power in the hands of the President." [49]

So the compromise that had seemed possible in December did not work out: the House Select Committee on the Rebellious States, overestimating its strength and underestimating Lincoln's, failed to secure the revised Wade-Davis Bill, while the administration and its supporters were unable to readmit Louisiana. Later, when President Andrew Johnson and the Republican

[48] *Cong. Globe*, 38 Cong., 2 sess., 1107–1109 (Feb. 25, 1865); 1129 (Feb. 27, 1865); Cincinnati *Daily Commercial*, Mar. 2, 1865.

[49] *Cong. Globe*, 38 Cong., 2 sess., 1429 (Mar. 7, 1865); 1011 (Feb. 23, 1865). Louisiana's senators presented their credentials and sought admission at the special executive session of the Thirty-ninth Congress, which convened directly after the close of the Thirty-eighth, but the Senate did not admit them.

party had become irreconcilably divided over policy toward the rebel states, the failure of the executive and Congress to agree on a plan of reconstruction before the war ended seemed unfortunate indeed.[50] But in the spring of 1865 only a few men felt an urgency in the situation such as would be warranted by subsequent events. Henry Winter Davis, for example, angrily predicted in February 1865, when it was evident that the House would not pass the reconstruction bill, that representatives and senators from the southern states would be in Washington seeking admission upon the opening of the next Congress in December. And should they get that far, said the fiery Marylander, they would "cross the threshhold of the House." Lyman Trumbull felt equally strongly that a resolution of the reconstruction question ought to be achieved before Congress adjourned, but he spoke from the opposite point of view. Proposing to readmit Louisiana, Trumbull urged, "If it is of importance to lay a foundation for the restoration of this Union, for a peace that will be worth having, we must fix it at some time." [51] Few others, however, believed that the situation was quite so urgent or shared the sense of misgiving that committed proponents of either the revised congressional plan or the President's policy felt when Congress adjourned.

Because the revised Wade-Davis Bill had not gone far enough toward ensuring Negro political equality, abolitionists did not regret its failure. Without a provision for full Negro suffrage, wrote Gerrit Smith of the reconstruction bill, its passage "will justify the continued fear that this nation is lost." Overlooking

[50] Isaac Arnold, Illinois Republican and a close friend of Lincoln, wrote in 1866: "Since Mr. Lincoln's death, all who have appreciated the great national misfortune resulting from the separation of President Johnson from the men who elected him Vice-President, and his estrangement from Congress, must deeply regret that this bill, or some bill embodying the views of Congress, did not become a law before the accession of Mr. Johnson to the Presidency" (*The History of Abraham Lincoln and the Overthrow of Slavery* [Chicago, 1866], 475).

[51] *Ibid.*, 969 (Feb. 21, 1865); 1127 (Feb. 27, 1865).

the limited role allowed to Negroes in military service, Smith in a letter to James Ashley said the bill "not only shuts out black men . . . but . . . permits the great mass of disloyal white men to vote." The abolitionist *Independent* saw no harm in postponing the reconstruction question, because "reconstruction on a basis of color instead of simple citizenship . . . [is] undesirable and mischievous." Declaring that Congress "could not rise above the level of the word 'white,' " *The Independent* asserted that it was better to take no action than to take any which was so imperfect as to be unjust. The Boston *Commonwealth* applauded Sumner for preventing the recognition of Louisiana, observing that the result vindicated its own earlier opposition to the compromise bill, and looked with optimism to the organization of the rebel states on the basis of the Declaration of Independence. The Worcester *Daily Spy*, a journal of Massachusetts radicalism, without stopping to regret the failure of the reconstruction bill urged the rejection of Louisiana and pointed out that when the war was over, "the question of reconstruction will assume a magnitude and importance which it has not yet known." [52]

On the other hand, supporters of the administration on the Louisiana question were also sanguine about the future. The New York *Times* did not regard the failure to settle the question of the rebel states as significant, because it held that the "real responsibilities connected with the work of reconstruction rest with the next Congress." The *National Intelligencer* agreed that the problem of reconstruction properly belonged to the next Congress and believed that Lincoln's "wise and simple" policy would be implemented by the return of at least two southern states. The Boston *Journal*, while it would have welcomed the readmission of Louisiana, could see reasons for postponing action on reconstruction. "By another meeting of Congress,"

[52] Gerrit Smith to James Ashley, in *The Liberator*, Feb. 24, 1865; *The Independent*, Mar. 16, 1865; Boston *Commonwealth*, Mar. 11, 1865; Worcester *Daily Spy*, Feb. 24, 1865.

argued the *Journal*, "the path of duty will seem clearer and less obscured by clouds." John Sherman, in the Senate, spoke for most Republicans who favored the Louisiana government but were willing to put the question off, when he said that the Louisiana resolution was not of vital importance.[53]

Both sides in the reconstruction struggle, moreover, were inclined to watch the progress of events before deciding on a definite policy. This really meant waiting to see how the South would react to defeat. The correspondent of *The Independent* wrote that by the time that the next Congress met, "we shall doubtless understand a little better what is the real condition of Louisiana, Arkansas, and Tennessee." It was just as well, therefore, that the reconstruction bill did not pass. The New York *Times* explained that the kind of rule established over the defeated states "must depend largely upon the disposition cherished by the Southern people after active hostilities are over." Similarly, the Boston *Journal* favored letting reconstruction go until the next Congress, when the fighting would be over, "and we can better judge of the temper and loyalty of the people of the South." [54]

With the end of the war imminent and Congress adjourned, Lincoln could look forward to taking the initiative in promoting loyal state governments in the South. Nor was it a situation that many Union men, at least outside Congress, found disagreeable. The New York *Tribune*, which had supported territorial reconstruction in 1862 and the Wade-Davis Bill in 1864, exaggerated only slightly when it stated editorially, after the defeat of the revised reconstruction bill: "It is impossible to foresee and provide for all the contingencies of a clouded future. We . . . simply urge that it cannot now be determined, by any power

[53] New York *Times*, Feb. 28, 1865; *National Intelligencer*, Mar. 4, 6, 1865; Boston *Journal*, Mar. 3, 1865; *Cong. Globe*, 38 Cong., 2 sess., 1127 (Feb. 27, 1865).

[54] *The Independent*, March 2, 1865; New York *Times*, Feb. 28, 1865; Boston *Journal*, Mar. 3, 1865.

less than all-seeing, that other agencies may not be better adapted [than the reconstruction committee's plan] to the state of facts that may be found existing six, three, or even two months, hence." [55]

[55] New York *Tribune*, Feb. 23, 1865.

X

Reconstructing the Union,
April 1865

SIX weeks after Congress adjourned, the war ended, and reconstruction became the central and overriding issue in American politics. Although reconstruction had been a major policy problem for many months, the defeat of the Confederate armies in April 1865 placed it in a new light, from the standpoint of the administration, by raising the question of re-establishing civil government for millions of southerners who would now, according to the verdict of the trial at arms, resume what might be at best only a nominal allegiance to the Union. Lincoln of course wanted to retain the 10-per-cent governments already in existence and hoped that the mode of reconstruction undertaken in Louisiana would establish a pattern for other states to follow; to that extent he had been concerned with the postwar situation. But he also had conceived of reconstruction policy as an adjunct of over-all Union strategy, which prevented him from fully anticipating the postwar situation. In any case the 10-per-cent governments were obviously predicated on wartime conditions: in view of their limited actual jurisdiction, their practical dependence on the Union army, and the small proportion of their populations that was and had been genuinely Unionist, they were provisional governments in fact if not in law, at least as the administration viewed the law. The new circumstances created by Union victory therefore promised a severe test of Lincoln's plan of reconstruction. Hardly had there been time to evaluate the changed conditions, however, when Lincoln's assassination stunned the nation and drastically altered the political situation.

As Union armies drove to final victory in the spring of 1865, Lincoln turned increasingly to problems of peace. After achieving military victory, the President was primarily concerned to restore order and complete reconstruction, which to him meant organizing new governments and getting the states back into their customary relations with the Union.[1] With these objectives, he explored, and in an experimental way initiated, several expedients which, if they were successful, he could support by more direct means, but which, if they were unsuccessful or politically not feasible, he could reject. It is in light of these goals that Lincoln's final actions, some of which were apparently contradictory, must be viewed.

The Sherman-Johnston peace convention, announced three days after the assassination, resulted from initiative taken by Lincoln in the last days of the war. Sherman's terms to the Confederate general were exceedingly liberal, including the recognition of existing southern governments, universal amnesty, the

[1] Alexander K. McClure, a Pennsylvania publisher and politician who was in close touch with the President in the last year of the war, wrote that Lincoln "feared almost universal anarchy in the South when the shattered armies of the Confederacy should be broken up, and, instead of a restoration of peace and industry or anything approaching friendly relations between the Southern people and the government, he anticipated guerilla warfare, general disorder, and utter hopelessness of tranquillity throughout the rebellious States" (*Abraham Lincoln and Men of War-Times* [Philadelphia, 1892], 243). Gideon Welles, in his *Diary* (ed. Beale, II, 279), offered a similar view: "Civil government must be reestablished [Lincoln] said, as soon as possible; there must be courts, and law, and order, or society would be broken up, the disbanded armies would turn into robber bands and guerillas, which we must strive to prevent."

permission to store arms in state arsenals, and a promise of Supreme Court jurisdiction over conflicting claims by rival state governments, as in Louisiana.[2] These terms went far beyond what Lincoln had approved as reconstruction policy, but it is not necessary to accept Sherman's assertion that he was acting on Lincoln's express instructions to believe that the President, when he met with his military commanders at City Point, Virginia, in late March, had urged on them the importance of demobilizing the opposing forces quickly and of effecting peace in a way that would put a stop to the hostilities and disorder that he feared might continue.

It is probable that Lincoln spoke to Sherman about dealing with the existing rebel governments, for this was one of the points raised in a conference the President had shortly before the end of the war with John A. Campbell, the Confederate Secretary of War. On April 5, after the capture of Richmond, Lincoln presented Campbell with the Union's peace terms: the restoration of national authority in all the states, the prohibition of slavery, and the cessation of hostilities upon the disbanding of all rebel forces. In addition, by Campbell's account, Lincoln said that "he had been thinking of a plan for calling the Virginia Legislature, that had been sitting in Richmond, together, and to get them [to] vote for the restoration of Virginia to the Union." Campbell said that Lincoln wished the legislature to recall the Virginia troops from rebel service, but that his main object was to "test its disposition to co-operate with him in terminating the war."[3] Campbell may have exaggerated the scope of Lincoln's intentions, but it is true that the President was considering working through the Virginia legislature. On April 6 he notified

[2] Raoul S. Naroll, "Lincoln and the Sherman Peace Fiasco—Another Fable?" *Journal of Southern History*, XX (Nov. 1954), 459–483; Thomas and Hyman, *Stanton*, 406.

[3] John A. Campbell to J. S. Speed, Aug. 31, 1865, in "Papers of John A. Campbell, 1861–1865," *Southern Historical Society Papers*, n.s., no. 4 (Oct. 1917), 69–71.

General Weitzel, who was in Richmond, that "the gentlemen
who have acted as the Legislature of Virginia, in support of the
rebellion, may now . . . desire to assemble at Richmond, and
take measures to withdraw the Virginia troops, and other support from resistance to the General government." He instructed
Weitzel to give them permission and protection should they
attempt to convene. After Lee's surrender on April 9, Lincoln
pursued the idea further with members of the Cabinet. According to Gideon Welles, Lincoln "wished prominent Virginians
who had the confidence of the people to come together and turn
themselves and their neighbors into good Union men." Fearing
that disbanded rebel armies might turn into guerilla bands, Lincoln wanted them to "undo their own work" and assist in re-
establishing civil government.[4]

Although it might have made sense to try to work through
the established leadership in the South, such an approach was
politically impossible. Republicans in general strongly opposed
recognition or legitimization of rebel authority in any form.
George Julian and other members of the joint Committee on the
Conduct of the War, in Richmond at the time, "were all
thunderstruck" when they learned of Lincoln's order to Weitzel
concerning the Virginia legislature. They were "thoroughly
disgusted," Julian said, "by this display of misguided magna-
nimity." Conservative Union men also objected. Gideon Welles
thought that the government would be embarrassed by recognizing and treating with the rebels, now that it was able to prescribe what should be done. He feared, in addition, that the
former rebels might be encouraged to make terms the government could not accept. The Cabinet as a whole disliked the idea
of letting the Richmond legislature assemble—Secretary of War
Stanton and Attorney General Speed led the opposition—
because it would have amounted to a recognition of rebel
authority. In the face of this critical response Lincoln retreated.

[4] Lincoln to Godfrey Weitzel, Apr. 6, 1865, in *Collected Works of
Lincoln*, VIII, 389; Welles, *Diary*, ed. Beale, II, 279–280.

On April 12 he revoked the instructions to Weitzel concerning
the members of the Virginia legislature and told the Cabinet that
he had perhaps made a mistake and was ready to correct it.[5]

Turning to other expedients, Lincoln authorized Stanton to
prepare a plan for governing Virginia and North Carolina that
would maintain order and enable the federal government to resume operations there. Accordingly, on April 14, Stanton presented a plan for a single military government over both states,
which the Cabinet approved, with the exception of Gideon
Welles, who objected to placing two states under a single government. This violated the traditional rights and individuality of
the states, he said, and was the more objectionable in view of the
existence of the Pierpont government, previously recognized
as the legitimate government of Virginia by the United States.
Lincoln agreed with Welles's criticism and asked Stanton to revise the plan to provide for dealing with the two states sep-
arately. For the rest, however, Lincoln endorsed Stanton's
proposal, describing it as substantially the same as that which
had been discussed in previous Cabinet sessions. That Lincoln
approved the plan, now that his idea for working through the
former rebel leaders had been rejected, is hardly surprising, for
in essence it continued the wartime policy of military government. Stanton's plan was not really intended as a program for
reconstruction—one of the most vital issues, Negro suffrage,
was purposely avoided—but was to be a means of securing the
stability and order that Lincoln saw as the first necessities if a
sound reconstruction was to follow.[6]

The Negro question—the "everlasting" Negro question as

[5] George W. Julian, *Political Recollections*, 254; Welles, *Diary*, ed.
Beale, II, 280; Gideon Welles, *Civil War and Reconstruction*, comp. by
Albert Mordell (New York, 1959), 186–187; Thomas and Hyman,
Stanton, 354–356; Lincoln to Godfrey Weitzel, Apr. 12, 1865, in *Col-
lected Works of Lincoln*, VIII, 406–407.

[6] Frederick W. Seward, *Reminiscences of a War-Time Statesman and
Diplomat, 1830–1915* (New York, 1916), 256–257; Thomas and Hyman,
Stanton, 357–359; Welles, *Civil War and Reconstruction*, 190–193.

conservatives termed it—was of course central to reconstruction. Granting political privileges to the freedmen was part of the problem, but equally important, and perhaps from Lincoln's point of view more urgent, were the physical safety and security of the former slaves—and of the whites with whom they would be living in the South. So great did the difficulties of race relations seem to Lincoln that he was prepared to consider overseas colonization, which he had supported until 1863 but which had failed and been discredited, as at least a partial solution. In conversation with Benjamin F. Butler in early April, Lincoln expressed his fear of a race war in the South. If Negro soldiers went back to the South, Lincoln said, they would "be but little better off with their masters than they were before, and yet they will be free men." As Butler recalled, the President then said: "I fear a race war, and it will be at least a guerilla war because we have taught these men how to fight." There were plenty of people in the North, moreover, who would furnish Negroes with arms if white southerners oppressed them. From this perspective Lincoln suggested the possibility of colonizing Negro soldiers, and responded favorably to Butler's counterproposal to employ them on an overseas canal project. According to Butler, Secretary of State Seward, whom Lincoln wanted Butler to consult about the diplomatic aspects of the project, said he knew the President's anxiety on this score and had heard it expressed several times.[7] Butler's low reputation among historians and the glaring contradiction between exploring colonization and advocating suffrage rights for Negro soldiers, a proposal which Lincoln made a few days later, have kept these statements of Butler from being generally accepted. Yet the fear of violence and of continued fighting was in accord with views Lincoln expressed elsewhere concerning reconstruction. His main objective was to secure peace and order, then to proceed with solving

[7] Benjamin F. Butler, *Autobiography and Personal Reminiscences of Major-General Benjamin F. Butler: Butler's Book* (Boston, 1892), 903–907.

the political problems of the relations between North and South, and if partial colonization could promote these ends, he was willing at least to investigate its possibilities.[8]

Lincoln's last public speech, in which he blended the seemingly contradictory positions of support for the government of Louisiana and flexibility in policies toward other states, was characteristic of his experimental, nondoctrinaire approach to reconstruction at the end of the war. Having opposed the Wade-Davis Bill because it threatened the loyal government in Louisiana, and having maintained this position in the recently completed congressional session, Lincoln was quite thoroughly committed to recognition of the new state government. Too much had been gained, moreover—"nearly all the things the nation wants," said Lincoln—to allow a turning-back in Louisiana. The chief object, therefore, was to restore the state to its relations with the Union, and the question was whether this could be done sooner by supporting or by rejecting the reorganized government. "Concede that the new government of Louisiana is only to what it should be as the egg is to the fowl," the President reasoned, "we shall sooner have the fowl by hatching the egg than by smashing it." Enumerating the objectives that had not been achieved, he cited the failure to extend the franchise to at least some Negroes. "I would myself prefer that it were now conferred on the very intelligent, and on those who serve our cause as soldiers," he declared. He thought that this goal could more easily be reached, however, "by saving the already advanced steps toward it, than by running backward over them."

---

[8] Colonization, historically a means by which slaveholders sought to strengthen the system of slavery by removing free Negroes, hardly seems reconcilable with a genuine regard for the freedmen. Yet it is possible that Lincoln approached colonization from humanitarian considerations. If so, and if the project discussed with Butler had failed, Lincoln might have used federal power to protect Negroes when racial conflict erupted in 1865. On Lincoln's views on colonization, see Paul J. Scheips, "Lincoln and the Chiriqui Colonization Project," *Journal of Negro History*, XXXVII (Oct. 1952), 418–453.

It would be better also, Lincoln added, if the popular base on which the Louisiana government rested were 50,000 rather than only 12,000 citizens.[9]

At the same time Lincoln stressed the importance of a flexible approach toward the other rebel states. Reiterating that he had "presented *a* plan of reconstruction" and had "distinctly stated that this was not the only plan which might possibly be acceptable," he even said that the decision to support Louisiana was not irrevocable. "As to sustaining it [Louisiana], my promise is out," he said, but added, "As bad promises are better broken than kept, I shall treat this as a bad promise, and break it, whenever I shall be convinced that keeping it is adverse to the public interest." For the rest, he felt that "so great peculiarities pertain to each state, and such important and sudden changes occur in the same state; and, withal, so new and unprecedented is the whole case, that no exclusive, and inflexible plan can safely be prescribed as to details and collaterals." Observing that important principles must be adhered to, Lincoln concluded, "In the present '*situation*' . . . it may be my duty to make some new announcement to the people of the South." [10] Taken as a whole, the speech was a masterly interweaving of assurance to supporters of the administration's reconstruction policy that the same course would be pursued, and of concessions to critics of executive reconstruction in the form of support for limited Negro suffrage, a broader popular base for reorganized governments, and a suggestion that changes in reconstruction policy were in the offing.

Lincoln was assassinated before he had charted a definite course for dealing with the new conditions produced by the end of the war. Holding ostensibly to the wartime policy of encouraging 10-per-cent governments, he nevertheless expressly qualified his commitment to this policy and for the time being

[9] Last public address, Apr. 11, 1865, in *Collected Works of Lincoln*, VIII, 403–404.

[10] *Ibid.*, 401–402, 404–405.

attempted to take one approach, then another, in trying to conclude hostilities and create a stable peace. Lincoln's failure to commit himself to a definite policy makes it impossible to say whether Andrew Johnson carried out Lincoln's reconstruction plans, fascinating though the inquiry may be. It is possible, however, to evaluate the situation at Lincoln's death in order to see what had been accomplished in planning for peace and where the United States government seemed to be headed in its efforts to reconstruct the Union.

The changing attitudes of the President and Congress toward reconstruction during the war provide a perspective for such an analysis. After an initial period in 1861 during which restoration of the old Union seemed possible, the leaders of congressional reconstruction endorsed the thoroughly radical alternative of territorialization, then retreated in 1863 to a more moderate solution that respected the existence of the states. Starting from the same premise of restoring the old Union, Lincoln, on the other hand, adopted more radical policies toward the rebel states. Throughout the war, however, the President and Congress were one in extending national power into areas of policy traditionally reserved for the states.

The Crittenden and Johnson resolutions of July 1861, declaring the purpose of the war to be the restoration of the Union with the rights of the states intact and disavowing any intention of subjugating them, expressed the congressional view of reconstruction at the start of the war. At this time Congress cooperated with the President in recognizing the loyal government of Virginia, which had been organized by the Unionist movement in the western part of the state, and saw in this development a method by which other seceded states might be brought back with a minimum of political and social change. James Ashley later said of this period, "If the rebellion had been suppressed at once, if the people in rebellion had laid down their arms, then every gentleman here and all who served with me in the Thirty-Seventh Congress knows very well that they would have been welcomed back to their former positions at once." [11]

As it became clear that Southern Unionism was a negligible force in the rest of the rebel states, however, radical antislavery men such as Ashley, who from the first had sought a thoroughly reconstructed, not a restored Union, won support for their plan to make territorialization the organizing principle of reconstruction. Relying on an understanding shared by some conservatives as well, they reasoned that although the southern states had no right to secede, their acts of rebellion and war had caused their constitutional and political destruction as states, and in law and in fact had reduced them to territories. In March 1862 the House Committee on Territories, under Ashley's chairmanship, reported a reconstruction bill which declared the rebel states destroyed, placed them under territorial governments with boundaries to be determined by the President, and prohibited the proposed territorial governments from passing any act protecting or recognizing slavery. The bill also confiscated rebel property and distributed it to loyal soldiers and citizens, both Negro and white; excluded from political privileges former United States officers, lawyers, and ministers who had supported the rebellion; and prepared the way for the granting of Negro political rights by omitting any racial qualification for suffrage and jury service under the territorial government. Emancipation and confiscation, Ashley later admitted, referring to this reconstruction bill, were "undoubtedly my purpose, and there are today, thousands of thinking men, who now believe that Congress was criminally guilty, because it failed to do this act of prudence and justice." [12] Although a majority of the Republicans supported the bill, a coalition of moderate Republicans and Democrats defeated it in March 1862.

Following this setback, and after military governments created by Lincoln had stirred protest for their policies toward

[11] *Cong. Globe*, 39 Cong., 2 sess., 783 (Jan. 26, 1867).
[12] James M. Ashley to Benjamin W. Arnett, Nov. 1892, in Ashley, *Orations and Speeches*, 361.

Negroes, congressmen concerned with reconstruction brought forward the less radical proposal of Senator Ira Harris of New York. As originally introduced in February 1862, Harris' bill called for territorial governments in the rebel states, with power to deal with "all rightful subjects of legislation"—a formula that authorized interference with slavery. But when the Senate judiciary committee reported it back in July, it had been amended to prohibit interference by the provisional governments with the laws and institutions of the states. Under the influence of Lyman Trumbull and Harris, the committee thus produced a moderate bill proposing genuine interim or transitional governments that would respect the *status quo* in the occupied states. There was of course no express guarantee of slavery (just as there was not in the Crittenden and Johnson resolutions), but the chief purpose of this effort was to assert congressional authority over reconstruction by superseding Lincoln's military governments and to protect free Negroes, not specifically to abolish slavery. Ironically, conservative Democrats killed this moderate measure, which might have provided a basis for cooperation between the executive and Congress on reconstruction. They objected to the territorial form of government as a violation of state rights and feared, despite the bill's amendment, that it would lead to interference with slavery.

Faced with strong opposition to territorialization in any form, Republicans concerned with reconstruction altered their approach in 1863. Rejecting territorialization, they proposed to base reconstruction legislation on the constitutional guarantee of a republican form of government to each state in the Union. This was a change toward moderation for it meant regarding the states as constitutionally still in the Union, though they had been deprived of state governments which the United States could recognize. In policy terms, congressional plans of reconstruction now emphasized the reorganizing of state governments based on new constitutions prohibiting slavery, instead of simply providing interim local government. These changes resulted in part from Lincoln's adoption of a policy of military emancipation, which made territorialization less vital to the antislavery purposes of Congress. But the alteration in theory and policy was anticipated before the Emancipation Proclamation was issued and was a moderate development designed to make congressional reconstruction appeal to a wider range of opinion.

A bill introduced by Senator Ira Harris in February 1863, which closely anticipated the Wade-Davis Bill of the following year, first presented the new solution. Harris provided for a provisional governor in each state, charged with administering civil affairs according to existing state laws, except those relating to slavery. In accordance with the Emancipation Proclamation, Harris required that new state constitutions guarantee the freedom of all persons. His bill also excluded former rebel military and civil officers from voting or holding state office and repudiated all rebel debts. Although these were radical steps not found in earlier legislation, they were more than offset by a major step away from the radicalism of Ashley's bill, in the form of a racial qualification. In Harris' bill and in later reconstruction bills, political rights, and suffrage in particular, would be restricted to white men.

While these new ideas were emerging in the winter of 1862–1863, the effort to initiate a congressional reconstruction policy centered for a short time on a proposal for holding congressional elections in Louisiana and Tennessee. The implications of this approach, namely, that the states were still in the Union and could be represented, even without state governments recognized by the United States, were also contrary to territorial theory. The House passed this moderate bill, but once again conservative Democrats in the Senate, fearful of the extension of federal power into matters reserved traditionally to the states, defeated it. Like Harris' moderate reconstruction bill of July 1862, this measure might have furnished a basis for cooperation between executive and Congress. By the time the Thirty-eighth Congress convened the following winter, however, events had superseded this limited method of beginning reconstruction with Harris' more comprehensive policy of looking to the creation of state governments based on new constitutions prohibiting slavery.

Continuing the attempt to find a congressional solution to the problem, and in part responding to executive actions, the House in December 1863 created a Select Committee on the Rebellious States. Straightaway, James Ashley, a member of the committee, introduced a bill that adhered closely to Harris' plan and that also embodied substantial elements of the plan announced in Lincoln's Proclamation of Amnesty and Reconstruction. The bill which the reconstruction committee reported and Congress passed in July 1864—the Wade-Davis Bill—retained the main features of Ashley's proposal but, taking its political character as a result of reaction to executive reconstruction in Louisiana, was a decidedly antiadministration measure.

The reconstruction committee, under Henry Winter Davis, eschewed the theory of territorialization in favor of a guarantee of republican government. Accordingly, it held that the seceded states had not been destroyed but that their governments had been overthrown and that the states existed in a disorganized condition. The Wade-Davis Bill provided for constitutional conventions to form new state governments, a remedy acceptable to moderates who considered the states still in the Union but out of their proper relation to the federal government, and to radicals who believed that the war had affected the condition of the states in a fundamental way, if it had not reduced them to territorial status. The conditions to be met in forming a new constitution were the prohibition of slavery, the exclusion of high-ranking rebel officers, both state and Confederate, and a repudiation of the rebel debt. These were substantially the same as in Harris' and Ashley's recent bills. The committee made some changes of a more radical nature, for example, insisting on the "iron-clad" oath to determine who would form the new government, requiring approval of a reorganized government by a majority of its citizens, and excluding from United States citizenship high-ranking rebel officers. On the other hand, the Wade-Davis Bill called for the enforcement of existing state laws, except those relating to slavery, and was conservative on the question of Negro political rights, extending suffrage to white men only. The bill was no less radical constitutionally than the early territorial bills in asserting national power over the rebel states. But on balance, being based on the guarantee clause of the Constitution and conceding nothing to Negro political equality (while protecting the freedom of the former slaves by guaranteeing the right of habeas corpus), the bill was sufficiently moderate, in contrast with the territorial committee's bill of 1862, to earn the support of moderate Republicans, whose votes enabled it to pass.

After Lincoln's pocket veto of the Wade-Davis Bill and his election to a second term, congressional strategists on reconstruction temporarily adopted a still more moderate position. In December 1864 the reconstruction committee reported a bill identical to the one passed the previous summer, but with a section recognizing the executive-inspired governments of Louisiana and Arkansas. The President in turn was supposed to approve the reconstruction bill applying to the other seceded states. The revised bill extended voting rights to Negroes in military service, but this was a concession to radical opinion that Lincoln himself would soon go on record as supporting. In January 1865, however, Winter Davis' committee practically reverted to its position of the previous year by making recognition of Louisiana and Arkansas conditional upon their acceptance of certain requirements of the bill. Since Lincoln would accept nothing less than the readmission of Louisiana, and since he could now command the support of a majority of Republicans on this issue, the committee's action eliminated the possibility of compromise. The House voted overwhelmingly to postpone the reconstruction bill in this form, which was tantamount to killing it. Thereafter the reconstruction committee returned to the

Wade-Davis Bill, revised to allow Negro soldiers to vote and amended in other respects in accordance with criticisms by moderate Republicans. Objectively the bill differed little from the Wade-Davis plan, but Lincoln's re-election had so altered the political situation that it was too radical for most Republicans.

After the House reconstruction committee failed to get its bill passed, the Senate judiciary committee failed in its attempt to get Louisiana readmitted, despite the support of a majority of the Senate. A handful of senators, led by the radicals Sumner and Wade, filibustered to prevent the Louisiana resolution from coming to a final vote. Thus at the end of the session, six weeks before the end of the war, most Republicans wanted congressional supervision of reconstruction, either by means of a detailed plan or of a general assertion of minimum principles, as well as recognition of executive reconstruction in Louisiana. But because a minority of conservative Republicans opposed any form of congressional action and because a minority of radicals opposed recognition of Louisiana, no formula for congressional reconstruction could be agreed upon.

In contrast to Congress, President Lincoln adopted more radical positions toward the rebel states and reconstruction, in relation to those he started with, as the war progressed. On the proposition that the Union was perpetual and the states indestructible, Lincoln first sought to restore the pre-existing Union and to this end recognized the Pierpont government as the legitimate government of Virginia. The loyal people were the state, he declared in his special message to Congress of July 4, 1861. When, in the next several months, however, southern Unionism and reconstruction by the loyal population, as in Virginia, proved to be unsuccessful, Lincoln asserted federal power directly to govern occupied rebel states. Acting under the pressure of the congressional attempt to impose territorial governments upon the South, he established military governments in four rebel states in the spring of 1862. Trying to forestall the up-

heaval threatened by territorialization efforts, Lincoln appointed
men inclined to respect the *status quo* with regard to slavery and
charged them, as military governors, to administer the civil
affairs of their states until the citizens could organize local governments. This conservative purpose notwithstanding, the resort
to military government represented a radical extension of federal
authority into the internal affairs of the states. At the same time
Lincoln recommended to Congress a policy of compensated
emancipation, in response to antislavery pressures that were becoming irresistible. He was beginning to depart from the policy
of restoring the old Union with the pre-existing powers of the
states intact. The Emancipation Proclamation of January 1,
1863, marked a decisive change in this respect, for at the least it
meant that the states would lose their power to protect slavery.
What else it might mean, with regard to the growth of national
power, for example, also became an open question.

In the winter of 1862–1863 Lincoln tried to promote the
reorganization of state governments by holding congressional
elections, and succeeded in getting two Louisiana representatives
admitted to the House. He soon moved beyond this limited
approach, however, and encouraged the creation of new state
governments in accordance with the Emancipation Proclamation. Specifically Lincoln urged the forming of new state constitutions prohibiting slavery, which were the chief demand of
the leading antislavery men; he was therefore taking the radical
approach to reconstruction at this time. Throughout 1863, Lincoln followed this pattern. He supported the efforts of radical
Unionists in Louisiana to hold a constitutional convention, and
in December 1863 issued a Proclamation of Amnesty and Reconstruction which incorporated many of the radical ideas that
had developed up to that time. Though he had exempted parts
of several rebel states from the effect of the Emancipation
Proclamation, trying to induce them to return to the Union, in
his proclamation on reconstruction Lincoln made emancipation a
condition of readmission for all the states. Further, a loyalty test

would be required of all persons who wished to take part in the reorganization of state government, irrespective of past loyalties. This plainly refuted the earlier notion that those who had remained loyal constituted the state, and to some southern Unionists seemed to put all the citizens of a state, loyal and disloyal, into a kind of alien-enemy category. The President also excluded leading Confederate officers from amnesty. On the other hand, he said he would recognize governments approved by only 10 per cent of the 1860 electorate. While often cited as an illustration of Lincoln's generous and liberal spirit toward the South, the 10-per-cent plan was primarily intended as a means of weakening the rebellion by providing a rallying point for Unionist sentiment and action.

Throughout 1864, Lincoln maintained this reconstruction policy. In December he contemplated further concessions to radical views—a compromise by which he would approve the Wade-Davis Bill in return for congressional recognition of the Louisiana and Arkansas governments. The reconstruction committee withdrew the compromise offer, however, and the House went on to defeat the revised Wade-Davis Bill. Though it was more radical than his own plan, Lincoln was willing to sign the bill if he could get Louisiana into the Union at the same time. He wanted to make a start, to establish a precedent for the other states vindicating executive power, and to trust to his influence with Congress, reconstruction legislation notwithstanding.

Though he issued no further proclamations on reconstruction, Lincoln clarified his position on certain points that warrant consideration in evaluating the situation at his death. Of first importance was his endorsement of limited Negro suffrage. In August 1863, Lincoln authorized the enrollment of all loyal citizens in Louisiana, without regard to color. In his December proclamation, however, he introduced a racial qualification, limiting participation in reconstruction to persons eligible to vote in 1860. But in March 1864, in a letter to the governor of the new loyal government in Louisiana, he moved in the opposite direction, suggesting that intelligent Negroes and those in military service be allowed the suffrage. In discussing the proposed compromise on reconstruction in December 1864, Lincoln declared that he was opposed to universal enfranchisment of freedmen, not to a limited suffrage for certain classes of them. And in his last public address he declared himself in favor of suffrage for the "very intelligent" freedmen and those who had served in the military.

Second, though he believed that reconstruction was largely an executive function, especially during the war, Lincoln consistently recognized the part Congress would play. At the very least Congress held the power of decision in readmitting states. Accordingly, as Isaac Arnold expressed it, Lincoln regarded a 10-per-cent government as "a permissive, subordinate Government . . . requiring the action of Congress, before [it] would be entitled to resume its former relations, and be entitled to representation in Congress and to vote in the electoral college." [13] Related to this understanding were Lincoln's concern to avoid commitment to a single, inflexible plan of reconstruction and his view that his was only one possible approach to the problem. Having practically invited Congress to evolve a plan in his message of December 1863, Lincoln pocket-vetoed it, but he did so because it would have bound the government to a single plan (in addition to undermining the Louisiana government), not because he thought Congress had no power to legislate on reconstruction. In the last winter of the war there were several suggestions of a change in administration policy, such as Lincoln's appointment of a commission to investigate the administration of civil affairs in Louisiana, his statement that the door of amnesty probably would be closed, and the tentative agreement to a compromise with Congress. And the last thing Lincoln said in public about reconstruction was that he was considering making a new announcement to the people of the South.

At Lincoln's death the differences between the administration

[13] Arnold, *The History of Abraham Lincoln and the Overthrow of Slavery*, 652–653.

and Congress stood out most sharply, for of utmost significance when Andrew Johnson assumed office was the deadlock on this now paramount issue between the two political branches of the government. There were, nevertheless, similarities in the positions of Lincoln and the planners of congressional reconstruction. There was a split, but it was not complete and irreconcilable.

The constitutional situation of the rebel states was a difficult question which Lincoln sought to avoid but on which he in effect took a position substantially the same as that of the congressional plan. After arguing for territorialization or "state suicide," the reconstruction committee retreated to the guarantee of republican government, according to which the states, though disorganized, were in the Union. A middle ground was necessary, from which the right of secession could be denied and the states seen as still in the Union (territorialization seemed to concede something to the secession argument), yet which would also accommodate the view that the war had caused a change in the condition of the states. The Wade-Davis Bill and subsequent variations of it fulfilled these requirements. In his own imprecise and indirect way Lincoln came essentially to the same conclusion. Starting with the proposition that the states could have no other legal status than that of members of the Union—a doctrine of state indestructibility, in other words—he later conceded, in effect, that they were something less than full-fledged states in possession of their usual powers. By referring, in his Proclamation of Amnesty and Reconstruction, to the subversion of, and need to re-establish or create state governments, Lincoln took the stand that states could exist without republican governments. He placed the states in the same limbo-like condition when he said in his last speech that reconstruction must begin with "disorganized and discordant elements."

On the other hand, though eager to establish that the rebel states were in some sense still in the Union, both the President and Congress wished to assert an unprecedented degree of national power over them. They were equally radical on this constitutional issue. Military government over an American state was as inconsistent with state rights as territorialization would have been, and when General Banks told the citizens of Louisiana that martial law was the law of the state, he illustrated the point. In Congress, meanwhile, Union men derived as much power from the clause guaranteeing republican government as they had from the territorial principle, or as the executive found in the military role of commander-in-chief. The United States had plenary power over the rebel states, said Henry Winter Davis, and few Republicans doubted it.

On the Negro question there were many shades of opinion within the Republican party, and the issue was anything but settled. Yet at the end of the war the President and Congress— including the radical-led Select Committee on the Rebellious States—had gone the same distance in meeting the challenge created by emancipation. Congress had passed, and the President had signed, the Freedmen's Bureau bill, and while they had not gone very far toward the granting of Negro political equality, they had traveled an equal distance along this road. Although a number of radicals desired universal suffrage, the most that the reconstruction committee would agree to was voting rights for Negroes in military service. Congress did not approve the revised reconstruction bill containing this modicum of Negro suffrage, but it was not this but the failure to recognize Louisiana which the Republican majority opposed. Lincoln meanwhile went on record in favor of the same degree of Negro suffrage. True, he was talking about a single state, Louisiana, which had had an unusually large free Negro population before the war.[14] But an endorsement of limited voting rights such as Lincoln made in his last address would have been hard to confine to a single state, in view of the growing demand among Republicans for some form of Negro suffrage.

[14] Ludwell H. Johnson, "Lincoln and Equal Rights: A Reply," *Civil War History*, XIII (March 1967), 71.

Both Lincoln and the reconstruction committee displayed a degree of ambivalence toward rebel leaders and the possibility of dealing with them in establishing peace. At one point in February 1865 the House committee on reconstruction proposed recognizing the rebel states if they would give up the fight and ratify the antislavery amendment to the Constitution. "Some gentlemen think it strange that such a section should emanate from me," James Ashley said of this proposal. Nevertheless, he explained, his objective was to secure stable governments and sustain the executive amnesty proclamation, which similarly was aimed at getting the rebels to quit the war. In this way, Ashley said, "the President may lawfully and rightfully treat with them [rebel officials] and recognize them as the existing government." [15] A few months later Lincoln had much the same idea when he authorized members of the rebel Virginia legislature to meet. At the least they would facilitate the withdrawal of troops, and possibly take part in the settlement of reconstruction issues.

On the other hand, inconsistent with the idea of working through the established leadership of the South was the disposition of the President and Congress to exclude former rebels from political activity. Here the stronger passions of radical congressmen caused the congressional plan of reconstruction to be harsher than Lincoln's, going so far as to bar from United States citizenship top Confederate and state officers, while the executive plan denied amnesty only to high-ranking Confederate officials. Yet the rationale in each case was to guarantee safety for the future—in Lincoln's words, "to separate the opposing elements, so as to build only from the sound." By the end of the war the reconstruction committee had agreed to drop the exclusion-from-citizenship clause, though the "iron-clad" oath still barred more former rebels from reconstruction than did the presidential plan. The advent of peace, however, might have

15 *Cong. Globe,* 38 Cong., 2 sess., 969 (Feb. 21, 1865).

lessened the difference between the two plans even more in this respect. Amnesty, a means of weakening the rebellion in wartime, could be a means of bringing about the political security Union men desired in peacetime. Lincoln was kind and generous, but, as he suggested in his message of December 1864, he might have been more stringent in granting amnesty and pardon after the war. So despite differences in degree, the President and Congress broadly agreed on the need to exclude top rebels from reconstruction, if to deal with them directly was politically impossible.

This does not mean that Lincoln and Congress or the Select Committee on the Rebellious States saw eye to eye on reconstruction. A majority of Republicans in Congress would admit Louisiana but might demand something more with regard to other states, and though unable to secure appropriate legislation, wanted Congress to supervise, or set general standards for, reconstruction. The reconstruction committee, for its part, at the close of the session supported a bill that was in many respects harsher toward the South than the executive plan. The chief difference, however, was that Lincoln designed his plan as an element of wartime strategy, while the reconstruction committee shaped its plan for the postwar situation. Once the war ended, therefore, some of the specific points of contrast appeared in a different light. For example, Lincoln would recognize state governments based on as few as 10 per cent of the white electorate, while the reconstruction committee insisted on governments supported by a majority of the enrolled white citizens and Negro soldiers. This was a great difference, but with the end of the war it lost much of its significance. The reorganized governments in Louisiana and Arkansas rested on slender popular bases and depended mainly on the military for support. Not possessing constitutional legitimacy because they had not been recognized by Congress, it was doubtful that they would possess political legitimacy either. That is, it was questionable whether they would be able to withstand the opposition that would be almost certain to emerge against them when the mass of white southerners returned to allegiance and found men running their states who had been loyal to the Union during the war. In this context congressional warnings that 10 per cent of the people could not rule the majority took on added significance. Lincoln at the end of the war renewed his pledge to Louisiana, but not to Arkansas, and it is not unlikely that he would have accepted the majority-rule requirement for other states, as indeed Andrew Johnson did when he faced the postwar situation.

Related to the question of 10 per cent versus 50 per cent was the loyalty-oath problem. The presidential plan required only a prospective oath; the reconstruction committee's plan required the prospective oath of a majority of the enrolled citizens before the rebuilding process could begin, but also the "iron-clad" oath of those who would vote for, or be delegates to, a constitutional convention. This was a substantial difference, but again one that the end of the war placed in a different light. For just as it would be difficult to maintain the 10-per-cent feature of the executive plan, so would it be difficult to insist on the "iron-clad" oath. If the attempt were made "to discriminate the loyal from the disloyal and exclude from voting all who have given aid and comfort to the rebellion," Henry Winter Davis wrote in May 1865, in what amounted to a description of the "iron-clad" oath, "a mere handful of the population will remain, wholly incompetent to form or maintain a State government." [16] Rigid application of the "iron-clad" oath was thus not a practicable means of guaranteeing political security during reconstruction. The next logical step, from the Republican point of view, was to balance former rebels with former slaves, that is, enfranchise the freedmen in proportion to the number of former rebels permitted to enjoy political rights. Here, then, was another key difference between the executive plan and the plan of the reconstruction

[16] Henry Winter Davis to Edward McPherson, May 27, 1865, McPherson Papers, Library of Congress.

committee which appeared less significant once the war was over.

A more substantial difference between Lincoln and the planners of congressional reconstruction was evident in a jurisdictional conflict: Was reconstruction a subject for legislative or for executive action? Neither branch saw the problem as exclusively its own but rather as a question of which had the greater constitutional authority to shape policy toward the seceded states. Viewing this authority in relation to over-all Union strategy, Lincoln considered it fundamentally an executive function. Although in December 1861 he was willing to turn the problem of administering justice in occupied areas over to Congress, he soon altered his approach to reconstruction issues and treated them as within the sphere of executive power. And although on numerous occasions he acknowledged the power of Congress to decide whether states could be readmitted—leading Isaac Arnold to conclude "that in his [Lincoln's] judgment, whether the people of a State which had been in rebellion were in a condition to be represented in Congress, and take part in the Government, and upon what terms they should be represented, was a question for the determination of Congress"—there is no evidence that Lincoln was prepared to allow the initiative in reconstruction to pass to Congress.[17] In December 1864 he was even willing to sign a reconstruction bill if it included recognition of Louisiana, confident that he could still control the process in the other states. He did not question the authority of Congress to legislate on reconstruction, but he was sure of his own authority and wanted to remain in control of federal policy. Hence the significance of Louisiana; he continued to support it in April 1865, because by getting it recognized, he would establish a precedent and retain the initiative, even if policy toward the other states might differ in certain details in response to pressures within the party and in Congress. And that

[17] Arnold, *Lincoln and the Overthrow of Slavery*, 654.

was why, at his last Cabinet meeting, Lincoln said that he was glad the war had ended when it did, so that he could deal with reconstruction without interference from Congress.[18]

On the other hand, the Select Committee on the Rebellious States, and Congress as a whole, regarded reconstruction as a legislative question. The prosecution of the war was basically an executive task, the efforts of the joint Committee on the Conduct of the War notwithstanding, but the reorganization of new state governments and their restoration to the Union was fundamentally a matter for Congress. This constitutional understanding was present from the start of the war, even among Republican moderates like Ira Harris of New York and Henry L. Dawes of Massachusetts, who did not differ with the administration's slavery policy. It formed the basis for the election committee's bill of 1863 providing for congressional elections in two rebel states, which was intended to supersede executive with congressional authority over reconstruction, and for the Wade-Davis Bill of 1864, which had the same purpose. At the close of Congress in March 1865 a majority of Republicans wanted to admit Louisiana, but they also wanted to assert congressional control over reconstruction. The power to guarantee republican government to each state and the power to judge the elections and qualifications of its own members were the specific foundations on which Congress claimed to supervise the process. Congressional partisans recognized that the President enjoyed an advantage in initiating policy, and they sometimes applauded him, as when he issued the Proclamation of Amnesty and Reconstruction. But they firmly upheld the power of Congress "to alter, revise, or supplement his work," as Edward L. Pierce, the friend and biographer of Sumner, put it.[19] This constitutional understanding was evident during Lincoln's administration and

[18] Nicolay and Hay, *Abraham Lincoln*, X, 283; Welles, *Civil War and Reconstruction*, 190–191.

[19] Edward L. Pierce, *Enfranchisement and Citizenship: Addresses and Papers*, ed. A. W. Stevens (Boston, 1896), 151.

later provided a link between radical and moderate Republicans when opposition to President Johnson's policies developed in 1866.

Although Lincoln and the reconstruction committee in effect placed the rebel states in the same constitutional limbo, their attitudes toward the states were also a source of conflict within the party. Lincoln thought that whether the states had been in or out of the Union during the war was immaterial; more important was getting them back into their relations with the Union. This image of Lincoln—as the practical, nondoctrinaire statesman cutting away constitutional abstractions to get to the heart of the matter—has always seemed appealing and persuasive. Yet there were many Union men for whom the issue which Lincoln consciously tried to avoid had profound implications. To say, as Lincoln did, that the condition of the states was irrelevant was to overlook an entire dimension of the conflict. Secession was illegal and could not be permitted; but to stop at that and not answer the question, What was the status of the states? was to overlook their acts of rebellion and war. All Republicans agreed on the need to get the states back into their places in the Union, but many wanted to establish clearly the condition of the states, since that related to the origins of the war and was a way of placing responsibility for the conflict. Edward McPherson, during the war a Republican representative from Pennsylvania, dwelt on this very problem in discussing reconstruction in late 1865. "I believe it is the sentiment of his best friends, as it will be the judgment of history," McPherson wrote of Lincoln, "that with all his noble qualities of head and heart, and all his patriotic devotion to the cause of his country, he never came up to his duty, in holding rebels responsible for the consequence of their own acts, and in no case did he more unfortunately fail, than in recognizing, in theory, the doctrine of State indestructibility, while he was obliged, every day, to repudiate it in his practice." [20]

[20] Edward P. McPherson, "Reconstruction of Rebel States," 3, MS, McPherson Papers, Library of Congress.

The status of the states was important because it involved the very nature of the war. But it was also important for practical reasons. For if the states were considered to be in the Union, without qualification, a strong case could be made for letting them resume their former positions and powers. Foremost among the powers that many Republicans wanted to withhold for the time being was the states' traditional power over civil rights in general and citizenship and suffrage in particular.[21] But Lincoln's failure to clarify the condition of the rebel states made this effort more difficult. Edward McPherson believed that had there been a clear statement of the position of the states, explaining that if defeated they would lose all political rights as states, "every emergency, not only of the war, but of subsequent reconstruction, would have been fully provided for, so that loyal men could have given a sound reason for every necessary measure attending either; which, upon the hypothesis of State indestructibility, they cannot do." [22]

The most significant difference between Lincoln and elements in Congress, though not Congress in general, concerned fundamental aims. All Republicans wanted guarantees for the future: they wanted to ratify the antislavery amendment, protect the freedom of the former slaves to the extent necessary to make that freedom meaningful, and prevent a resurgence of southern political power that would threaten the Republican party itself. Lincoln supported these aims, and most Republicans in turn supported his goal of achieving, within this framework, a rapid reconstruction with as little social and economic dislocation and disruption as possible. The radical wing of the party, however, definitely wanted something more—in short, a revolution in the social, political, and economic life of the South. These men—Ashley, Stevens, Sumner, Wade, Chandler, Julian,

[21] See, for example, Richard H. Dana, Jr., *Speech at Faneuil Hall . . . to Consider the Subject of Reorganization of the Rebel States* (Boston, 1865), 2; and Joseph P. Thompson, *Abraham Lincoln: His Life and Its Lessons . . .* (New York, 1865), 35.

[22] McPherson, "Reconstruction," 3-4.

Beaman, and others, numbering about twenty-five in the House and less than ten in the Senate—hoped to break up the southern plantation system, distribute land to the freedmen, exclude former rebels from politics, and enfranchise the former slaves. Clearly, these goals were incompatible with Lincoln's. Yet, small in number and themselves not agreed on specific measures to achieve their goals, the radicals did not control Congress.[23] They had managed to defeat Louisiana recognition and would exert pressure on the administration in an attempt to secure at least some form of Negro suffrage and keep former rebels out of Congress. But their reconstruction bill had not passed, and whether they would exercise much influence in the future depended largely on how the South would adapt itself to defeat and the changes it produced. Ben Butler revealed the weakness of the radicals when he wrote to Ben Wade in July 1865, "The most vivid hope I have is that the rebels will behave so outrageously as to awaken the Government and the North once more out of the dream of brotherly union where brotherly love is not." [24] Finally, the response of the South to the postwar situation would depend in large measure on the reconstruction policy of the President in the long interval before the next Congress convened.

Though personally shocked and aggrieved by Lincoln's death, politically the radicals considered the event a stroke of good fortune. Having struggled throughout the war to get Lincoln to move at a faster pace, yet having found that he remained master

[23] W. R. Brock, *An American Crisis: Congress and Reconstruction, 1865–1867* (London, 1963), 66–69; Joseph B. James, *The Framing of the Fourteenth Amendment* (Urbana, Ill., 1956), 11; Eric McKitrick, *Andrew Johnson and Reconstruction* (Chicago, 1960), 54; LaWanda and John H. Cox, *Politics, Principle, and Prejudice, 1865–1866* (New York, 1963), 208; David Donald, "Devils Facing Zionwards," in Grady McWhiney, ed., *Grant, Lee, Lincoln, and the Radicals* (Evanston, Ill., 1964), 72–91.

[24] Benjamin F. Butler to Benjamin F. Wade, July 26, 1865, Wade Papers, Library of Congress.

of the political situation even when he gave in to their demands, as he did on emancipation, the radicals saw in Andrew Johnson a committed enemy of the rebellion who would be a more willing agent for their purposes. Consequently, they welcomed him and expressed relief, if not satisfaction, that Lincoln was no longer President. According to George Julian, the radicals "regarded his death as a providential means of saving the country." Henry L. Dawes wrote to his wife the day after Lincoln's assassination, "Would you think it possible for men of our own party to say that they are *glad* he [Johnson] is there. I have heard it more than once today! Such is the madness and fury of men." [25]

Radical well-wishing for Johnson was effusive. Ben Wade and members of the joint Committee on the Conduct of the War, on which Johnson had served, were confident of the influence they would wield. "Johnson, we have faith in you," Wade said. "By the gods, there will be no trouble now in running the government!" James Ashley, who trusted Johnson so much that he expressly urged him not to call a special session of Congress, wrote, "The prayer of every loyal heart in the nation is, that God will bless, preserve, and keep you from all harm." B. Gratz Brown of Missouri, assuring Johnson of his "most zealous support," said, "God in His providence has called you to complete the work of rebuilding this nation that it might be stamped with the idea of radical democracy in all its parts." Since Johnson denounced treason in the most radical terms, he seemed especially reliable on the question of policy toward former rebels. From Missouri, Charles Drake, urging that martial law was necessary for protection against a resurgence of rebellion, wrote to Johnson, "I cannot allow myself to believe that one who knows rebels as well as you do, will consent to withdraw it from us." Even Henry Winter Davis, who was more skeptical

[25] "George W. Julian's Journal—The Assassination of Lincoln," ed. Grace Julian Clarke, *Indiana Magazine of History*, XI (Dec. 1915), 337; Henry L. Dawes to Electa Dawes, Apr. 16, 1865, Dawes Papers, Library of Congress.

than other radicals about the new President's personal qualities, felt that "Johnson if sober will bring a very different spirit into the dealings with the rebels." On the issue of Negro suffrage, too, Johnson gave the appearance of supporting at least some degree of radicalism. Salmon P. Chase, now Chief Justice of the Supreme Court but still heavily involved in Republican politics, prepared a public address for Johnson to deliver in which he had the new President declare his support of Negro citizenship and suffrage. Johnson did not take Chase's advice, but after the two talked it over in late April, the Chief Justice said he "almost hoped the President's reluctance was conquered and that the new and crowning proclamation would be issued securing equal and universal suffrage in reorganization." In mid-May, Wade and Sumner reassured a meeting of Republicans that Johnson was in favor of Negro suffrage and was not in danger of coming under conservative influence on this score.[26]

But the honeymoon between Johnson and the radicals ended when the President, on May 29, 1865, issued a proclamation on North Carolina reconstruction which excluded Negroes from suffrage. Profoundly disappointed, the radicals did not give up relying on him or start opposing the administration, but their disenchantment with him began. And the more it grew, as Johnson liberally pardoned former rebels, allowed them to hold political office, and recognized their governments and the black codes which they enacted, the more the radicals were willing to reassess Lincoln's value to the party and the Union cause. In short, the worse the situation under Johnson, the better it seemed to have been under Lincoln.

[26] Julian, *Political Recollections*, 255; James M. Ashley to Andrew Johnson, Apr. 15, 1865, B. Gratz Brown to Johnson, Apr. 17, 1865, Andrew Johnson Papers, ser. 1, Library of Congress; Henry Winter Davis to S. F. Du Pont, Apr. 15, 1865, S. F. Du Pont Papers, Eleutherian Mills Historical Library; Draft of an Address to the People of the United States, Apr. 16, 1865, Johnson Papers, ser. 1, Library of Congress; Chase, *Inside Lincoln's Cabinet*, 271–272; Julian, *Political Recollections*, 263; correspondence of the Boston *Advertiser*, in Cincinnati *Gazette*, June 23, 1865.

James Ashley demonstrated the typical results of this intellectual process in an address many years later to the Ohio Republican League. Though not denying that the radical wing of the party opposed the authority with which Lincoln proposed to reorganize the southern state governments, Ashley insisted, "Through all these earnest discussions [with Lincoln], sometimes waxing warm, as they of necessity did, there never was any estrangement between us, nor an unkind act to be recalled or regretted." Ashley was sure that "had Mr. Lincoln lived he would eventually have adopted the views held by a majority of the Republicans in Congress." Even Henry L. Dawes, more critical than most of his colleagues, could write that Congress, including the radicals, "never doubted Lincoln" with regard to securing the gains of the freedmen. "But in his successor," wrote Dawes, completely overlooking the initial enthusiasm for Johnson, "there was never from the beginning any such confidence." [27]

Such assessments of Lincoln owe a good deal to the passage of time and are not the most reliable authority for understanding the relationship between Lincoln and the Republican party. Yet they were not constructed out of whole cloth. At the time of his death many Republicans, radicals included, thought that Lincoln was becoming more radical on the crucial issue of Negro suffrage and were confident that in matters affecting reconstruction in general he would respond to pressures generated within the party, as he had during the war. Salmon P. Chase, a leading advocate of equal voting rights, was encouraged after Lincoln's speech of April 11 because "he at length openly avow[ed]" his support for limited Negro suffrage. Chase subsequently wrote to Theodore Tilton, editor of *The Independent*, that in his last conference with Lincoln about suffrage for the freedmen of the South, "he [Lincoln] was nearer right on this subject, according to my views of right, . . . than on any other day before." At-

[27] James M. Ashley, "Abraham Lincoln," *Magazine of Western History*, XIV (May, 1891), 31; Henry L. Dawes, "Recollections of Stanton under Johnson," *Atlantic Monthly*, LXXIV (Oct. 1894), 498–499.

torney General J. S. Speed told Chase that at the last Cabinet
meeting Lincoln had "never [before] seemed so near our views,"
and Secretary of War Stanton was similarly encouraged to believe that the President was beginning to appreciate the need for
Negro suffrage. Many abolitionists also, remembering Lincoln's
progress in taking action against slavery, anticipated his conversion to a policy of supporting Negro suffrage. Wendell Phillips
told the Massachusetts Anti-Slavery Society in January: "I have
no doubt, any more than the most sanguine among us, that if the
same pressure could be continued upon the administration which
we have enjoyed hitherto, and which has made 1864 out of
1861, we should compel liberty out of the present aspect of
affairs." Lydia Maria Child wrote to George Julian a few days
before the assassination, "I think we have reason to thank God
for Abraham Lincoln. With all his deficiencies, it must be admitted that he has grown continually." Though Charles Sumner
criticized the lack of a disposition in Lincoln to accept general
principles and follow them logically, he admitted, "The more I
have seen of the Prest the more his character in certain respects
has risen." A few months later Sumner wrote in reference to
Johnson's reconstruction program, "I cannot believe that Prest
Lincoln, if alive & seeing the anarchy & insecurity which it en-
tails & its defiance of just principles, would have given his hand
to any such policy." Describing the slain President's funeral
procession, George Julian remarked on Lincoln's hold on the
Negroes "and indeed on the whole country, including even
those who regarded his death as a providential means of saving
the country." [28]

[28] Chase, *Inside Lincoln's Cabinet,* 265–268; Boston *Commonwealth,*
May 20, 1865; Thomas and Hyman, *Stanton,* 355; McPherson, *Struggle
for Equality,* 314; Lydia Maria Child to George W. Julian, Apr. 8, 1865,
Giddings-Julian Papers, Library of Congress; Boston *Commonwealth,*
Feb. 18, 1865; Charles Sumner to Salmon P. Chase, Apr. 12, 1865, Chase
Papers, ser. 2, Library of Congress; Sumner to Henry L. Dawes, July 20,
1865, Dawes Papers, Library of Congress; "George W. Julian's Journal,"
ed. Clarke, *Indiana Magazine of History,* XI, 337.

Not Lincoln as a "Moses with commandments" moved by a "questing spirit," as one historian has written,[29] but Lincoln as head of the Republican party, concerned to maintain its institutional existence, unity, and power, provides the best key to an understanding of the situation at the end of the war. The Republican party, founded only eleven years before as a single-issue organization, had fought the war for Union and emancipation and in April 1865 was in the process of committing itself to an additional objective—the safety and welfare of the former slaves. How far the party would go on this issue, whether it would stop with a guarantee of the privilege of the writ of habeas corpus or go on to guarantee equal civil rights and perhaps political equality, was precisely the question. Lincoln did not favor universal suffrage, but on the other hand he was committed to protecting the freedom of the Negro and preventing his virtual re-enslavement. Between these two extremes there was much room to maneuver, but that Lincoln and the party in Congress would remain united in working out a solution was the opinion of many contemporaries. Isaac Arnold felt justified in concluding, on the basis of Lincoln's "whole administration, from the tone of his proclamation on the [Wade-Davis] bill, from his uniformly kind, courteous and respectful treatment of Congress, . . . that there would have been no division between Congress and himself" concerning reconstruction. Even congressional insistence on the "iron-clad" oath was not an impediment, according to Arnold, because while Lincoln did not say, " 'Rebels must take the back seats,' . . . he placed loyal men in the front seats." "No man ever received office from him who could not take the 'Iron clad oath,' " Arnold asserted. George Julian later wrote, "It was forgotten in the fever and turbulence of the moment [i.e., the assassination], that Mr. Lincoln, who was never an obstinate man, and who in the matter of

[29] Harold M. Hyman, "Lincoln and Equal Rights for Negroes; The Irrelevancy of the 'Wadsworth Letter,'" *Civil War History*, XII (Sept. 1966), 266.

his Proclamation of Emancipation had surrendered his own judgment under the pressure of public opinion, would not have been likely to wrestle with Congress and the country in a mad struggle for his own way." The characteristic that Julian described—Lincoln's interest in party unity—also impressed George Boutwell. It "may not be amiss to look at Mr. Lincoln as a politician and partisan," Boutwell pointed out in retrospect. "These he was, first of all and always. He had political convictions that were ineradicable, and they were wholly partisan." Hugh McCulloch, the conservative Secretary of the Treasury at the time of the assassination, thought Lincoln would have favored a constitutional amendment indirectly enfranchising the freedmen by requiring that representation be based on the number of eligible voters. More important, McCulloch believed that Lincoln "would not have quarreled with his party," and, commanding the confidence of the people, "could, therefore, have given direction to reconstructive legislation." [30]

At the end of the war the executive and Congress were deadlocked on reconstruction, but they were not split as Johnson and Congress were to be a year later. A basic conflict existed between executive and congressional understanding of constitutional power over reconstruction, as well as a conflict between Lincoln's objectives and those of the radical wing of the party. But this did not mean that adjustment and accommodation were impossible. The President and Congress, including the Select Committee on the Rebellious States, almost reached an accord in December 1864, when the issue was not yet paramount and there was more room to maneuver than there would be later. Lincoln was under no illusion about the radicals but was prepared to deal with them on the basis of concrete proposals, not of deep-seated motivations. When Montgomery Blair de-

[30] Arnold, *Lincoln and the Overthrow of Slavery*, 474–475, 655; Julian, *Political Recollections*, 256; George S. Boutwell, *The Lawyer, the Statesman and the Soldier* (New York, 1887), 126; A. T. Rice, ed., *Reminiscences of Lincoln*, 421–422.

nounced the proposed compromise of December 1864 as a radical plot to undermine the President's position, Lincoln told him, "It is much better not to be led from the region of reason into that of hot blood, by imputing to public men motives which they do not avow." [31] The radicals were unwilling to compromise at that time but after Congress adjourned, they were in a weaker position, for the initiative clearly lay with the President, who could determine the influence the radical wing of the party would have by his leadership and guidance of the South. It is in this respect that Andrew Johnson was too successful for his own good: he took the initiative, but his policy allowed the outrageous acts to occur that some radicals had predicted would be necessary if they were to have more influence on the course of reconstruction. It is difficult to believe that Lincoln, committed to the welfare and unity of the Republican party, to the maintenance of national power, and to minimum guarantees of Negro freedom, would have allowed such action as the promulgation of the black codes and the violent intimidation and injury of Negroes and Unionists to go unchecked, all of which destroyed the possibility of reconciliation that had existed at the end of the war. Wartime planning for reconstruction had not produced a definitive solution, but the President and Congress had arrived at certain understandings concerning party, national power, and minimum guarantees for the freedmen from which a solution could have emerged.

[31] John Hay, *Lincoln and the Civil War*, 246.

A Bibliographical Essay

THE best one-volume work on the Civil War, James G. Randall and David Donald, *The Civil War and Reconstruction* (2d ed.; Boston, 1961), also contains the best critical guide to the literature in this field. The present bibliographic listing, needless to say, is selective.

Government Documents

Manuscripts

The legislative branch of the National Archives maintains a file of original bills and resolutions introduced into the Thirty-seventh and Thirty-eighth Congresses. Since not all proposed legislation was printed, it is often necessary to consult these manuscript records. Even then it is not always possible to learn the contents of a bill or resolution, for the original copies of some measures never found their way into the records of Congress. Other materials on deposit at the National Archives that were useful for this study are the papers of the House Committee on Territories, the Committee on Elections, and the Committee on the Judiciary, for both war congresses. The papers of the Select Committee on the Rebellious States of the Thirty-eighth Congress consist only of a small number of petitions from radical antislavery organizations. Papers of Senate committees were generally of less value than those of the House, although the records of the judiciary and territories committees were occasionally useful.

Printed Documents

The printed bills and resolutions of the Thirty-seventh and Thirty-eighth Congresses were of course an indispensable source. The Library of Congress has a very nearly complete file of printed bills, and what it lacks the Senate Library in the Capitol is able to provide. The Library of Congress is presently engaged in microfilming a complete file of printed bills and resolutions. The part of the project dealing with the Thirty-seventh and Thirty-eighth Congresses has been completed. The *Congressional Globe*, the record of debates in Congress, is also indispensable for the study of wartime reconstruction. Its limitations are well known to scholars, yet it remains an invaluable source of information. It should be used in conjunction with the *House Journal* and the *Senate Journal*, which are more authoritative for determining the actual order of business and more convenient for counting votes (and occasionally more accurate). The House and Senate journals also contain indexes giving the titles and legislative history of all bills and resolutions introduced into Congress. Reports of committees of the House and Senate contain much information about reconstruction during the war. The House Committee on Elections issued numerous reports on election cases from southern states, while the Senate judiciary committee performed this function with respect to the election of senators. *House Miscellaneous Documents* and *Senate Miscellaneous Documents* contain evidence relating to elections and to reconstruction efforts generally in occupied rebel states. The development and operation of military government can be followed in the basic source relating to the army, *The War of the Rebellion: A Compilation of the Official Records of the Union and Confederate Armies*, ed. R. N. Scott *et al.* (130 vols.: Washington, 1880–1901). *Statutes at Large of the United States of America, 1789–1873* (17 vols.; Boston, 1850–1873) is of course a basic source in congressional and legislative history.

Collections of Manuscripts

Collections of letters and private papers of members of Congress and other public officials were helpful in understanding the emergence of reconstruction as a major political issue but of considerably less value in explaining developments in Congress or the executive branch. Although in most manuscript collections at least a few letters from constituents or correspondents dealing with reconstruction could be found, only a relative few contained evidence relating directly to the formation or implementation of the reconstruction policies of either the President or Congress. Except where otherwise indicated, the following collections are in the Library of Congress. Among the most useful are the papers of Nathaniel P. Banks and Salmon P. Chase, which contain letters from congressmen and from persons involved in Louisiana reconstruction. The Henry L. Dawes Papers were also useful. Dawes, the chairman of the Committee on Elections, commented on the political situation in letters to his wife and received letters from Unionists in Louisiana. After his retirement from politics in the 1890's, he wrote numerous essays on the war and reconstruction, most of which have remained unpublished and are in the Dawes Papers. The Joshua R. Giddings-George W. Julian Papers were occasionally useful. Julian was not deeply involved in reconstruction, but received letters on the subject from abolitionists. The Andrew Johnson Papers are a valuable source, especially for understanding the outlook and expectations of radical Republicans after Lincoln's death. The Robert Todd Lincoln Collection of the papers of Abraham

Lincoln is obviously of major importance, containing letters of advice on reconstruction from members of Congress, Cabinet officers, and other persons in politics. Occasional items of significance are included in the papers of Edward McPherson—a representative from Pennsylvania in the Thirty-seventh Congress and Clerk of the House in the Thirty-eighth Congress—Thaddeus Stevens, and Benjamin F. Wade. There is a valuable collection of Henry Winter Davis letters in the Samuel Francis Du Pont Papers in the Eleutherian Mills Historical Library, Wilmington, Delaware.

Newspapers

Reconstruction was important enough to merit comment and analysis from the beginning of the war, so it was possible to discern public reaction to executive and congressional proposals by consulting a variety of newspapers. Among the most useful sources was the Boston *Commonwealth*, which took a strong interest in reconstruction, reporting and editorializing from a radical-abolitionist point of view. The Boston *Journal*, a Republican paper, was useful chiefly for the reports of its Washington correspondent, Benjamin Perley Poore. The Cincinnati *Gazette* carried the equally valuable correspondence of Whitelaw Reid, who was close to a number of antislavery Republicans. The *Gazette* often editoralized on reconstruction from a radical standpoint. The Democratic approach to reconstruction was expressed by the Columbus *Crisis* and the Detroit *Press*. *The Independent*, an abolitionist paper published in New York, was useful both for its editorials and its Washington correspondence. The same was not true of *The Liberator*, the organ of the Garrison wing of the abolitionist movement, which contained only an occasional editorial or letter about reconstruction. The New York *Herald*, edited by James Gordon Bennett, was a valuable source of Democratic criticism of the administration and radicals in Congress. Three major Republican newspapers which followed reconstruction closely were the New York *Evening Post*, the New York *Times*, and the New York *Tribune*. The Philadelphia *Press*, published by John Forney, was useful mainly for the articles that Forney wrote under the by-line "Occasional" or "Observer." The Springfield, Massachusetts, *Weekly Republican* was a persistent critic of radical schemes of reconstruction, as was the Toledo *Blade*, which kept a close watch on James Ashley. The Washington *Chronicle* and the Washington *National Republican* represented Republican views and occasionally editorialized on reconstruction. Similarly helpful was the Washington *National Intelligencer*, conservative Unionist in outlook. The Worcester *Daily Spy* published Washington correspondence and editorials expressing a radical Republican attitude toward reconstruction.

Printed Primary Sources

Published Correspondence, Collected Writings, and Diaries

The Diary of Edward Bates, ed. Howard K. Beale (Washington, 1933), is a useful source for learning about conservative attitudes toward reconstruction in 1863. *Private and Official Correspondence of General Benjamin F. Butler*, ed. Jessie Ames Marshall (5 vols.; Norwood, Mass., 1917), contains letters relating to the anti-Lincoln political maneuvering in 1864 and the Wade-Davis Manifesto. The diaries of Salmon P. Chase are of considerable value for information on wartime reconstruction. Most important is *Inside Lincoln's Cabinet: The Civil War Diaries of Salmon P. Chase*, ed. David Donald (New York, 1954). "The Diary and Correspondence of Salmon P. Chase," American Historical Association, *Annual Report, 1902* (Washington, 1903), contains letters relating to Treasury Department operations and politics in Louisiana. Adam Gurowski, *Diary* (3 vols.; Boston, New York, Washington, 1862–1866), comments on congressional affairs and the changing views of antislavery leaders, with some of whom Gurowski was on good terms. *Lincoln and the Civil War in the Diaries and Letters of John Hay*, ed. Tyler Dennett (New York, 1939), reports Lincoln's opinions on reconstruction not found in his public speeches of 1864 and 1865. Lincoln's speeches and correspondence are available in various forms. The authoritative edition is *The Collected Works of Abraham Lincoln*, ed. Roy P. Basler, assistant eds. Marion Dolores Pratt and Lloyd A. Dunlap (9 vols.; New Brunswick, N.J., 1953–1955). Charles Sumner, *The Works of Charles Sumner* (Boston, 1870–1883) contains essays and speeches on reconstruction, as well as information about Sumner's political relations. *The Diary of Gideon Welles*, ed. Howard K. Beale (3 vols.; New York, 1960), is valuable for information about developments concerning reconstruction, despite its strong antiradical bias.

Memoirs, Autobiographies, and Reminiscences

George S. Boutwell, *Reminiscences of Sixty Years in Public Affairs* (2 vols.; New York, 1902), reviews the disagreement in the Republican party over theories of reconstruction in 1864. Noah Brooks, *Washington in Lincoln's Time* (New York, 1895), contains valuable accounts of some dramatic scenes in Congress, as well as interviews with Lincoln concerning reconstruction. Benjamin F. Butler, *Autobiography and Personal Reminiscences* . . . (Boston, 1892), comments on Lincoln's interest in colonization at the end of the war. Henry L. Dawes published a portion of his voluminous writings on the Civil War and reconstruction in the following articles: "Recollections of Stanton under Lincoln and Johnson," *Atlantic Monthly* (Feb., Oct. 1894), 162–169, 494–504; and "Two Vice-Presidents: John C. Breckinridge and Hannibal Hamlin," *Century Magazine*, n.s., XXVIII (July, 1895), 463–467. George W. Julian, *Political Recollections, 1840–1872* (Chicago, 1884), is an important account of radical dissatisfaction with Lincoln's reconstruction policy. Ward Hill Lamon, *Recollections of Abraham Lincoln, 1847–1865*, ed. Dorthy Lamon (Chicago, 1895), and Alexander K. McClure, *Abraham Lincoln and Men of War-Times* (4th ed.; Philadelphia, 1892), are useful for understanding Lincoln's approach toward reconstruction at the end of the war. Albert G. Riddle, *Recollections of War Times: Reminiscences of Men and Events in Washington, 1860–1865* (New York, 1895), tells about congressional developments and conversations with Lincoln. John Sherman, *Recollections of Forty Years in the House, Senate, and Cabinet: An Autobiography* (2 vols.; Chicago, 1895), was occasionally helpful, although it contains inaccuracies concerning the origins of the Wade-Davis Bill.

Pamphlets, Books, Speeches, and Articles

General accounts by contemporaries that comment to a significant extent upon reconstruction are Isaac N. Arnold, *The History of Abraham Lincoln and the Overthrow of Slavery* (Chicago, 1866); James G. Blaine, *Twenty Years of Congress: From Lincoln to Garfield* (2 vols.; Norwich, Conn., 1884–1886); Samuel S. Cox, *Three Decades of Federal Legislation, 1855 to 1885* (Providence, 1885); Edward P. McPherson, ed., *The Political History of the United States during the Period of Reconstruction* (Washington, 1871); and Henry Wilson, *History of the Rise and Fall of the Slave Power in America* (3 vols.; Boston, 1872–1877). Wilson's *History of the Antislavery Measures of the Thirty-seventh and Thirty-eighth United States Congresses, 1861–65* (Boston, 1865) is a useful summary, though lacking in analysis and insights into congressional actions.

The war produced a vast literature of speeches, essays, and pamphlets, many of which dealt in part with reconstruction. James M. Ashley, *Orations and Speeches: Duplicate Copy of the Souvenir from the Afro-American League of Tennessee to*

Hon. James M. Ashley of Ohio, ed. Benjamin W. Arnett (Philadelphia, 1894), is a most important source. It contains Ashley's speeches in and out of Congress, a copy of his reconstruction bill of 1862, and letters concerning wartime reconstruction. Major statements of the conservative approach to reconstruction are Montgomery Blair, *Speech on the Revolutionary Schemes of the Ultra Abolitionists, and in Defense of the Policy of the President* . . . (n.p., 1863), and Blair's *Speech on the Causes of the Rebellion and in Support of the President's Plan of Pacification* . . . (Baltimore, 1864). Another valuable expression of the Democratic attitude toward reconstruction is *Congressional Address: By Members of the 38th Congress, Politically Opposed to the Present Federal Administration and Representing the Opposition Union Sentiment of the Country* (Washington, 1864). Henry Winter Davis, *Speeches and Addresses* (New York, 1867), reflects the shift in Republican constitutional theory to the concept of the guarantee of republican government. Thomas J. Durant, *Letter . . . to the Hon. Henry Winter Davis, October 27, 1864* (New Orleans, 1864), is an account of the struggle to control Louisiana reconstruction. The issue of Negro suffrage and reconstruction is dealt with in *The Equality of All Men before the Law Claimed and Defended; in Speeches by William D. Kelley, Wendell Phillips, and Frederick Douglass* . . . (Boston, 1865). William D. Kelley, *Replies . . . to George Northrup* (Philadelphia, 1864), suggests that recontruction was, in some cases at least, an explicit issue in the campaign of 1864. Robert Dale Owen, *The Conditions of Reconstruction; in a Letter . . . to the Secretary of State* (New York, 1863), reflects the insistence on emancipation as a condition of reconstruction in 1863. Henry J. Raymond, *The Administration and the War* . . . (n.p., 1863), expresses the reluctance of conservatives to accept emancipation as a condition of reconstruction. Several essays by Gideon Welles on reconstruction, written in the 1870's, have been reprinted in two volumes, *Civil War and Reconstruction* and *Lincoln's Administration*, both compiled by Albert Mordell (New York, 1960). These essays have the same virtues and defects as Welles's diary.

Of numerous books and articles dealing with reconstruction in its constitutional dimension, the following were the most useful from the standpoint of combining insight into the problem with analysis of developments and tendencies in Congress and the executive branch: Joel Prentiss Bishop, *Secession and Slavery: Or the Effect of Secession on the Relation of the United States to the Seceded States and to Slavery* . . . (Boston, 1864); Orestes Brownson, "The President's Message and Proclamation," *Brownson's Quarterly Review*, Nat. Ser., I (Jan. 1864), 85–112, and "The Return of the Rebellious States to the Union," *ibid.*, 3d New York Ser., IV (Oct. 1863), 483–511, which may be supplemented with Brownson's larger work, *The American Republic: Its Constitution, Tendencies, and Destiny* (New York, 1866); Alpheus Crosby, *The Present Position of the Seceded States and the Rights and Duties of the General Government in Respect to Them* (Boston, 1865); William M. Grosvenor, "The Law of Conquest the True Basis of Reconstruction," *New Englander*, XXIV (Jan. 1865), 111–131; John C. Hurd, "Theories of Reconstruction," *American Law Review*, I (Jan. 1867), 238–272, and *The Theory of Our National Existence* (Boston, 1881); William Beach Lawrence, "International Law," *Monthly Law Reporter*, XXVI (Nov. 1863), 12–22; an unsigned article, "The Legal Status of the Rebel States Before and After Their Conquest," *ibid.* (Aug. 1864), 537–557; Joel Parker, "Constitutional Law," *North American Review*, XCIV (April 1862), 435–463; Charles Russell, "Our Domestic Relations; or, How to Treat the Rebel States," *Continental Monthly*, V (May 1864), 511–516; Henry Everett Russell, "Reconstruction," *ibid.*, IV (Dec. 1863), 684–689; Charles Sumner, "Our Domestic Relations; or, How to Treat the Rebel States," *Atlantic Monthly*, XII (Oct. 1863), 507–529; Emory Washburn, "Reconstruction: The Duty of the Profession to the Times," *Monthly Law Reporter*, XXVI

(July 1864), 477–484; and William Whiting, *The Return of the Rebellious States to the Union: A Letter . . . to the Union League of Philadelphia* (Philadelphia, 1864).

Secondary Materials

Biographies

Lincoln biography is of course a major field in itself. Excellent bibliographies on Lincoln may be found in James G. Randall, *Lincoln the President*, Vol. II: *Springfield to Gettysburg* (New York, 1945), 343–400, and Vol. IV: *Last Full Measure* (New York, 1955), 380–398. Isaac N. Arnold, *The Life of Abraham Lincoln* (Chicago, 1885), is a useful if somewhat uncritical study by a close political associate and friend of Lincoln. James M. Ashley, "Abraham Lincoln," *Magazine of Western History*, XIV (May 1891), 23–36, relates the radical-conservative split in the Republican party to its Democratic and Whig origins and places Lincoln in this context. The works previously cited by Ward Hill Lamon and Alexander K. McClure give worthwhile accounts of Lincoln. John G. Nicolay and John Hay, *Abraham Lincoln: A History* (10 vols.; New York, 1890), is an important source despite its semiofficial, apologetic tone and point of view. It contains much information about wartime reconstruction policies. Henry J. Raymond, *The Life and Public Services of Abraham Lincoln* (New York, 1865), includes a chapter on reconstruction under Lincoln. A number of useful brief accounts are presented in Allen Thorndike Rice, ed., *Reminiscences of Abraham Lincoln by Distinguished Men of His Time* (New York, 1886). The best recent works on Lincoln are Richard N. Current, *The Lincoln Nobody Knows* (New York, 1958); David Donald, *Lincoln Reconsidered: Essays on the Civil War Era* (2d ed.; New York, 1961); James G. Randall, *Lincoln the Liberal Statesman* (New York, 1947), and *Lincoln the President* (4 vols.; New York, 1945–1955; Vol. IV completed by Richard N. Current); Benjamin P. Thomas, *Abraham Lincoln: A Biography* (New York, 1952); and T. Harry Williams, *Lincoln and the Radicals* (Madison, Wis., 1941). Williams' thesis—that the radical wing of the Republican party was Lincoln's main political enemy—stimulated a re-examination of Civil War politics; David Donald's essay, "The Radicals and Lincoln," in *Lincoln Reconsidered*, was the first significant dissent from what had become the standard view. Donald argued that the differences between Lincoln and the radical wing of his party were not as great as had been thought. Recent attempts to explain Lincoln's political position are William D. Mallam, "Lincoln and the Conservatives," *Journal of Southern History*, XXVII (Feb. 1962), 31–45; Hans Trefousse, "A Radical Reconsidered: Ben Wade, Lincoln, and the Civil War," *Topic*, I (Fall, 1961), 16–29; and, engaging in a second round of debate, David Donald, "Devils Facing Zionwards," and T. Harry Williams, "Lincoln and the Radicals: An Essay in Civil War History and Historiography," in Grady McWhiney, ed., *Grant, Lee, Lincoln, and the Radicals: Essays on Civil War Leadership* (Evanston, Ill., 1964), 72–117.

There are biographies of nearly all the major and many of the second-level figures of the Civil War era. Most of these studies are useful in a general sense and some are of special interest for those investigating reconstruction during the war. Fred H. Harrington, *Fighting General: Major-General N. P. Banks* (Philadelphia, 1948), is excellent on Louisiana reconstruction. Fred Nicklason, "The Early Career of Henry L. Dawes, 1816–1871," an unpublished dissertation (Yale University, 1967), is a valuable study of the chairman of the elections committee, who was involved in reconstruction during the war. Edward L. Pierce, *Memoir and Letters of Charles Sumner* (4 vols.; Boston, 1877–1893), contains several letters dealing with reconstruction and is the best study of Sumner during and after the war. J. W. Schuckers, *The Life and Public Services of Salmon Portland Chase* (New York, 1874), includes letters bearing on reconstruction. William E. Smith, *The Francis Preston Blair Family in Politics* (2 vols.; New York, 1933), recounts the attempts of the Blairs to forestall radical plans of reconstruction throughout the war. There is a distinct need for a thorough study of Henry Winter Davis, Montgomery Blair's archrival. Until one is forthcoming, the best work on this important figure remains Bernard C. Steiner, *Life of Henry Winter Davis* (Baltimore, 1916). Benjamin P. Thomas and Harold M. Hyman, *Stanton: The Life and Times of Lincoln's Secretary of War* (New York, 1962), explains much about the role of the army in reconstruction. Hans Trefousse, *Benjamin Franklin Wade: Radical Republican from Ohio* (New York, 1963), is a competent study which presents a thorough revaluation of radicalism. It is disappointingly thin, however, on the Wade-Davis Bill and wartime reconstruction.

Monographs, Articles, and Miscellaneous Works

Many studies of Civil War politics and of Lincoln briefly examine reconstruction, while works on postwar reconstruction usually go back to review Lincoln's proclamation of amnesty of 1863 and the Wade-Davis Bill of 1864. Consequently, wartime reconstruction has been a relatively neglected field of study. Eben G. Scott, *Reconstruction during the Civil War in the United States of America* (Boston, 1895), was the first work to deal with the subject, and even then Scott devoted more than half of the book to a constitutional history of America from the colonial origins to the secession crisis. Scott's thesis was that under radical Republican influence the original objective of restoring the Union was transformed into an attempt to reconstruct it which departed completely from any constitutional sanction or authority. The beginning of a more systematic, though narrower, study appeared a few years later in Frederick W. Moore, "Representation in the National Congress from the Seceding States, 1861–65," *American Historical Review*, II

(Jan., April, 1897), 279–293, 461–471. This was followed by Charles H. McCarthy, *Lincoln's Plan of Reconstruction* (New York, 1901), a sympathetic interpretation of Lincoln which saw him adhering consistently to a lenient policy toward the South— the same, indeed, that Andrew Johnson carried out. McCarthy's book, which surveyed developments in the southern states as well as congressional action on reconstruction in 1864–1865, remained the standard work on the subject until the appearance of William B. Hesseltine, *Lincoln's Plan of Reconstruction* (Tuscaloosa, Ala., 1960). Hesseltine challenged the view that Lincoln had a consistent policy for reconstructing the South, arguing instead that he tried several approaches, none of which was successful. Hesseltine's book was essentially a restatement of the main theme of his earlier work, *Lincoln and the War Governors* (New York, 1948), in which he concluded that Lincoln "made a nation." In his 1960 work Hesseltine concluded that Lincoln "reconstructed the nation." According to both books, Lincoln achieved his result by destroying state rights.

Certain constitutional aspects of reconstruction during the war have been the subject of study. The most obvious presidential power involved in reconstruction is examined in Jonathan T. Dorris, *Pardon and Amnesty under Lincoln and Johnson: The Restoration of the Confederates to Their Rights and Privileges* (Chapel Hill, N.C., 1953). Harold M. Hyman, *Era of the Oath: Northern Loyalty Tests during the Civil War and Reconstruction* (Philadelphia, 1954), discusses the origin and operation of the "iron-clad" oath. Charles O. Lerche, Jr., "Congressional Interpretations of the Guarantee of a Republican Form of Government during Reconstruction," *Journal of Southern History*, XV (May, 1949), 192–211, in part deals with wartime developments. Harold M. Hyman, "Reconstruction and Political-Constitutional Institutions: The Popular Expression," in Hyman, ed., *New Frontiers of the American Reconstruction* (Urbana, Ill., 1966), 1–39, makes a beginning toward understanding the progress of constitutional thought during the war.

Military government was an important constitutional development for which the starting point of any study is William Whiting, *War Powers under the Constitution of the United States* (43d ed.; Boston, 1871), written from an extreme nationalist point of view by the chief legal advisor to the War Department. Seminal studies in this area are A. H. Carpenter, "Military Government of Southern Territory, 1861–1865," American Historical Association, *Annual Report, 1900* (2 vols.; Washington, 1901), I, 467–498; and James G. Randall, *Constitutional Problems under Lincoln* (rev. ed.; Urbana, Ill., 1951), ch. x. See also the previously cited biography of Stanton by Benjamin P. Thomas and Harold M. Hyman.

The development of policies concerning the freedmen as an aspect of wartime reconstruction is dealt with in George R. Bentley, *The Freedman's Bureau* (Philadelphia, 1955); James M. McPherson, *The Struggle for Equality: Abolitionists and the Negro in the Civil War and Reconstruction* (Princeton, 1964), and *The Negro's Civil War* (New York, 1965); Willie Lee Rose, *Rehearsal for Reconstruction: The Port Royal Experiment* (Indianapolis, 1964); John G. Sproat, "Blueprint for Radical Reconstruction," *Journal of Southern History*, XXIII (Feb. 1957), 25–44. The extent to which the granting of Negro civil rights formed a part of Lincoln's reconstruction policy at the end of the war is discussed in Ludwell H. Johnson, "Lincoln and Equal Rights: The Authenticity of the Wadsworth Letter," *Journal of Southern History*, XXXII (Feb. 1966), 83–87; and Harold M. Hyman, "Lincoln and Equal Rights for Negroes: The Irrelevancy of the 'Wadsworth Letter,'" *Civil War History*, XII (Sept. 1966), 258–266.

Besides studies of individual states, references to which may be found in the footnotes, numerous general works deal in part with reconstruction during the war. Old but still important are John W. Burgess, *Reconstruction and the Constitution, 1866–1876* (New York, 1902); C. E. Chadsey, *The Struggle between President Johnson and Congress over Reconstruction* (Baltimore, 1897), which contains an able analysis of Lincoln and Congress; and William A. Dunning, *Essays on the Civil War and Reconstruction and Related Topics* (New York, 1898). A judicious and perceptive account of wartime reconstruction may be found in Carl Russell Fish, *The American Civil War*, ed. William Ernest Smith (New York, 1937). Studies of Lincoln by Nicolay and Hay, T. Harry Williams, James G. Randall, and Richard Current contain chapters on wartime reconstruction. Professor Randall made a more detailed investigation of the subject in *Lincoln and the South* (Baton Rouge, La., 1946). Recent accounts of reconstruction under Andrew Johnson which contain insights into the wartime problem include W. R. Brock, *An American Crisis: Congress and Reconstruction, 1865–1867* (New York, 1963); John and LaWanda Cox, *Politics, Principle, and Prejudice, 1865–1866* (New York, 1963); David Donald *The Politics of Reconstruction, 1863–1867* (Baton Rouge, La., 1965); Eric McKitrick, *Andrew Johnson and Reconstruction* (Chicago, 1960); Rembert W. Patrick, *The Reconstruction of the Nation* (New York, 1967); and Kenneth Stampp, *The Era of Reconstruction* (New York, 1965). A useful collection of documents which shifts attention to reconstruction during the war is Harold M. Hyman, ed., *The Radical Republicans and Reconstruction, 1861–1870* (Indianapolis, 1967).

Index

329

Winner of the 1966
Beveridge Award

Reconstructing the Union

Theory and Policy
during the Civil War

HERMAN BELZ

Reconstruction as a problem that concerned both the President and Congress from the beginning of the war is the subject of this valuable addition to Civil War literature. Focusing on the theories and policies, the attitudes and actions, of the executive and legislative branches in Washington, and treating peripherally efforts in the several southern states, the author views from a new perspective the entire struggle over rebuilding the Union.

Closely connected with reconstruction were other issues, among which the freedom and status of emancipated slaves were most important. Mr. Belz studies these complex sets of problems and the response of the Union's political leaders to them, from the opening of hostilities in April 1861 to their conclusion four years later.